Tools ↳ Salesforce Pardot
↳ HubSpot

Marketing Automation FOR DUMMIES®

A Wiley Brand

Prospect Score: How interested they are in your service based on the activities they engage in

by Mathew Sweezey

Prospect Grade: Indicates whether they fit your ideal prospect profile, determined by comparing their demo info w/ the criteria you set (job title, industry, location, etc.)

Marketing Automation For Dummies®

Published by: **John Wiley & Sons, Inc.,** 111 River Street, Hoboken, NJ 07030-5774, www.wiley.com

Published simultaneously in Canada

For general information on our other products and services, please contact our Customer Care Department within the U.S. at 877-762-2974, outside the U.S. at 317-572-3993, or fax 317-572-4002. For technical support, please visit www.wiley.com/techsupport.

Wiley publishes in a variety of print and electronic formats and by print-on-demand. Some material included with standard print versions of this book may not be included in e-books or in print-on-demand. If this book refers to media such as a CD or DVD that is not included in the version you purchased, you may download this material at http://booksupport.wiley.com. For more information about Wiley products, visit www.wiley.com.

Library of Congress Control Number is available from the publisher.

ISBN: 978-1-118-77222-5

ISBN 978-1-118-77222-5 (pbk); ISBN 978-1-118-77227-0 (ebk); ISBN 978-1-118-77230-0 (ebk)

Manufactured in the United States of America

C10004931_100218

Contents at a Glance

Table of Contents

Introduction

The marketing world has changed more in the last few years than in the entire 100 years prior. Technology has given rise to an ultra-connected world and a new way in which people operate, communicate, and find things. This fundamental change has also given rise to new and better ways to reach your consumer. Marketing automation allows a business to reach people in a personal and scalable way, increasing your marketing's effectiveness — and your revenue.

In this book, I tell you all about marketing automation: what it is and why it is something you should strongly consider putting to use for your company. I show you how to find a marketing automation tool to suit your needs, how to set it up, and how to create better campaigns than ever before.

About This Book

This book exists to help you understand this new technology called marketing automation. Whether you need to run marketing campaigns for your company, work on the sales side, or employ the people doing those things for you, having a strong understanding of the most critical marketing process is a must. The reason marketing automation has become such a critical piece of the marketing world is that it solves the issue of how to be relevant at scale. This book gives you a look at marketing automation that's unlike any other publication on the topic. I've laid this book out to teach you the why, the what, and the how.

The book uses a step-by-step approach to guide you through every aspect of working with this technology. Here are some conventions used in the book that you should know before jumping in:

- Web addresses and programming code appear in `monofont`. If you're reading a digital version of this book on a device connected to the Internet, note that you can click the web address to visit that website, like this: `www.dummies.com`.
- I've included Twitter handles of key people and companies when possible, and I've included them so that you can take action and follow them. Being successful with this technology requires constant learning. These are the best people to learn from.

Foolish Assumptions

The most foolish of assumptions is that you already know how to do automated marketing. The concepts that are the basis for current marketing methodologies do not translate directly into the work of marketing automation. Marketing automation is just as much of a mind shift as it is a new technology, and throughout this book I show you how to think correctly about marketing automation and how to best execute programs to meet your goals.

For those of you who are beginners to the field of marketing, I encourage you to learn the basics and stay with low-level techniques for a while. Don't try to run too fast without fully understanding how to walk. Also, realize that you most likely have *lots* of work ahead of you. I have, however, organized this book to make the workload as easy as possible to tackle.

For those of you who are advanced marketers, make use of the information that's appropriate for you and leave the rest. Also, realize that an advanced technique for you may be a basic technique for someone else. It's all about context, and I give you plenty of that in the book.

Finally, if you have a marketing automation tool, you *must* read this book. I can't tell you how many people have already tried working with marketing automation tools and still have no clue how to use them correctly. I see people still struggling to accomplish their basic goals a year after they've purchased their marketing automation tool, and I see people who are successful with their tool in very short order. The difference between the two is how they approach a new technology.

If you approach marketing automation without understanding it, and you use an outdated approach, you will not accomplish your goals and will likely end up having to hire a consultant to help you use your marketing automation tool. Reading this book will save you lots of money and months of work just by showing you the basic elements to focus on, how to think about setting them up, and how to improve your automated programs over time.

Technology is moving fast, and new tricks, tips, and tools emerge every day. Knowing which ones are important is necessary so that you don't get caught chasing fads.

Icons Used in This Book

The Tip icon marks tips (duh!) and shortcuts that you can use to make this process easier.

Remember icons mark the information that's especially important to know. Make sure to take the time to read these. I've included them because these are critical items to understand when working with marketing automation.

The Warning icon tells you to watch out! It marks important information that may save you headaches, so do NOT skip Warning paragraphs.

Beyond the Book

I have written some extra content that you won't find in this book. Go online to find the following:

- **Online articles covering additional topics at**

  `www.dummies.com/extras/marketingautomation`

  Here you'll find a Top 10 guide to creating great content, tips for automating follow-ups, help with data management, and more.

- **The Cheat Sheet for this book at**

  `www.dummies.com/cheatsheet/marketingautomation`

  Here you'll find additional articles about lead scoring as well as how to create the perfect nurturing email. Consult the cheat sheet when you are reviewing your lead scoring model, creating a lead score for the first time, or creating any drip nurturing programs.

Where to Go from Here

This book isn't written for you to start at the beginning and work your way through. It's written so that you can use it as a reference and get all the information you require in a chapter. The best way to use this book is to keep it with you and, of course, have it handy when you are either planning or executing your marketing automation programs.

Part I

getting started with Marketing Automation

For Dummies can help you get started with lots of subjects. Visit `www.dummies.com` for more great content online.

In this part . . .

- Get introduced to the modern buyer and learn why marketing automation is so effective.
- Create a business case for a marketing automation solution.
- Find out the basics of setting up a marketing automation tool.

Chapter 1

Introducing the Concepts of Marketing Automation

In This Chapter

- Defining marketing automation
- Defining the modern buyer
- Knowing why companies implement marketing automation
- Starting the conversation about marketing automation

Marketing automation is a buzzword in the marketing world. This chapter explains what it means and why marketing automation has made such a big difference in so many companies.

I show you what defines marketing automation and why it's such a big deal. I list the major reasons that companies are implementing marketing automation solutions and show you how to start conversations about it at your company. I also dig into the changes in the modern buyer that have made marketing automation so popular.

Defining Marketing Automation

The term *marketing automation* got its start in the mid to late 1990s when a few people were combing their databases with automated code to make it easier to segment their databases into more granular segments based on more data. Since then, it has turned into a massive industry and has been called the fastest-growing software segment in the CRM space.

In short, *marketing automation* refers to the process of using a single platform for tracking leads, automating personal marketing activities, and being able to produce full closed-loop reports on the effectiveness of all marketing activities.

There are also many other ways to refer to the processes that marketing automation encompasses. Each company that sells marketing automation software calls it something slightly different, and even the analysts call it something different. Here's a list of terms you may hear in place of marketing automation:

- Demand generation
- Lead performance management
- Revenue performance management
- Automated lead management
- CRM lead management

Marketing automation (or whatever name you call it) really consists of three parts:

- The first is lead tracking, which consists of tracking a lead across all marketing channels.
- The second is automated execution, which enables you to have automated processes take place either as marketing campaigns or as internal changes based on these tracked actions.
- Finally, the third part allows for closed-loop reporting for proving the value of your marketing efforts down to every dollar those efforts bring in.

Full marketing automation vs. piecemeal marketing automation

Marketing automation has many levels, an idea that you need to grasp before you dig deeply into this book. Currently, many options are available to help you automate marketing activities. Depending on your goals, you may just need a single tool to add to your existing toolbox, or you may need to replace your entire toolbox with a full marketing automation platform.

For example, say that you're using a form on a website and you can now easily have form submissions dropped right into your CRM without your having to lift a finger. This is an example of a single automation. A single tool can do this for you if this is all you require. I call a single tool working to do one action "piecemeal marketing automation." But if you need those form submissions to score your prospects so that you can determine who is the most sales ready, you need a full marketing automation platform. Removing tasks is considered a level of automation, but it is a single-point solution and doesn't meet all three of the criteria I mention in this chapter to qualify as full marketing automation.

As you go through this book, determine whether you need just piecemeal marketing automation or full marketing automation. Making this determination will help you to ensure that you get the tools you require and don't buy a technology just because it is a hot buzzword.

When thinking of marketing automation, many people may be confused, wondering whether it's a technology or a way of marketing. It's actually both. Marketing automation is just as much a new way of marketing as it is a new tool that most companies have never used before. There are also many levels of marketing automation. Throughout this book, I cover all levels of marketing automation and show you how to implement the new technology while thinking about marketing in a new way.

Recognizing the Relationship Between Marketing Automation and Online Marketing

Marketers are running the majority of their campaigns online. This fact makes many marketing activities easier to execute and track but also adds a lot of technical challenges. Marketing automation and online marketing have a symbiotic relationship. Think of marketing automation as an extension of online marketing. It needs online marketing to work, just as online marketing is made more effective by marketing automation.

Online marketing usually consists of many different channels and types of campaigns. Here are the marketing campaigns that can be made more effective with marketing automation:

- **Search Engine Optimization (SEO):** Marketing automation allows for the tracking of each keyword, and full closed-loop return on investment (ROI) reporting on every keyword.
- **Search Engine Marketing (SEM):** Marketing automation provides full lead tracking so that you can see each person and every paid advertisement that person has engaged with.
- **E-mail marketing:** E-mail marketing changes with marketing automation because you don't have to send blast e-mails, which are individually executed marketing pieces not tied to other prospect interactions. With marketing automation, you gain the ability to execute automated, personalized lead-nurturing campaigns that may last for months and dynamically change based on people's interactions with the emails they are receiving. So you move from a manual execution and scrubbing of lists to an automated campaign that can optimize itself for best results.
- **Content marketing:** Marketing automation gives you the ability to track every piece of content and see each person in your database who engages with your content.
- **Trade shows:** If you attend trade shows, marketing automation gives you the ability to track each lead from your booth and prove full ROI on each trade show.

- **Social media:** Tweets, blog posts, LinkedIn, Facebook, and all other social media channels can be tracked and reported on. So you can prove the ROI on social media down to the tweet and demonstrate how it influenced your last closed deal.
- **Website:** You can drive more value out of your website by knowing every page a prospect looks at, helping you to identify hot leads based on the prospect's level of engagement with key pages.

Marketing to the Modern Buyer

A European study in 2013 noted that the average consumer is in front of a screen 12 hours a day. More than 294 billion e-mails are sent each day, and more than 2 million new blog posts go online every day. The *Wall Street Journal* reports that more than 42 percent of holiday shoppers in 2013 did their holiday shopping online. Clearly, with the amount of time people spend online, if you're not online, you're going to be left behind.

Most of this is not news to you. You probably have a website, an e-mail tool, and a Twitter account. You have started to blog and create content for your website. You've learned about the benefits of SEO and optimized your content for search results. The next sections explain how to engage with the modern buyer in more granular detail so that you can easily see how marketing automation helps you better engage online with your consumers.

Feeding the need for content

Content marketing has become another buzzword in the marketing world. It has sparked the *New York Times* bestselling book *Youtility,* by Jay Baer, and spawned new institutes such as the Content Marketing Institute. Content marketing even changed the way Google's algorithm ranks websites in natural searches. The Internet is now made up of content, and marketers are clued in. We're creating more content than ever before, and it's because we have to.

Today's buyers want to get help and are looking to your company for that help — and they should be getting help from your content, too. This is one of the key messages Jay Baer puts forth in *Youtility*. It's also the message of Joe Pulizzi, founder of the Content Marketing Institute. Your content needs to be helpful to get people to engage with it, and you need to provide a lot of it, as well.

The need for all this content has put a strain on a marketer's day and made distribution of content a massive problem. Marketing automation helps to solve a lot of this content problem by giving marketers an automated way to distribute their content and by opening up more time in their day to create more content instead of managing a database. The need for content isn't going away. Content is only getting more important, which means that the problem of distributing content, and following up with people after they have engaged with your content, is only getting harder as well. Marketing automation makes content distribution and follow-up very easy.

With the new release of Google's Hummingbird, the content imperative has been driven to a new level. *Hummingbird* is the latest release on the Google algorithm for sorting search engine results. It now puts more emphasis on content, helping people answer questions rather than just supplying keyword matches. Most marketers are creating many forms of content. Here are just a few of the many types of content you should be considering:

- Webinars
- Videos
- Infographics
- White papers
- Research reports
- Surveys
- ROI calculators
- How-to guides
- Buyers' guides
- Ebooks
- Blog posts
- Newsletters

Prospects are searching for answers

People are beginning their research process on Google. Many marketers have turned to search engine optimization (SEO) and search engine marketing (SEM) to capitalize on these searches and help drive more leads into their pipeline.

SEO and SEM refer to the practices of optimizing your website for search engines. *SEO* refers to the natural way you rank in these searches, and *SEM* refers to the paid listing in these searches. Figure 1-1 shows the difference between a natural (SEO) listing in a search result and a paid (SEM) listing in the same search.

If you ever want to think about how big SEO and SEM are, just look at the profits from the largest SEM provider, Google AdWords. Google AdWords made Google more than $42 billion in profits last year. This profit was made on the 1.2 trillion searches preformed on Google in 2012.

Search marketing likely is not new to you; however, being able to prove the ROI on search engine marketing may be. Closed-loop reporting on any marketing channel, including SEO and SEM marketing, is one of the larger benefits of marketing automation.

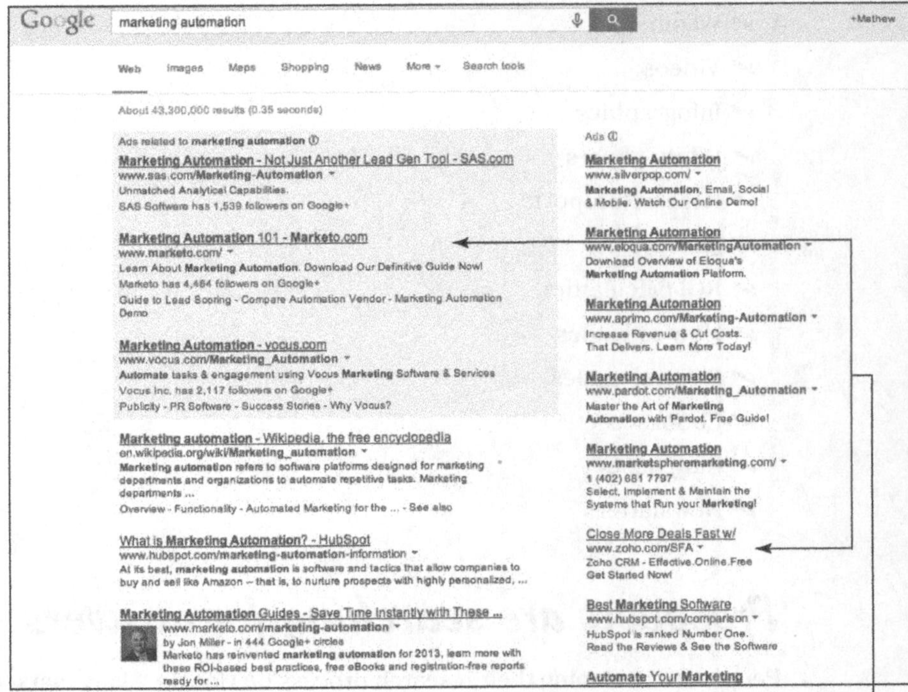

Figure 1-1: SEO is a natural ranking; SEM is paid.

Consumers are engaging over a life cycle

The concept of the buyer's life cycle is nothing new. It has been written about for years, and even implemented in just about every organization's sales department. I imagine that your sales team has opportunity stages during which salespeople talk differently to a buyer and have different goals to meet. This same thinking has not made its way to the marketing side of the house because there used to be no way to track a buyer's life cycle before that buyer was in the hands of the sales team. Marketing automation has changed this situation with lead tracking.

Consider how a buyer purchases things. This becomes the basis of all modern buyer theory and marketing theory. Dissecting how a buyer buys tells you where to market, what message to use, and what your next marketing move should be. When you do the research, you'll find out a few key things about the modern buyer, such as the following:

- **93 percent of all buying journeys begin online.** *Search Engine Journal* states that 93 percent of all buying cycles begin with a search. This may be a search on Google, Bing, Yahoo!, or other search engines.
- **Buyers don't want to talk to you right away.** Buyers searching online don't want to talk to a person right away. They prefer to gather information and then talk to the companies they feel are the best to talk to. This is why content marketing and online marketing have become so important.
- **Buyers are hypereducated.** The amount of information we are putting online has educated consumers on a completely new level. Buyers now hold the power of the sales process in their hands. They can read every tweet and review and find out all the pros and cons of your solution before they talk to you.
- **Buyers are hypersensitive.** With more than 294 billion e-mails sent every day, buyers are not engaging with e-mails or content unless it is 100 percent relevant to them. This is another reason that automated marketing has increased companies' bottom lines. By tracking leads and automating communications, companies can now get relevant with every communication they have.
- **Buyers go back to Google 2–3 times.** The buyer's life cycle was proved in a study I conducted in 2012 and published in an article on CLickz.com. The study found that buyers go back to search engines 2–3 times before they want to engage with sales and enter the sales cycle.

The concept of a buyer's journey helps marketers to be relevant with their communications. Marketing automation is the tool being used to stay relevant over the buyer's journey and the sales cycle. Understanding the fact that there *is* a journey is the first step in tracking where someone is in his or her journey. That tracking takes place through marketing automation.

Everyone is socializing online

Social media dominated online marketing over the past few years. Figure 1-2 shows the rise of social media after the rise of SEO and just before the rise of mobile. Social media has taken on a new meaning in the past few years. Social has quickly become known as anything online.

Consumers and businesses are getting more social every day. Two years ago, you may not have even heard of Twitter. In 2013, Twitter had an estimated user base of 215 million active users who send more than 400 million tweets per day, and it has become a mainstay in the social world. Other businesses are learning the power of Facebook and LinkedIn for business. With the rise of social media and social platforms, many companies are finding strong uses for social media.

Social media was designed to facilitate communications and has turned into a distribution channel with a massive reach. Authors such as Jeff Rohrs, author of *Audience* (John Wiley & Sons, 2014), speaks about the need for companies to build their own audiences on social media. This is a complete change from just a few years ago when many companies would buy audiences through mass media.

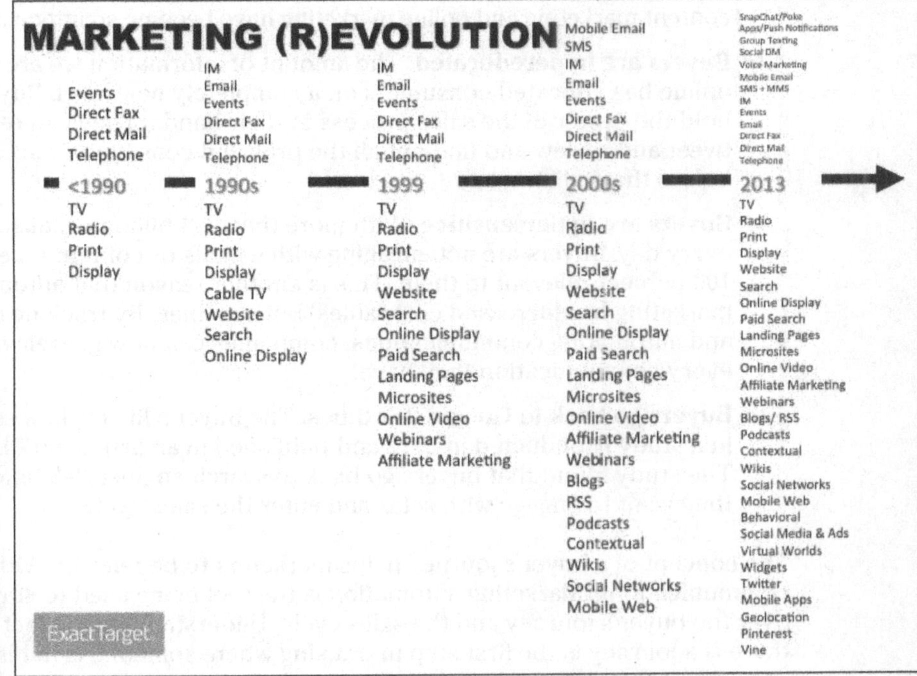

Figure 1-2: The rise of social media is a recent trend, preceded by SEO and mobile.

The main challenges of social media marketing are managing the massive level of communications, and proving the value of your efforts. Marketing automation has been the driving force for many companies to prove the value of social media by giving companies the ability to keep a consistent message across channels, tie social activity to actual revenue generated, and easily manage the multitude of social activities through automated programs.

Marketing in the ultra-connected world

Mobile doesn't really change marketing all that much. Before you dismiss that idea, hear me out. Mobile is just a device. Getting access to someone via mobile was a challenge in previous years. This is not the case now, with 42 percent of all email being opened on a mobile device and the large majority of social media being controlled from a mobile device.

If you market internationally, consider that more people have cell phones than have electricity or access to clean drinking water. If you look at the world this way, it's easy to see why mobile will soon be the number-one device your content is being read on, rather than being a different channel that you have to master.

The original idea for mobile marketing was to have an app because it gave you the ability to reach someone 24/7, with relevant messages to drive engagement. This is a great idea and works for many companies, but for many others, an app strategy is not a good idea. It's very hard to work your way onto a person's phone and keep that person engaging with your app if you're not pushing content to it constantly, but it is much easier to just send an email that gets read on the smartphone.

So instead of creating an app, you should try to figure out how to get content into people's hands 24/7 in the most relevant way possible. Marketing automation allows you to turn people's Inbox into your "app" that can push the correct content at the correct time and have it reach people wherever they are in the world.

Just think of it as having automated emails being opened on a different-sized computer. Speaking of the iPhone, Steve Jobs said something to the effect of, "This isn't a phone; it's a computer that can make phone calls." Think of your mobile strategy in the same light. Consumers are using their phones as devices to access your content, speak with you, or learn more about you. Marketing automation, through its ability to track every marketing interaction, can help you keep up with your prospects and then automate the correct message at the correct time, helping you to reach your consumers 24/7 with relevant content. This is the real goal of a mobile strategy, and it's accomplished much easier with marketing automation than with an app strategy.

Chapter 2

Creating a Business Case for Marketing Automation

In This Chapter

- Writing a business case for marketing automation
- Understanding the return on marketing automation investments
- Discussing marketing automation with internal stakeholders

When you're new to marketing automation, one of the first things you need to consider is how to show the value of marketing automation to the people who write the checks in your company. Even if you're the one with the budget, getting a consensus for your purchase decision is a good idea because marketing automation typically impacts a range of business operations.

With the idea of building a business case in mind, this chapter uncovers marketing automation's potential impact to your organization. I show you where your organization will gain the most value from automation, and I explain how to justify to your boss or other decision maker the expenses for bringing marketing automation in-house.

Writing a Business Case Document

Writing a business case document helps sell the value of marketing automation to other stakeholders who may not be involved in all aspects of the decision. You can use the other sections of this chapter to help fill in the sections of your business case. Your business case should include the following sections.

- **Executive Briefing:** Write a high-level overview of all following sections. This should be a summary no longer than one typed page.
- **Summary Recommendation:** Summarize all your options and your final recommendation based on the rest of your document.

- **Business Drivers:** Describe the reasons for adopting the new technology. Make sure to include multiple business drivers. These should be very high-level objectives that align with your company's main goals.
- **Scope:** Chart the time required to identify a marketing automation solution and implement the solution. List the required resources to realize the value you describe.
- **Costs:** List all upfront and recurring costs. Include time to set up, costs of long-term use, future upgrades, and contract lengths.
- **Benefits:** List the gains you'll realize from using the technology. Think in terms of business benefits such as being able to drive more revenue faster into the organization, or being able to create a more predictable lead pipeline.
- **Risks:** Consider all risks, including the risk of not using automation technology. This is a great place to use case studies of others in your industry to show what the risk of doing nothing is.
- **Strategic Options:** Detail all the possible options and explain the pros and cons of each option. Use an Excel spreadsheet to list and score each feature.

Knowing Why Companies Implement Marketing Automation

Everyone today is more social, more connected online, and more involved in reading online content than ever before. These are some of the key reasons that marketing automation has come to the forefront of the marketing world. With the increase in the amount of engagement, consumers are also expecting better engagement. They expect personal engagement, and the only way to have personal engagement at scale is through marketing automation.

Today's marketers need the ability to manage content in all online contexts and prove the value of these efforts. Marketers also need to produce lots of different types of content for their prospects and customers to get involved with.

Understanding how other companies implement marketing automation solutions can help to inform your business case. Here are some of the main reasons that other companies decide to get involved with marketing automation:

- **Generating more leads with the same budget.** Marketers typically have a lot to do and not a lot of budget to do it. Companies with limited budgets use marketing automation tools to automate many of the manual tasks that marketing demands so that marketing departments can spend more time being creative and generating more leads.

- **Proving the value of marketing efforts.** Marketing is an expensive activity, so many companies demand financial justification. Marketing automation allows companies to track leads and report on the return on investment (ROI) of marketing activities associated with those leads by tying marketing efforts to the sales opportunities that result. The beauty is that this is all done automatically.
- **Empowering marketing users to build online campaigns.** Some marketers may feel comfortable working with HTML and CSS to design landing pages, while other marketers have no interest in touching the code. Many marketing automation systems include "what you see is what you get" (WYSIWYG) builders that help nontechnical users create their own assets without coding from scratch. These features eliminate the need to engage front-end developers and can save your company time and money. Campaigns get out the door faster, and marketing users can make live changes to campaigns without waiting on another department for help.
- **Managing the lead funnel more effectively.** Most marketing departments have a lead funnel to communicate with prospects and determine when a lead gets passed to sales. With the full lead-tracking capabilities of marketing automation, qualifying leads and passing them to sales when they are ready to begin a sales cycle is much easier.
- **Aligning sales and marketing.** Sales and marketing get along better when they have full visibility into lead generation, qualification, hand-off to sales, and follow-up. With marketing automation, sales and marketing can easily see which leads are not being followed up on and automatically bring those leads back into marketing campaigns.
- **Consolidating multiple tools.** Online marketing, customer relationship management (CRM), social media, mobile marketing, retargeting, e-mail marketing . . . I could go on for a while. In a recent survey published by Salesforce.com, the best-of-breed companies use more than ten tools each in their marketing departments. Consolidating marketing tools makes it easier to launch cross-channel campaigns and report on the results of all the marketing tools used.

14 quick stats in favor of marketing automation

When you compare the results of the various approaches to marketing, you can present to your company a compelling business case for using marketing automation.

Marketing

- On average, leads that have been nurtured generate 20 percent more opportunities than non-nurtured leads. (Demand Gen Report, 2008, Andrew Gaffney)
- Companies with mature lead generation and management practices have a 9.3 percent higher sales quota achievement rate. (CSO Insights, 2007)
- Companies that excel at lead nurturing generate 50 percent more sales-ready leads at 33 percent lower cost. (Lori Wizdo, Forrester Research)
- Nurtured leads make 47 percent larger purchases than non-nurtured leads. (Aberdeen, 2009)
- Companies that automate lead management see a 10 percent or greater increase in revenue in 6–9 months. (Gartner, "The Top Six CRM Marketing Processes for a Cost-Constrained Economy," 2009)

Sales

- Ninety percent of business buyers say that when they're ready to buy, they'll find you. (Demand Gen Report, 2012)
- Research shows that 35–50 percent of sales go to the vendor that responds first. (Steve Watts, 2010, InsideSales.com)
- Seventy-one percent of the buying process is now complete by the time a prospect is ready to engage with sales. (SiriusDecisions, 2011)

Marketing Automation

- The adoption of marketing automation technology is expected to increase 50 percent by 2015. (Jay Famico, 2012, SiriusDecisions)
- A quarter of all B2B Fortune 500 companies are already using marketing automation, along with 76 percent of the world's largest software-as-a-service (SaaS) companies. (Mathew Sweezey, Pardot, 2013)
- Eighty-four percent of top-performing companies are using or plan to start using marketing automation between 2012 and 2015. (Gleanster, September, 2012)
- Marketing automation platform users have a 53 percent higher conversion rate from marketing response to marketing-qualified lead than nonusers. (Aberdeen Group, 2010)
- Sixty-three percent of survey respondents indicate that the ability to set measurable objectives for each of their campaigns is the biggest value driver of marketing automation. (Gleanster, 2012)
- Seventy-seven percent of CMOs at top-performing companies indicate that their most compelling reason for implementing marketing automation is to increase revenue. (Gleanster, 2012)

Starting the Conversation about Marketing Automation

As with any new investment in technology at a company, implementing marketing automation requires a lot of steps. The first step is to get the conversation going in your organization, and this section shows you a variety of ways you can get people talking to start generating interest and momentum.

Identifying the stakeholders

The stakeholders for marketing automation are a pretty wide bunch of people. You've got your marketing team, your CRM team, your website team, and your sales team. Getting all these people together can be a challenge, so here are a few keys to identifying and approaching these stakeholders:

- **Marketing team.** This goes without saying, so I keep it simple. Your e-mail, blog, website, social, mobile, and offline strategists will all need input on your marketing automation tool, so make sure that you include everyone on your team.
- **Customer relationship management (CRM) team.** Integrating to your CRM is a big aspect of marketing automation. If you do not have a CRM tool, you can use one of the many marketing automation tools that have a built-in CRM. If you do have a CRM, you need your CRM admin to be involved at each step.
- **Website team.** You *must* have a website if you use marketing automation. If you do not have a website, take care of getting that first. Your website will usually need to be updated with new forms, landing pages, and some JavaScript added to it. This means that your web admin needs to be involved in conversations so that he or she knows what changes will need to take place and whether these changes are possible with your current technology setup.
- **Sales team.** The sales team can be the most vocal, so you *have* to involve them. I suggest that you begin with your highest-ranking sales staff and get them to buy in. It will not be hard if you can easily prove that their staff can cover more ground, get better leads, and close more deals. Do make sure to keep their knowledge focused on only the sales-facing technologies, such as CRM integration and sales enablement, and on what they will need to know and see. I would not involve them in general demonstrations, but rather have a specific sales demo done by your vendor just for the sales team.

Marketing automation isn't just for marketing

When you're asking upper management for another tool, you have a better shot at getting it if you can build a buzz around the impact to the organization as a whole, not just to your department. One of the best ways to do this is to share the ways marketing automation can help your colleagues in other departments. Here are the departments and topics you need to discuss in each department:

- **Lead intelligence for the sales department:** Marketing automation has a big impact on the sales department. Talk to the sales staff about the value of lead tracking and lead scoring, and let them talk to each other about all the things they can do with the information, such as:
  - Know when hot prospects are on the website
  - Know what white paper a lead read
  - Know every page a lead checked out on your website
  - Know in real time when a lead is researching your products
- **Activity reporting for the services department:** Invite your services team to discuss the ways the team might use lead visibility reporting to help mitigate churn rates by using lead tracking. This allows the services staff to see which customers are not using the product so that they can proactively reach out to ensure that they retain these customers. Ask them for input on using lead nurturing tools to stay in front of clients during a long life cycle.
- **Revenue prediction for executives:** Being able to predict future revenues is important for C-level executives in every company. To get your executive team talking, ask a colleague or a sales rep selling marketing automation tools to provide a sample revenue forecast from her marketing automation tool. Then ask your executive team to evaluate the benefits of knowing more details about how much money they are going to make next quarter and how the information might be useful in board meetings and business projections.

Marketing automation has many more benefits to get your organization talking about, but you need to start with these three keys. I also suggest that you find webinars to help spread the idea of marketing automation. Many vendors have webinars, white papers, and ROI calculators to help you. Figure 2-1 shows an ROI calculator provided by Pardot.com to help companies determine the potential increase in revenue with the addition of marketing automation.

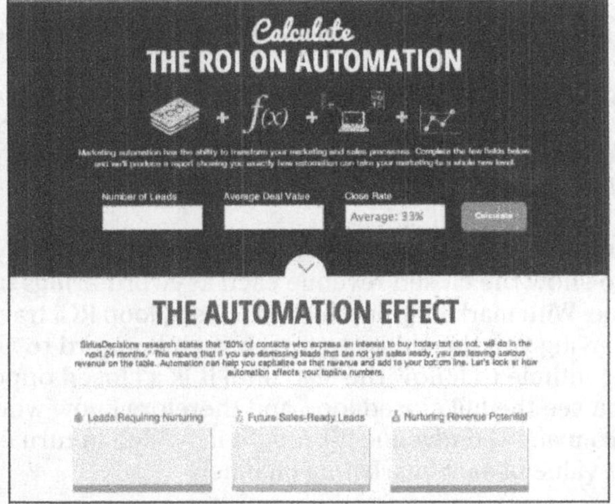

Figure 2-1: An ROI calculator can help you determine the impact of marketing automation on your business.

Driving More Revenue from Your Investment in Online Marketing

Companies are investing more into online marketing every year. Google reported a net profit of $43 billion dollars in 2012, which was an increase by $7 billion dollars from 2011. This increase clearly shows that companies are investing more in online marketing.

Whether your investment in online marketing is increasing or staying the same, marketing is always expected to drive more revenue from those investments, and marketing automation is helping many companies to drive more revenue from all their online marketing efforts. See the "Furthering your investment in online marketing" sidebar for more information on how you can get more value out of your online marketing budget with marketing automation.

The following sections show you where marketing automation can impact revenue in a variety of marketing channels so that you can include those channels in your business case and show how marketing automation adds to the value of your entire marketing program. I discuss combining marketing automation with other online marketing programs in more detail in Chapter 11.

Invigorating search engine marketing

Search engine marketing (SEM) combines placing paid ads on search engines with optimizing web content to display organically in search engine results. Connecting marketing automation to your paid search campaigns gives you three main benefits:

- **Closed-loop ROI tracking:** *Closed-loop ROI tracking* provides you with the ability to show the closed revenue each keyword brings in over a period of time. With marketing automation, closed-loop ROI tracking tracks every lead, giving you the ability to attach each keyword to a prospect record and continue to follow the lead until it is a closed opportunity in the CRM. You see the full closed loop and therefore know where each lead came from and the revenue it brought in, which in turn enables you to prove the value of each marketing channel.
- **Better intelligence for sales:** Because every lead passed to sales through marketing automation has a full history report, including the keywords a prospect searched for, the sales department can use this data to improve its sales process. For example, if your lead searched for your competitor's keyword, a sales representative can assume that it is a competitive deal, and even know who his competition is.
- **More relevant campaigns:** Because marketing automation shows you the keywords that are important to each prospect, you gain the ability to use this information for segmentation, nurturing, and changing your paid search campaigns to match the prospect's interests. These three main benefits of marketing automation for SEM give you the ability to prove your value, identify where your money should be spent, and increase the sales from your SEM budget. As a result, you'll spend less and get more.

Furthering your investment in online marketing

Marketing automation does not work without online marketing, and online marketing is not as effective without marketing automation. You need to continue to invest in both to ensure your success. You should consider investing time for testing new online marketing methods and continually creating new content.

Before you ramp up your online marketing campaigns, do the opposite. Consider putting your online marketing efforts on hold for your first month with a marketing automation tool. This will give you the ability to create a baseline from which you can measure future campaigns.

Read Seth Godin's book *Permission Marketing* (Simon & Schuster, 1999), as well as Peppers and Rogers' *The One to One Future* (Doubleday, 1993), before you begin. These books lay out the foundation of modern marketing for you.

Removing the guesswork from SEO

A website's ability to be found and ranked highly by a search engine is both an art and a science, and achieving it can also require a large investment of time and money. Because all your search engine optimization (SEO) efforts are costly, it's important to prove the value of these efforts, which can easily be tracked with marketing automation.

Most SEO efforts are evaluated on the basis of how many unique visitors you generate and how high your website is ranked when listed on a search results page. Both of these metrics are great, but they are very subjective without the ability to connect them to actual closed business.

Marketing automation allows you to track ROI down to each keyword over a given time frame because the leads and their search terms are being connected, as shown in Figure 2-2.

Natural Search Report

Query Date: All Time   Filter: Tools

Keyword	Unique Searches	Prospects	Opportunities	Opportunity Value	Revenue
Marketing Automation	49,690	3,452	843	$915,252.00	$364,262.00
Marketing Automation Tips	3,182	53	4	$4,000.00	$0.00
Lead Nurturing	2,086	220	48	$42,674.00	$16,406.00
Lead Scoring	1,319	31	0	$0.00	$0.00
Email Marketing	1,288	124	39	$35,340.00	$11,740.00

Figure 2-2: Report showing the ROI on SEO efforts.

Keyword reporting is a basic feature in most marketing automation tools. Connecting a search term to a closed deal is very basic, and you can easily set up tracking so that every lead shows a history of search terms that follows the lead all the way to a closed deal in your CRM. This history of search terms leads to reporting closed business and connecting the cause of the business to every search term, piece of content, and web page. These features can easily give you the information you need to prove the return on your investment and take the subjectivity out of SEO.

Reinforcing your investment in content marketing

Content marketing is one of the hottest topics within B2B marketing today. Creating content involves coming up with new content ideas, creating the content, distributing the content, and tracking its impact to your bottom line. Many of these steps are made easier with marketing automation, helping marketers show the value of content marketing in new ways that weren't possible before.

Creating content involves curating, creating, and producing. Marketing automation gives marketers the ability to test different content, see real-time engagement, and host their online content. The real-time insights such as which content is being read by whom, and how it is influencing people's buying cycles, are insights that can be obtained only when a marketer has a marketing automation tool that can look at each person and his or her engagement with content. The visibility that marketing automation gives a marketer helps remove the guesswork from content creation. Marketing automation also is a single tool that helps people create and publish these content campaigns.

Publishing your content is another time-consuming part of content marketing that marketing automation makes easier. Publishing content through email, blog posts, webinars, and nurturing campaigns all becomes easier when you can use a single tool rather than have to combine multiple tools to execute your content campaigns. Marketing automation allows marketers to create cross-channel, fully tracked, content-promotion campaigns in a single step, saving a lot of time trying to connect disparate channels and tools. You can more easily publish content with deeper insights that provide marketers with better feedback than ever before on their campaigns.

The feedback obtained is then used to help refine and curate as well as to prove the value of the content marketing campaigns. ROI reporting allows a marketer to tie revenue back to the content that either influenced or generated the revenue directly. Marketers can therefore prove the value of their more resource-heavy campaigns.

Trying to ask for a budget for a new piece of content is difficult. It is hard to justify paying a speaker $15,000 for a webinar if you cannot track sales associated with the webinar. Likewise, it's hard to justify creating a $10,000 ebook if you can't prove that it will deliver sufficient closed business. Using marketing automation in conjunction with your content strategy will make justifying future content efforts easier, as well.

Making sense of social marketing's impact to your bottom line

The largest barrier that companies face before investing in social marketing is their ability to prove its value. Marketing automation can easily solve this problem as well by looking at social media as a publishing platform for your content.

Through marketing automation, you can track each person's engagement with your social posts and combine the engagement activity such as lead scoring, with other data in your marketing automation system (see Figure 2-3).

Prospect Activities

Activity	Type	Campaign	Score	Date / Time
Custom Redirect: SugarCRM	Click	blog.pardot.com	2	Mar 28, 2011 4:39 PM
Visit: 23 page views Google Natural Search - search term: pardot forms Twitter	Visit	blog.pardot.com	23	Mar 28, 2011 4:40 PM
Page View: Pricing - Pardot	View	Pardot.com general tracking	5	Mar 28, 2011 8:18 PM
Form: Marketing Automation Buyer's Guide	View	Pardot.com general tracking	0	Mar 28, 2011 8:20 PM
Email: Marketing Automation Buyer's Guide Link	Sent	Pardot.com general tracking	0	Mar 28, 2011 8:20 PM

« Previous Page 36 of 89 Next »

Figure 2-3: Showing a prospect's engagement with Twitter and its effect on that prospect's lead score.

You can track any social channel, such as LinkedIn, Twitter, Facebook, or other channels in the same way. You can also connect each interaction on social media to a lead record that can then show the ROI of social media and prove its value to your organization.

Proving marketing's contribution to revenue

Before marketing automation, most marketers were looked at as an expense, not as a source of revenue. The problem was mainly attributed to the fact that the only reports available for marketing were subjective. When each tool operates in its own world, it is very hard to share data, and to connect marketing activities to closed revenue, because no clear paper trail exists. Just consider any report that you have to create whose data comes from two different places. With email and closed revenue, for example, many email tools can show you how many opens you had, but very rarely can you tie those opens directly to revenue because no connection exists between the two data sets. Any marketing automation tool can now combine these two data sets into one standard report because you're using a single tool that shares all the same data.

When looking to find money for your marketing automation solution, you can easily cut back on a single campaign and reinvest this money in a marketing automation solution. The visibility of the reporting alone will help you better invest the remaining monies in the most effective campaigns. I've seen plenty of companies cut back their paid search by a small margin to reinvest this money in marketing automation. As a result, they were able to drive significantly more leads with less but more effective spending.

Marketing automation systems can produce quantifiable reports showing the revenue generated from each campaign so that a marketer can prove value to the organization. Figure 2-4 shows the reporting that is available if you have a single marketing automation platform for execution of online campaigns.

The ability for a marketing automation tool to connect to a CRM is also a key component to allow for ROI tracking. ROI tracking can become an automated report that does not require a marketer to move, manipulate, or tabulate data. Removing the frustration of reporting is a smaller value of marketing automation. The larger value is being able to create reports that you simply could not create before. The example I give earlier in this section about seeing the actual revenue generated from an email campaign is a great example of a report that was not previously available but is now a standard report for just about any marketing automation tool.

After a CRM is connected to your marketing automation solution, it becomes very easy to see which side of the house is driving more revenue. This also takes marketing from being a cost center to a revenue center.

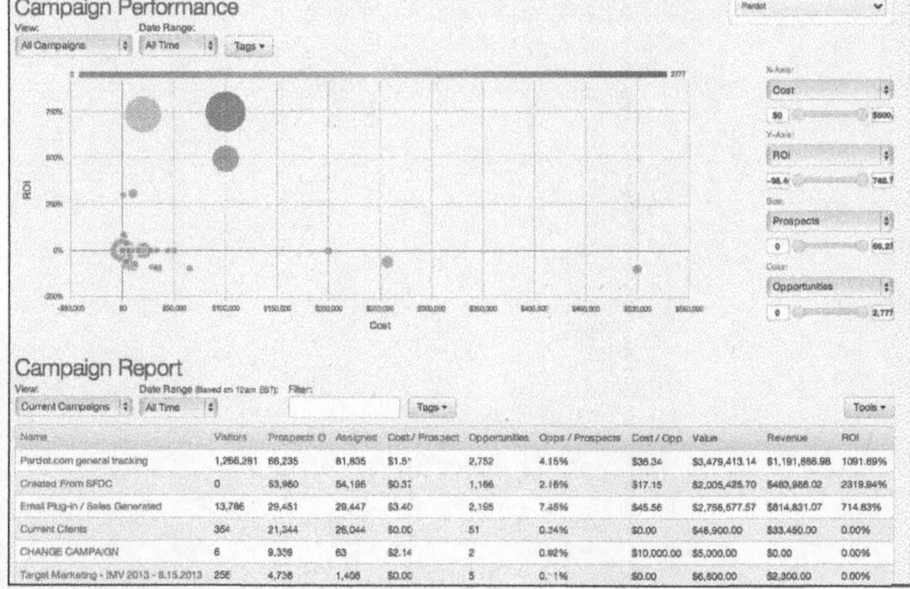

Name	Visitors	Prospects	Assigned	Cost / Prospect	Opportunities	Opps / Prospects	Cost / Opp	Value	Revenue	ROI
Pardot.com general tracking	1,266,281	66,235	81,835	$1.5	2,752	4.15%	$36.34	$3,479,413.14	$1,191,666.98	1091.69%
Created From SFDC	0	53,960	54,196	$0.37	1,166	2.16%	$17.15	$2,005,425.70	$483,966.02	2319.94%
Email Plug-in / Sales Generated	13,786	29,451	29,447	$3.40	2,195	7.45%	$45.56	$2,756,677.57	$614,831.07	714.83%
Current Clients	354	21,344	26,044	$0.00	51	0.24%	$0.00	$48,900.00	$33,450.00	0.00%
CHANGE CAMPAIGN	6	9,339	63	$2.14	2	0.02%	$10,000.00	$5,000.00	$0.00	0.00%
Target Marketing - IMV 2013 - 8.15.2013	256	4,736	1,406	$0.00	5	0.1%	$0.00	$6,600.00	$2,300.00	0.00%

Figure 2-4: ROI reporting shows marketing's contribution to revenue.

Chapter 3

Choosing a Marketing Automation Solution

In This Chapter

- ▶ Aligning your solution with key marketing goals
- ▶ Estimating investments in time and effort
- ▶ Choosing the right level of technology

Assuming that you've bought into the idea of getting a marketing automation solution at this point, now it's time to show you how to pick the correct one. I don't talk about vendors, because these will come and go over time. Instead, in this chapter, I tell you how to identify your core goals, set realistic expectations, and judge the actual time it will take to implement a solution. From here, you should be able to identify the vendors who are the best fit for your company.

Aligning a Solution with Core Marketing Goals

Marketing automation can offer a wide range of benefits, but most companies are content to buy marketing automation to help achieve one or a few marketing goals in the short term. You should focus on a few short-term goals and a few key features of marketing automation for the best results initially. The rest of your goals can wait until you master your tools and the details of marketing automation. Knowing which benefits of marketing automation are key to your marketing goals is the first major step in getting a marketing automation solution. The most common goals are the following:

- **Generate more leads:** If you start looking at marketing automation to generate more leads, stay focused on the ease of creating lead-nurturing campaigns and reporting on those campaigns.
- **Do more with the same size marketing team:** If your team is small, stay focused on the support, ease of use, flexibility of the platform, and training the company provides.

- **Consolidate multiple marketing tools:** If you are looking to streamline your marketing department, stay focused on integrations with your core marketing channels and on ease of use.
- **Better align sales and marketing:** If you are looking to better align sales and marketing, stay focused on CRM integration and sales enablement.
- **Prove the value of marketing efforts:** If you need more data to report on the impact of your marketing programs, focus on reporting and data collection.

Getting into marketing automation is a process, and each step builds upon the ones before it. So, start small and go *slowly*. That way, your goals can grow with your tool. Don't forget, your world isn't going to stop to let you buy a tool. You will continue to evaluate solutions and take care of your other daily responsibilities as well. So, easing into it will help you keep all your hair.

Setting realistic expectations

Gartner reports that companies using lead nurturing generate 451 percent more qualified leads than companies who don't. Although that is an amazing statistic, you shouldn't expect that you can buy a marketing automation solution today and generate an exponential increase tomorrow.

Marketing automation is a discipline just as any other form of marketing is. It requires a full understanding of the technology, the techniques, and the consumer behaviors that drive higher levels of engagement. Setting clear expectations over time helps you judge your performance and pace your implementation. To set realistic expectations, keep the following ideas in mind:

- **Marketing automation is a continuous process.** Becoming proficient at marketing automation takes a lot of time, although the effort required to begin is small. Focus on getting up and running today, and then focus on improving over time. Don't try to be perfect at each step. Instead, improve at each step by getting a little better than you were before.
- **Time is required to be successful.** Whatever your goals may be, success will take time no matter what solution you choose. You have to spend a lot of time on the front end before and during implementation, and less time as you become more proficient with your tool. Consider spending a few weeks to set up your tool, and a few hours per week for making improvements after you're set up.
- **CRM is a limiting factor.** Your CRM is a major part of what you will be able to accomplish with a marketing automation tool. If you have an in-house CRM, make sure that you understand how your in-house capabilities will define your integration requirements. If you are using an off-the-shelf CRM solution, you need to understand your product's limits and connection types, have access to your CRM administrator, and know that he or she is ready and able to help. Your CRM connections will likely be the most complicated piece of your setup, as well as the most limiting if your CRM can't support the connections you need or the programs you want to run. I explain CRM setup in Chapter 5.

Tips from Scotland's leading marketing automation experts on picking a tool

You may be asking, why Scotland? Well, consider that Scotland is a very small geographic area. Companies that operate in a specific geographic region are just like many businesses that have small addressable markets. These tips should help you see some key points for smaller companies, or those in international markets. They also show you the impact that marketing automation is already having around the world as it becomes an increasingly global trend. I've been fortunate enough to speak with McRae & Company, Scotland's leading marketing automation experts, and they have a few suggestions for companies just getting started with marketing automation:

Tip #1: Ensure that you have executive sponsorship.

First and foremost, marketing automation is the business response to the changing behavior of the modern customer. Whereas sales teams were once the gatekeepers of product information, these days the empowered buyer conducts her own research and speaks to a salesperson only when she is ready. Understanding the self-guided nature of the buyer's journey is essential to grasping the significance of marketing automation for an entire organization, and it's imperative that this message be understood from the top. In truth, nothing hinders a marketing automation initiative more than missing executive sponsorship.

Without strong leadership, the investment appears inconsequential to many departments, and the necessity for alignment is significantly underplayed. At a time when executive teams are more ROI-focused than ever before, it's easy for marketing automation to be erroneously dismissed as yet another expense. Consequently, time and effort must be spent presenting the full business case to senior management to secure support and capture the imaginations of the rest of the organization as a result. If someone is not on board or simply does not understand the concept, it's crucial to address this in the planning stages and highlight the need for operational change in today's era of the empowered customer. Frankly, without a senior management mindset behind it, alignment will not succeed.

Tip #2: Consider what you really need.

As more vendors have entered the marketing automation arena, the temptation for small enterprises to progress with the first vendor they come into contact with (generally, those with the largest marketing budgets) can be easy to succumb to; this is always a risk. Rather than there being a one-size-fits-all solution, it's crucial to remember that most platforms are designed with specific budgets, resources, and priorities in mind. At the selection stage, it's important to consider areas like product complexity, market maturity, and sales cycle length.

Tip #3: Develop a demand generation strategy with both sales and marketing.

Many small and medium enterprises (SMEs) incorrectly view content creation as the most significant hurdle to overcome when planning for marketing. Yet, the reality is that prior to this stage, and perhaps even prior to the evaluation of a marketing automation solution, the marketing team, sales team, and executive sponsor should spend significant time crafting a demand generation strategy that aligns with the business objectives and considers precisely how a lead will move through an improved funnel. The better defined this strategy is in the planning stages, the easier it is to identify exactly the kind of content that is needed and to maximize its effectiveness. An all-encompassing demand generation strategy is the true king of modern marketing and should cover all areas — from scoring rules, lead-nurturing tactics, and renurturing loops to buyer personas, handover points, and key performance indicators (KPIs). This streamlining ensures that marketing's efforts are in line with the expectations of the sales team and underpinned by marketing automation, and it empowers small-staffed SMEs to achieve, and often outdo, the results of larger competitors.

Determining the need for a custom integration vs. an out-of-the-box connection

If you are using a popular CRM application such as Salesforce.com, SugarCRM, Microsoft Dynamics CRM, or NetSuite, it's easy to find a marketing automation tool with built-in connections. If you are using a custom-built CRM or an industry-specific CRM, you probably need a custom integration. Either way, you have three ways to evaluate your solution based on your chosen CRM against your marketing automation tool, from basic to advanced, as follows. The level of sophistication you require, and your tools, will dictate which is correct for you.

- **Basic: Manual import and export.** If you choose a marketing automation solution with this feature, you have the option of CRM alignment without any integration at all, but it limits your ability for dynamic interaction. This option is best if you have a custom CRM, no API option, or a CRM that is not supported by your marketing automation tools with an out-of-the-box connection feature.

  Manually importing and exporting requires a CSV file to share your data between your CRM and your marketing automation system. Importing via the CSV file type saves you 60–80 hours of custom API development and still gives you the ability to report marketing campaign ROI. This basic connection, however, limits your ability to pass leads back and forth between systems in real time. Manually importing data is also a great option to help keep your beginning marketing automation implementation simple while still achieving your goals regardless of whether your tool supports your CRM.

- **Standard: Out-of-the-box connection.** Most CRM connections can easily be installed without a lot of IT support because the marketing automation system is ready "out of the box," with connection features for nontechnical folks. This is the best of the three options when you can find it. However, the more customized your CRM needs to be, the less likely you are to find an out-of-the-box connection that works for your CRM. Check with your vendor to see whether this is an option for you.

- **Most Complex: Custom API integration.** An *application programming interface* (API) is developer-speak for a gateway that connects two software systems through a programming language. If you are not familiar with API programming, you need to find someone who is. This may be your IT team, or you may have to hire an outside consultant to help.

  Expect building out the API to take between 60 and 80 hours of custom work to integrate your solutions. This option is the best choice if you have a custom CRM and the resources to build the connections. Only about 10 percent of companies choose this route because of cost and complexities.

APIs are not just for big companies. If you have a smaller CRM, such as Zoho or others, you may find prebuilt APIs to help you integrate your CRM with your marketing automation tool without the need to invest in a large API project. Check out cloud connector services or prebuilt services such as Kevy.com.

Finding the correct level of technology

Because marketing automation inevitably involves bringing new technology in-house, your business case should recommend the technology with the right level of efficiency gains within your budget. Three levels of marketing automation technology are worth considering:

- **Basic automation:** Allows for connectivity of a few main channels — usually email, website, and a CRM. These tools allow for the basic campaigns to happen but do not lend themselves to large-scale campaigns. These tools are best suited for very small companies with fewer than five employees. The cost of these tools is also very low.
- **SMB automation:** Best for companies that need very easy-to-use tools but have an appetite for more advanced campaigns. Usually, companies that have 10–300 employees and do not have very advanced needs adopt these tools.
- **Enterprise automation:** For the very advanced companies that need ultimate customization, flexibility, and the most robust tool set they can afford. These solutions generally require you to hire additional people dedicated to running the marketing automation solution because of its complexities. Usually, enterprise companies use these solutions.

After choosing a marketing automation level to recommend to your company, you should consider the following individual factors to help you further refine your needs:

- **Database size:** The size of your database dictates the cost of your solution and the need for database features within your application. If your database is very large, you probably need more advanced features to tackle all the possible scenarios you'll likely face. Consider a small database as having fewer than 10,000 contacts in your database, and a large database as having more than 120,000 total contacts. Your database includes customers, prospects, and cold leads.
- **Users:** You need to decide how many users will have to have access to the solution to achieve the results you are looking for. Remember that if you want to increase the revenue coming into your organization, every salesperson might have to have a license for the software as well so that salespeople can take advantage of the lead-tracking tools. This is important to know because some tools charge you based on the number of users who use the application.

Don't overbuy; here's why

It's easy to get trapped into thinking that the more technology you buy, the more efficiency you will gain. That line of thinking can get you in trouble and cause you to overbuy and spend too much money on features you won't use. To avoid overbuying, understand your team's level of comfort with technology. If you're on a very tech savvy team, a more complex solution might be a good fit. But if your team is not tech savvy, stick to a solution that will allow you to execute your current campaigns using a less complicated approach. Remember to stay focused on the main goals you are trying to solve with marketing automation and you'll end up with the right level of technology.

- **Other integrations:** Make sure that your tool will connect with your CRM, content management system (CMS), and other marketing channels. Generally, the more connections you require, the higher your costs will become and the more efficient you can make your connections.

Estimating Your Total Investment in Marketing Automation

Investing in a solution involves a large commitment of time, resources, and new processes. Many people underestimate some of these investments when investigating marketing automation. Most companies adopt new tools rather quickly and fail to notice the fact that marketing automation is as much a new way of thinking as it is a new tool.

Marketing automation requires more than just spending money to buy a technology solution. The largest portion of spending happens through your time, effort, and indirect costs. The following sections outline the indirect investments that are the most often overlooked when preparing for marketing automation.

Judging the time required to build campaigns

When a vendor tells you that one of his product's features is "ease of use," it doesn't mean the same thing as "no time required." Marketing automation is a platform requiring work to set up and run.

Campaigns usually take a lot of time to set up initially and generally consist of multiple moving parts, each requiring differing amounts of time to create and manage. The most common parts of a campaign are forms, landing pages, emails, content, and reports. Here's some advice to help estimate the time required to set up the following items:

- **Forms:** Most campaigns involve a form to collect email addresses. With marketing automation, you can generally build a form and use it multiple times. The misjudgment of time comes in when people start adding complexities to their forms. Proper planning will help you identify the appropriate complexity and help you judge the time required to build your forms. Basic forms can take ten minutes, whereas complex forms can take an hour or more.
- **Landing pages:** Landing pages are generally used in conjunction with a form. Most marketing automation tools allow you to build your form and landing page at the same time. Most tools offer a variety of complex features for landing pages such as using dynamic forms, split testing multiple versions for maximum results, and offering personalized content. Make sure that you understand how your landing page and form builder work. If you are not HTML proficient, make sure to work in adequate time to play with the tool so that you understand the time and skill required to build what you need. These little features can make a big difference.
- **Emails:** Emails are the most overlooked asset in a marketing automation campaign, and they typically account for the largest misjudgment of time. Most companies think that marketing automation involves building one email at a time, but actually it's not uncommon to need to build ten emails at one time for a lead-nurturing campaign. Plan to invest one hour per email template when you begin. After you have a template set up, this time requirement should sharply decline. Before building your emails for lead nurturing, make sure to educate yourself on how to build an email for lead nurturing. That kind of email is very different from emails used for mass email blasting.
- **Content:** Emails, landing pages, databases, and reports all require someone to create content. For example, if you have ten emails in your lead-nurturing campaign, you need a minimum of ten pieces of content to send in those emails. Many companies cite this need for content as their biggest time sink in creating a campaign as well as the biggest reason people hold off on marketing automation.
- **Reports:** Creating the appropriate tracking for each campaign is usually overlooked because it hasn't been included in all your marketing campaigns before. Estimate about an hour for each campaign to set up the proper tracking and reporting. Use your time to make sure that your links, forms, and emails will give you the required information to evaluate your effectiveness.

Judging other time requirements

You shouldn't expect to put more than a few hours a week into managing a marketing automation application after it is up and running. The major investment of time is all on the front end. In addition to estimating the time it takes to set up your campaigns, you should also estimate time for education, training, planning, and database cleanup as follows:

- **Education:** The best time to invest in educating yourself on marketing automation techniques is before you buy a solution. That way, you are more likely to find out what you need as you learn to think completely differently about everything from email to content. The time to read and attend seminars and webinars should be added to your time estimate. I recommend focusing your education on the topics of lead tracking, behavioral data, and modern lead nurturing. Having a grasp of these topics will save you countless hours in the future. Estimate at least 10–20 hours of learning before you evaluate tools.
- **Training:** Training for you and all your stakeholders needs to be taken into account. Training yourself can range from ten hours to a full week, even for the easiest-to-use tools. No matter how easy a tool is or how intuitive it may be, you and your stakeholders need to be trained to use it. You should plan time for training your sales team as well. Vendors should provide this training as part of your solution. If not, ask for training during your purchase negotiations.
- **Planning:** You should spend a good amount of time outlining and planning for your needs before you buy a tool. Estimate five hours of planning before you buy a tool, and five to ten hours of planning for how to meet your needs with your specific tool after you have gone through your education. Remember the advice of "This Old House" host Bob Vila, who always said, "Measure twice and cut once."
- **Database cleanup:** Most companies forget to consider time spent cleaning up their database in their planning. Your database is likely very bad if you have not cleaned it up for a few years. On average, most companies I see have a database with bad email addresses accounting for 30 percent or more of their database. This is especially true for companies that have bought a list of email addresses at any time in the past. I discuss database cleanup in detail in Chapter 5.

Chapter 4

Setting Up a New Marketing Automation Tool

In This Chapter

- Developing a step-by-step plan
- Identifying efficiencies and quick wins
- Activating your solution and working with IT

Before you begin implementing a marketing automation program, you need to have your house in order and set up your tool. You're going to need buy-in from other stakeholders and commitments of time to develop content and integrate technologies. You'll be asking your organization to shift in a few different directions, and support from other departments is necessary to make your implementation a success.

In this chapter, I explain how to plan ahead and complete the preparation necessary to set you up for success. I also tell you what you need to know before you begin setting up your chosen tool. This chapter also covers the most common issues companies encounter when implementing marketing automation, and how to avoid them.

Listing Resources Needed for Initial Setup

You need a few specific items and resources to implement your solution. The following sections explain the steps involved and show you how to assemble your team. Setup preparation involves listing the resources you need, blocking time on your IT team's calendar, and getting the rest of your stakeholders on board.

Breaking down your integration into steps

Implementing your marketing automation tool can easily be broken down into three overarching steps, shown in Table 4-1.You should take the steps in the table in the order they appear if you have never implemented a marketing automation tool before.

Table 4-1 Basic Implementation Steps with Time Estimates

Step	*Items Required*	*Estimated Time*
Step 1: Connecting	IT resource	1 hour
	Authenticating email tool, creating CNAME	2 hours
	CRM admin, website admin	2 hours plus 5 minutes per custom field
Step 2: Importing	Email templates	25 minutes per template
	Nurturing templates	15 minutes per template
	Auto responder templates	20 minutes per template
	Landing page templates	1 hour upper template
	Data sets in CSV file (CLEANED)	10 hours of uploading
Step 3: Building	List of quick wins	1 hour meeting
	Nurturing program outlines	5–10 hours
	Sales lead qualification process and scoring process	5 hours of planning with your sales team
	Form layout	5 hours
	Segmentation ideas	2 hours

The connecting process includes various levels because each marketing channel and each data source requires a new connection. However, many of these connections aren't required for you to begin, and they can be implemented over time as you turn on additional functionality. Connecting your website, customer relationship management (CRM), and marketing channels is most important. In the connecting stage, you need to work hand in hand with your IT department. If you are your IT department, you'll need to have full access to your technical infrastructure. I suggest getting a hand from someone because these first steps can take a while if you're inexperienced, but they can be done in under an hour by an experienced IT professional.

After you are connected, you can begin to import your HTML and data sets. In the beginning, you need only a few basic templates. Plan to further develop the basic templates over time. This process is relatively easy and is completely based on how prepared you are before you get to this step. If you have spent adequate time educating yourself, you should have specific templates ready for your marketing automation tool and can quickly import them.

After your data sets are imported, you can start building your assets as well as your automations. This step involves specific knowledge of your tool and may require you to be trained on your tool before you begin. I cover the basics of how to build forms, landing pages, scoring models, and automations throughout the rest of the book.

Make sure that you have all your resources ready before you begin implementation. Many times, I see companies stall their implementation because they have not prepared their templates, don't know what data sets they want to use, and haven't thought out their automations yet. Don't forget your data sets, which include but are not limited to items such as a list of prospects, sales data, email lists, and any other set of information you need to run segmentation or an automation. Save time during implementation and have these items ready when you begin.

Committing to developing content

Most companies that engage in online marketing understand the value of creating content. Content provides search engine optimization (SEO) value, backlinks, and the benefits of thought leadership. When preparing for marketing automation, don't neglect to commit to an investment in content. Your commitment should include creating new content, testing new content mediums, and learning to use content in new ways. Here's what I mean in more detail:

- **Creating new content:** Your marketing automation tool will help you identify which content you should be creating, but you need to commit to the time and resources to build new pieces of content. Estimate creating a minimum of three to four new pieces of content per quarter.
- **Testing new content mediums:** New content also needs to be tested across new mediums. You will easily be able to test effectiveness with your marketing automation reporting functionality. For example, you should plan tests such as watching conversions to determine whether a video converts more prospects to customers when hosted on your site or on YouTube. You need to set aside time for constant testing, because testing leads to small increases in effectiveness of your programs over time.
- **Learning to use content in new ways:** A single piece of content can be used in many different ways. You can save time if your main content can be broken up into smaller pieces of content for use in emails and landing

pages. For example, a 15-page white paper can be divided into three separate five-page pieces targeted to a different step in the buying cycle. This breakdown will help you get more time savings out of a content effort and maximize your value at the same time.

Teaming up for best results

You need a team of people to make your implementation successful. Following is an overview of each person or group you are likely to need, and a brief description of what that person will be doing over the course of the implementation.

- **Marketing team:** Responsible for email creation, forms, landing page look and feel, lead flow process, nurturing program design, and PPC integration.
- **Webmaster:** Responsible for placing JavaScript tracking code within the element of web pages and for implementing iFrame code for your forms.
- **IT admin:** Responsible for creating vanity domain records (as in `www2.`*`yourdomain`*`.com`) and implementing email authentication with DKIM, Domain Keys, SPF, and SenderID. I discuss setting up email authentication in Chapter 10.
- **Marketing agency (if applicable):** Responsible for overall online marketing, lead management, and lead nurturing strategy, as well as for landing page and email asset creation.
- **Sales leadership:** Responsible for coordinating sales training, adopting of email plug-in, and working with marketing to set lead assignment processes.
- **CRM admin (if applicable):** Responsible for installing the marketing automation module into your CRM, setting up custom fields and layouts (should they be required), and adding any other required integrations, which may include iFrames and possibly custom code.

Furthering your investment in online marketing

Marketing automation does not work without online marketing, and online marketing is not as effective without marketing automation. You need to continue to invest in both to ensure your success. You should consider investing time for testing new online marketing methods and continually creating new content.

Before you ramp up your online marketing campaigns, do the opposite. Consider putting your online marketing efforts on hold for your first month with a marketing automation tool. This will give you the ability to create a baseline, from which you can measure future campaigns.

Read Seth Godin's book *Permission Marketing,* as well as Peppers and Rogers' *The One to One Future,* before you begin. These books lay out the foundation for modern marketing for you.

Targeting Efficiency in Your Implementation

Automating your marketing activities allows you and your company to remove many of the manual tasks performed on a daily basis. That way, you can become a much more efficient organization.

The next sections show you how to identify your efficiency gains and include them in your initial implementation. I also explain how to identify quick wins and bottlenecks in your marketing funnel so that you can focus your implementation on the efficiencies your organization needs in return for the money invested.

Identifying your quick wins and major pain points

When setting up your tool, start by focusing on quick wins. *Quick wins* are the first three or more efficiency gains that will return the largest benefits soonest after implementing your solution. By focusing on quick wins, your implementation will gain the most efficiency in the shortest amount of time.

The following list of quick wins contains the most common marketing activities that can be made more efficient through automation:

- Lead qualification
- Lead scoring
- List management
- List cleaning
- Lead assignment
- ROI reporting
- Lead nurturing

In addition to the aforementioned quick wins of marketing automation, there are also many benefits of automation to look forward to and to include in your initial implementation.

Efficiency equates to financial savings

Many analysts have measured financial savings after marketing automation is adopted by a company. Gartner Research reports a 15 percent savings on creative production as a result of implementing marketing automation.

A savings of 15 percent on the cost of creative production is very significant and usually will easily cover the cost of a solution. However, people don't buy marketing automation for cost savings. Look at cost savings as a bonus, and stay focused on building a sovereign department that can execute all your required activities without the need for external resources such as IT support.

After identifying your most compelling quick wins, you should define your largest business efficiency frustrations, using the following list as a guide. A company without marketing automation is likely to experience at least one of the following four major weaknesses, or "pain" points:

- **Lack of IT efficiency:** You experience inefficiency when creating, executing, reporting on, and managing online campaigns due to limited technical knowledge. Or, you may be beholden to your IT department for your HTML needs, website updates, or connecting data between tools because you can't execute these efforts without IT support. I explain how marketing automation removes the need for additional IT by giving you tools to work with these features without technical knowledge.
- **Disconnected marketing tools:** Manual efforts, such as data exporting or manual reporting, are frustrating due to the lack of connectivity between your marketing tools, and you find yourself often using spreadsheets to keep track of prospect interactions across tools.
- **Cumbersome lead generation:** You experience a lack of efficiency when managing, tracking, and increasing your lead flow with the same budget.
- **Lack of alignment between marketing and sales:** Your marketing and sales departments spend time and energy arguing over lead quality, lead flow, lead assignment, or campaign reporting.

Identifying quick wins and major pain points are the fastest ways to realize the value of your marketing automation tool and will provide you with a solid foundation for future expansion of that tool. As you evaluate marketing automation and prove its value over time, many aspects of it will provide you with continuous value.

Uncovering the bottlenecks in your marketing workflow

In order for your implementation to dig further into the value of efficiency gained through marketing automation, consider where automation is most likely to impact the bottlenecks in your marketing workflow. *Bottlenecks* are places in your marketing operations where an inefficient process causes a fast operation to slow down. Your implementation should focus on the specific places where automation will help you gain efficiency by eliminating bottlenecks. To identify your bottlenecks, follow these simple steps:

1. **Whiteboard your current marketing world.**

   Start by drawing your full marketing universe. Include every lead-generation channel, marketing channel, and tool that you use to execute these. Draw them on a whiteboard so that you can make sure you understand the flow of data and the processes you currently use.

2. **Circle your pain points.**

   With a different color, circle your pain points. Bottlenecks often happen one step before or after a pain point.

3. **Make a list of the bottlenecks that cause your pain points.**

   Prioritize the list by identifying which of your bottlenecks will have the largest impact on your main marketing goals when eliminated.

4. **Circle your pain points.**

If you can identify your largest bottleneck, and work just to solve that one issue during your first year of using a marketing automation tool, you will derive significant value from your purchase. Move on to smaller bottlenecks later. Identifying these bottlenecks before you purchase a solution also helps you to select the correct tool. I discuss choosing the right solution in Chapter 3.

First Steps to Activating Your Solution

After you've done your initial preparation, as described in the previous sections of this chapter, you should be ready to start playing with the technology. You want to take setting up the system very seriously. Doing the setup wrong will cause you a lot of frustration. I suggest making sure that you have all your team members ready to go and have time booked on the calendars of both your IT admin and your webmaster.

Creating your alias

Your *alias* is the "vanity name" you will be using. It is also referred to as a CNAME. The reason you need to set up an alias is that 99.9 percent of all marketing automation solutions are software-as-a-service (SaaS)-based technologies. This means that they are hosted online, not on your servers. Because your marketing automation tool is not on your servers, landing pages created in your tool will not appear to be hosted by your company unless you create a vanity URL to fix this. See Figure 4-1 to see the difference between a landing page that has a vanity URL and one that does not.

For example, if you are using Pardot.com as your solution, and your company is site.com, you need to set up a CNAME so that all landing pages and emails that are sent from Pardot.com reflect your company's name. So you will need to set up a CNAME, which might be `go.site.com`.

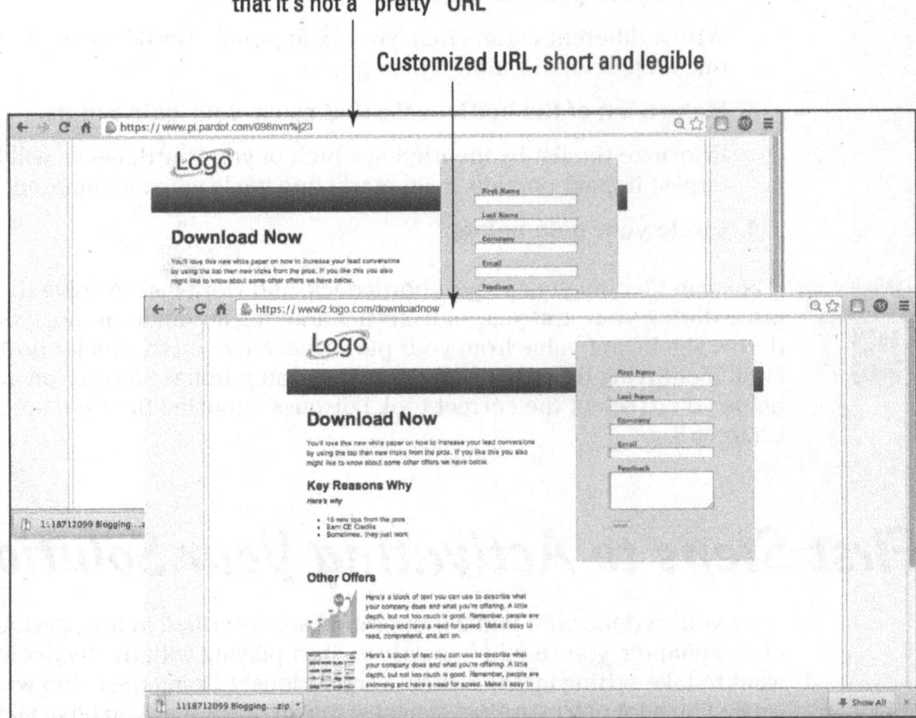

Figure 4-1: Landing page with a vanity URL vs. one without a vanity URL.

Here are the steps you should take to create your CNAME. Figure 4-2 shows an example of what you need for setup.

Alias (Examples)	Type	Points To
go.yoursite.com **www2**.yoursite.com **info**.yoursite.com	CNAME	go.pardot.com

Figure 4-2: Create a CNAME using an alias, type, and points.

You need access to your web hosting service to complete the following steps:

1. **Choose your CNAME/Alias.**

   This process is required by the majority of marketing automation tools; however, depending on your hosting service, details may vary from what I describe here. Hosting companies generally use the same process, but you might notice slight differences from these steps. You are free to choose any alias you'd like, but I recommend something unobtrusive to give your visitors the best possible user experience. For example, if your domain is `www.site.com`, I recommend `www2.site.com`, which is commonly used in marketing. Other options are

   - `go.site.com`
   - `content.site.com`
   - `info.site.com`
   - `news.site.com`
   - `marketing.site.com`

2. **Log in to your domain's DNS record.**

   Your *DNS record* is the record on your IP address that SPAM filters use to verify whether emails sent from your vendor are really okay to send. The DNS entry allows the SPAM filter to ping your IP address and verify that the emails are really being sent by you. This is to protect you from people hijacking your email tool and spamming the world. You need to set up three things inside your DNS record:

   - Alias
   - Type
   - Points to

3. **Wait for your DNS to propagate.**

   Keep checking your DNS record account. It may take up to 24 hours.

4. **Log in to your marketing automation tool to edit your account settings.**

   Each tool requires you to do this in a different way, but you need to insert the alias information in to your system.

5. **Verify that your CNAME is working correctly.**

   If everything is set up correctly and your DNS change has taken effect, entering your vanity into a browser should redirect to your home page. That is the easiest way to verify that your new CNAME is working correctly.

Adding tracking code to your website

Tracking code is a small piece of code you will be placing on your site. The tracking code places a cookie on each person's browser. A *cookie* is a small tracking beacon used to follow people's actions while on your site. The process of adding tracking code to your website will vary based on how your website is set up. If you are, like most companies, using a content management system (CMS) such as WordPress or Drupal, the addition of the tracking codes should be fairly easy. If you don't have a content-management system, you need your webmaster to assist you in this process. Adding the tracking code is a simple copy-and-paste operation. The trick is in knowing where to paste the code, as I explain in the upcoming steps.

Cookies can be controversial, especially depending on the country you're in. Many European countries have different laws regarding what you may or may not do with cookies. I suggest researching this issue first before you use them. In most countries (including the USA), it is sufficient to place a note in the terms and conditions of your website stating that your website uses cookies and that by using your website, users agree to your terms of use. However, you should check with your local laws to be sure.

Follow these steps to add tracking code to your website:

1. **Obtain your tracking code in your marketing automation tool.**

   The code is a piece of JavaScript, as shown in Figure 4-3. Depending on your tool, this piece of code may be short or long; the code varies from one tool to another.

```
<script type="text/javascript">
piAId = '1001';
piCId = '83807';

(function() {
    function async_load(){
        var s = document.createElement('script'); s.type = 'text/javascript';
        s.src = ('https:' == document.location.protocol ? 'https://pi' : 'http://cdn') + '.pardot.com/pd.js';
        var c = document.getElementsByTagName('script')[0]; c.parentNode.insertBefore(s, c);
    }
    if(window.attachEvent) { window.attachEvent('onload', async_load); }
    else { window.addEventListener('load', async_load, false); }
})();
</script>
```

Figure 4-3: Tracking code is JavaScript found in your marketing automation tool.

2. **Locate your global footer in your content management system.**

   For example, Figure 4-4 shows the global footer in a WordPress website. If you don't have a content management system, your webmaster needs to complete this step and the next step for you.

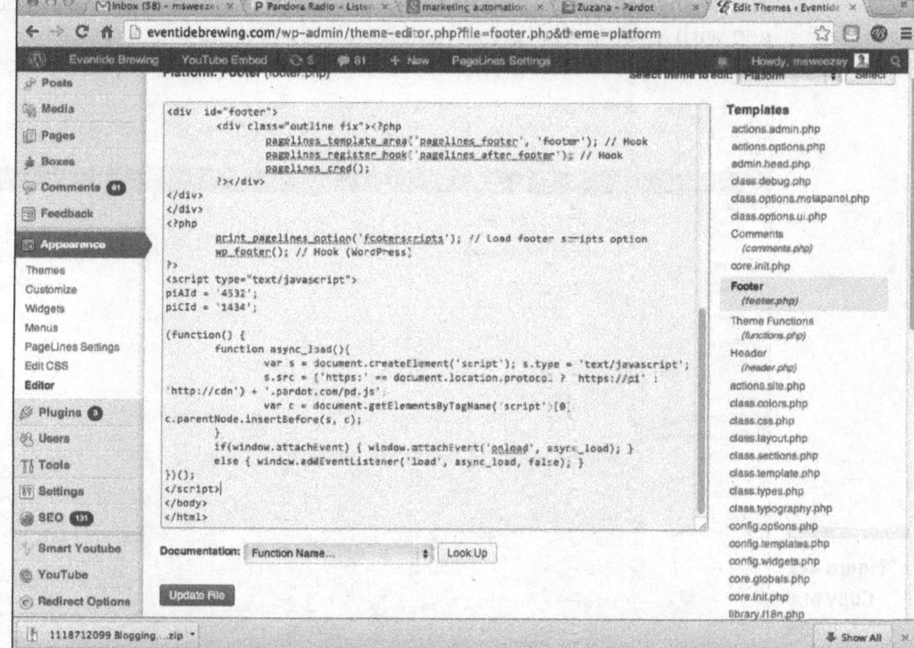

Figure 4-4: The global footer of a WordPress site, where your tracking code goes.

3. **When you have found your tracking code and located your global footer, copy and paste your tracking code into the footer.**

   Figure 4-5 shows tracking code from the Pardot marketing automation system properly placed in the global footer of a content management system. Make sure to paste the code into every web property you own.

Most marketing automation tools let you customize your code to allow for specific parameters to be passed through to your solution. For example, you can customize your code for scoring and segmenting directly on the page a person is on. You can code the page to increase a person's score directly if she visits the page, or change her lead source after visiting your blog so that you know which deals your blog influenced.

Importing assets into your marketing automation tool

The next sections show you how to import four different assets into your marketing automation tool. *Assets* are any piece of content that you plan to use with your marketing automation tool, such as

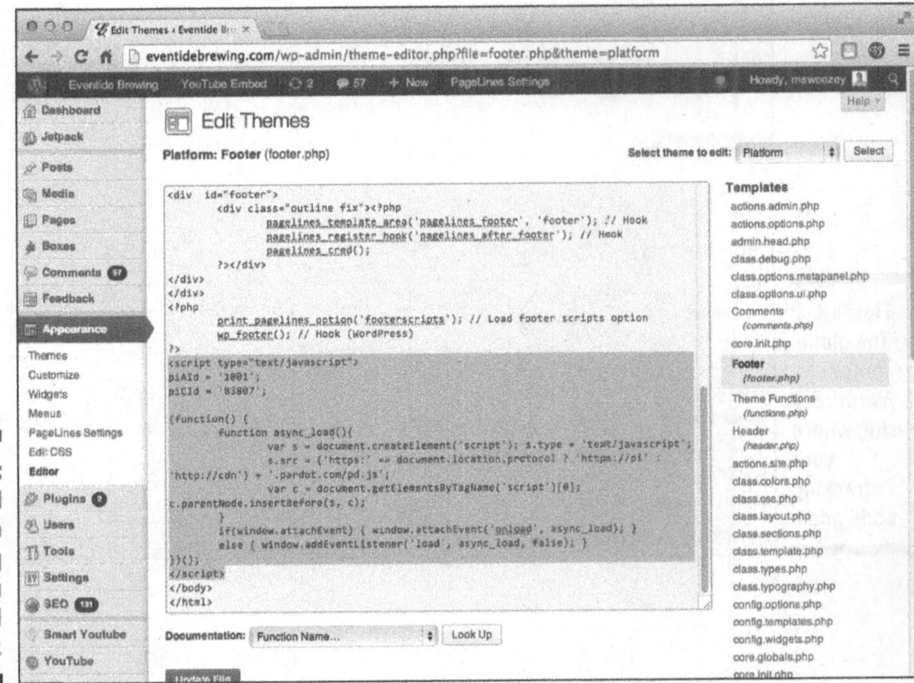

Figure 4-5: Copy and paste tracking code in the global footer.

- A form
- A template
- Web content

Assets are the key for lead generation. Make sure that you understand the difference between assets you host and those hosted on other sites, and how you need to connect these assets.

Uploading assets into your marketing automation platform is usually as simple as copying and pasting. The only difference is the fact that you might be asked to put some special automations on the asset. Although the steps you take after your asset is uploaded depend on your tool, it's usually easier than falling off a log.

Assets such as white papers, videos, forms, and landing pages that are hosted on your site are uploaded into your marketing automation platform. Your marketing automation platform allows you to publish these assets and track individual leads engaging with them. If you are hosting assets on another site, one that you don't control, you still upload the asset to your marketing automation tool, using a custom URL to paste to the other site.

The URL is the key item. Whether a site is hosted by you or by someone else, as long as you can obtain the URL and use a custom redirect, you can track the asset. You can therefore track many more assets than you can normally host on any given solution.

Integrating traceable content

Traceable content is any content that can be tracked when your audience engages with it. Tracking a user's interaction with your content allows follow-up automations to take place. There are many different types of content, including videos, white papers, podcasts, sales sheets, and so on. Treat all content the same to make this process easy.

All content that you upload into your marketing automation solution becomes accessible through a URL and traceable back to each person who interacts with the content. You can use your content URLs as links on your website or as links in a tweet on Twitter to promote your latest white paper.

Uploading content is as simple as uploading a picture to Facebook. If the content you want to use exists on a third-party site, your vendor needs to show you how to include that content in your tools with custom redirected URLs, as shown in Figure 4-6.

This is the Custom Redirect to use to track people going to the destination URL.

Name	Linkedin Campaign URL
Destination URL	http://www.eventidebrewing.com
Tracked URL	http://go.pardot.com/l/13332/2013-12-04/76q2w
Short URL	http://bit.ly/1cWxxzX
Unique Clicks	0
Total Clicks	0

Figure 4-6: Talk to your vendor about redirected URLs for tracking content not hosted on your site.

Setting up SPF/Sender ID

SPF stands for Sender Policy Framework, which is an industry-standard form of email authentication designed to prevent email spoofing. To implement SPF, you need to add a TXT record to your domain name server (DNS). A TXT record is a text record in your DNS that can verify a domain to send emails on your behalf. *Domain name server* is the technical term for the way your email domain name connects with your email server through various Internet protocols. You have different ways to set up your SPF record depending on how your email is currently configured. If you're not familiar with your SPF, consult your current email vendor to find out how to set it up. The following list helps you to know what your next steps are depending on your current situation:

- **If you do not have an SPF record:** Check with your vendor for your SPF TXT record. It is likely to look like the following:

```
v=spf1 mx include:aspmx.pardot.com ~all
```

- **If you already have an SPF record listed:** Consult with your IT staff or the person responsible for maintaining your domain's SPF statement. Let that person know that you'd like to add a new SPF record to your existing SPF statement. It's important to note that the SPF protocol allows a maximum of ten lookups total.
- **Sender ID will set up automatically:** The SPF record in your domain's DNS setup will automatically be used to authenticate mail servers through Microsoft's Sender ID program because SPF and Sender ID are now merged. You do have to make sure that the SPF information is complete and accurate.

Setting up DomainKeys

DomainKeys is an email authentication system designed to verify the DNS domain of an email sender to verify message integrity. This protocol is largely backed by Yahoo!. To implement DomainKeys, add two new TXT records to your DNS, as shown in Figure 4-7.

Figure 4-7: Setting up DomainKeys requires two TXT records.

For	Domain	Type	Entry
SPF	test.com	TXT	v=spf1 include:aspmx.pardot.com ~all
Domainkey_Policy	_domainkey.test.com	TXT	t=y; o=~;
Domainkey	pardot._domainkey.test.com	TXT	k=rsa; p=MIGfMA0GCSqGSIb3DQEBAQUAA4GNADCBiQKBgQDeKBUE+dvLpO/pda52BO/rVMNLohc2qzl+HkAMGRk+JO/ODq/WT

The first record contains the general DomainKeys settings:

```
domainkey.yoursite.com TXT "t=y; o=~;"
```

The second record is your actual key:

```
._domainkey.yoursite.com TXT    "k=rsa;
 p=MEwwDSJHJKoZIhvcNAQEBBQADOwAwOAIxANDl1x8anhySwnWoafyw
EUeuNoNbav9JrAdUAsqln8YYA0jkARmuox2EdWkU5fkrzQKJHSGB"
smtpapi._domainkey.yoursite.com TXT "k=rsa;
 t=s;
p=MEwwDSJHJKoZIhvcNAQEBBQADOwAwOAIxANDl1x8anhySwnWoafyw
EUeuNoNbav9JrAdUAsqln8YYA0jkARmuox2EdWkU5fkrzQKJHSGB"
```

Removing IT from Your Marketing Work Flow

The first goal of most marketing automation tools is to give a marketer a single tool to manage all marketing executions with minimal technical skills required. This feature of marketing automation solutions is very compelling to smaller organizations and to organizations limited by technical resources. The next sections show you how to remove IT from your marketing work flow.

Dragging and dropping IT out of your marketing work flow

All online marketing and content marketing require a significant amount of knowledge in HyperText Markup Language (HTML) and Cascading Style Sheets (CSS). The problem is, most marketers do not know how to write in these languages.

Most modern online marketing revolves around content marketing. Content marketing involves many moving parts, including HTML programming, to build and connect the following:

- A form to protect the content
- A landing page to host the form and the content itself
- Connections to social media
- Email marketing
- Other online marketing for promoting the content

Marketing automation tools still use HTML, but they allow marketers to have a single platform for execution of all online marketing campaigns without the need for programming HTML from scratch. That way, you gain the ability to easily create HTML without needing IT support.

Most marketing automation tools use a WYSIWYG editor that allows you to drag and drop content into emails, forms, and landing pages, as shown in Figure 4-8. *WYSIWYG* is an acronym that stands for What You See Is What You Get. When you drag or drop something onto your screen with a WYSIWYG editor, the editor creates the code automatically, saving you a trip to the IT department to ask for code support.

You can connect your entire campaign by using a WYSIWYG editor to drag and drop code in all the necessary places, thereby connecting your forms to your CRM system, email tools, and website. You can also build entire forms quickly and publish them online in a matter of seconds. You will never need IT again to build, launch, or maintain a marketing campaign. So if you add up all the hours you spend with IT before marketing automation, your implementation can demonstrate a savings of time and money based on the hours saved and devoted to more marketing-focused efforts.

When you are considering marketing automation, make sure that you are looking closely at the level of flexibility of the WYSIWYG application. Dragging and dropping content is limited by the WYSIWYG editor's features, so make sure that the application you choose allows you to build the programs you want to run. I discuss choosing a solution in Chapter 3.

Figure 4-8: Use a WYSIWYG editor to build landing pages without HTML coding.

The single prospect record

Marketing involves targeting groups of people and individuals within those groups. Without marketing automation, IT is usually responsible for making sure that mass-marketing efforts are tracked on an individual level. This is because large databases are involved to connect multiple data points from multiple marketing applications. Marketing automation solves this issue without IT because all efforts are executed from a single tool. Sharing a single database allows for all marketing efforts to be attributed to an individual in a database, creating a *single-prospect record* (see Figure 4-9).

Using marketing automation, a single-prospect record can easily show the prospect's individual engagement with sales and marketing, all on the same screen.

With marketing automation in place, the idea of a single-prospect record is no longer an issue for IT to solve. That's because a singular platform for execution allows for a single-prospect view of marketing engagement. Showing the value of automating single-prospect records to both marketing and sales will help you show a lot of value for your investment in marketing automation.

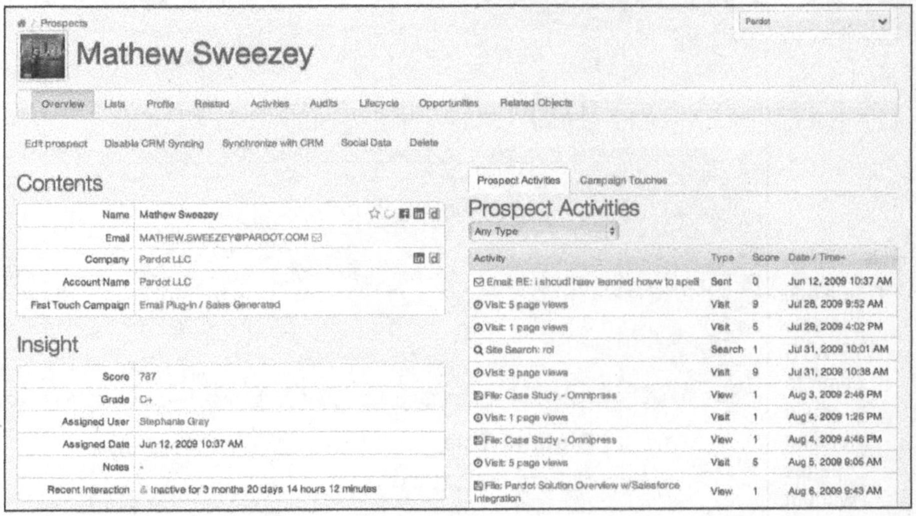

Figure 4-9: Single-prospect records can be generated without IT involvement.

Learning that sometimes automation needs a hand

Not everything can be automated. In fact, trying to go with 100 percent automation is not always best. I've worked for many companies that use automation and still manually inspect each lead using a member of the lead assignment team before the lead is sent to sales. This approach ensures that lead assignment rules are kept to a minimum and makes for an even better relationship between marketing and sales.

Also, sometimes not everything *can* be automated. Amazon.com proved this when it released a tool called Mechanical Turk. It is a way for you to have real people doing manual tasks that are too complicated to do through software. An example is finding contact information for people. If Amazon sees the value in manual tasks, you should, too.

Overautomating processes is one of the more frequent issues that companies run into. Whenever you think marketing automation should get you 100 percent automated, remember Frankenstein. You are building a monster when you do this, and overautomation will become the slave of your tool. The main causes of overbuilding are people who are new to marketing automation, or those who did not invest enough time in understanding marketing automation processes.

Single view is the future

The single view of a customer is the key to the future of marketing campaigns. The benefit of a single-prospect view is that it helps to connect both marketing and sales. It allows sales staff to see why a lead is being passed to them and how to follow up with the lead. It also gives them the upper hand to close the deal more quickly. For marketers, single-prospect view allows for better segmentation, personalization, and advanced automations. This single view makes all other automations possible. It is the life blood of marketing automation.

Consider also that the single view will include things you currently can't track, such as actions and behaviors. Your current database may include which emails were sent to a prospect, or the employee count of that prospect's company. The single-prospect view could also include which pages of your website were viewed and which keywords were searched on by your prospect. The single-prospect record can therefore provide a level of detail you've never had before in marketing or sales. This visibility into every action is what makes the single-prospect record so rich and marketing automation so powerful.

If you find yourself wondering why one simple task takes a number of interdependent rules, you are probably trying to overautomate, or you have a bad process in place.

Marketing automation tools are built with best practices in mind. If your processes are not following best practices, you need to rework your processes to fit into a new tool. Failing to do so can cause lots of issues with process flow.

If you find yourself in an overautomated environment, start changing the amount of automation by going back to your main goals. Work with your vendor to identify modern best practices for achieving your goals, and see whether your vendor can suggest a better way through a new process or a feature you're not aware of.

Part II

Working with Data and Leads

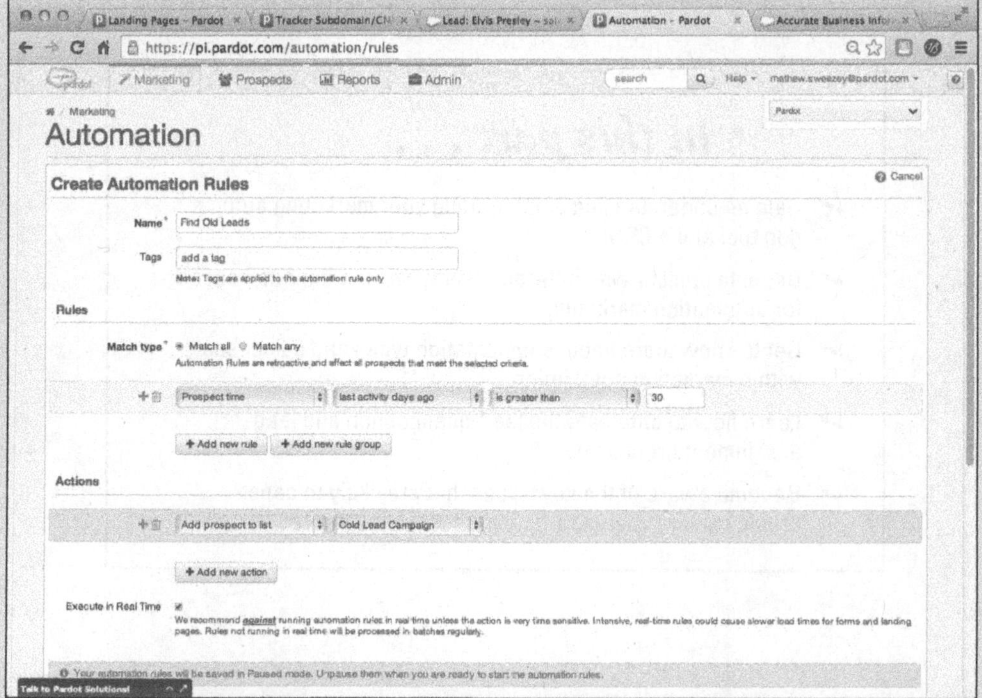

For some great tips on data management, check out `www.dummies.com/extras/marketingautomation`.

In this part . . .

- Gain an understanding of integrating your marketing automation tool and a CRM.
- Become familiar with different data types and their use cases for automation marketing.
- Get to know more about segmentation types and use cases within marketing automation.
- Learn how to automate the lead-qualification and lead-assignment processes.
- Become aware of the key issues that are likely to cause problems with your lead-flow process in the future.

Chapter 5

CRM Integration

In This Chapter

- Planning your CRM integration
- Connecting data and database fields
- Troubleshooting common issues with CRM

Connecting your customer relationship management system (CRM) and your marketing automation tool unlocks many of the powerful features that improve your communication between marketing and sales and allow you to move to more advanced marketing programs. It also enables closed-loop return-on-investment (ROI) reporting on marketing campaigns (you can see ROI contributions from sales and marketing in one report).

Connecting a CRM system and a marketing automation system is not a simple task. Of all of the problems typically seen with failed implementations, a bad CRM connection is in the top three reasons for failure. The issue is complicated by the fact that every company uses a CRM system in a different way, and not always in the way that CRM systems were intended to be used. In this chapter, I prepare you to look at your CRM system usage and take a flexible approach to make your integration work better.

I show you how to plan your integration between your marketing automation tool and your CRM system. I also cover how to go over your current CRM system to see whether you need to add fields and whether you will require additional tools to connect the two systems together.

Clearly Defining Your Wants and Needs for Marketing Automation and CRM

Your CRM system is key to your success with marketing automation. Also, many marketing automation tools are specifically made for one CRM or another. For example, Microsoft purchased MarketingPilot, which is tightly integrated into the Microsoft Dynamics CRM systems. Oracle purchased Eloqua, which is now the leading marketing automation solution for its CRM. Salesforce.com purchased Pardot to be the in-house solution for its CRM.

Many other notable solutions exist that tie into the most popular CRM applications. Remember, however, that the success of your tool is dependent on your CRM system and its abilities, so the better the connection is to your CRM system, the easier it will be to utilize and maximize the value of your investment.

CRM goals can get pretty detailed. To avoid getting caught up in the details, I suggest that you list your basic wants and needs first, and add more details after your basic wants and needs are defined, as shown in Table 5-1.

Table 5-1 Basic and Detailed CRM Needs and Wants

Need or Want	***Basic Goal***	***Detailed Goal***
Importing leads	Import new leads into the CRM	Real-time automation of lead to CRM importing. Do you need to import this as a lead or a contact?
Proving results	ROI reporting	Automated ROI reporting through tight integration with opportunity records in your CRM. Integrating with custom fields on a record to prove results.
Lead scoring	Identify hot leads	Does your tool allow for scoring from behaviors and actions, or just from data points within the CRM system?
Lead flow	Lead notifications sent to sales	Lead notifications within CRM. Do tasks need to be created for sales?

Your CRM wants and needs should be used in conjunction with diagramming your campaigns to identify which solution will best deliver the most wants and accomplish all needs.

Mapping out your CRM integration

Your integration should be mapped out with the following checklist and requirements:

- **Find your install module.** Most marketing automation tools have an *install module*, which is an automated program that you can run to set up some of your basic CRM connections. Your install module is probably found in your CRM's app center or provided by your vendor.
- **List the fields you need.** In order for your CRM integration to report on leads passed to sales and progress through the sales cycle, your fields need to match your process and goals. Make a detailed list of all Lead, Contact, Account, and Opportunity fields you think you need to sync between the two systems. Remember that you may not need to have all the fields you currently have in your CRM replicated into your marketing automation tool. You do not need to have a field if you don't plan to use the data for segmentation or automating processes.
- **Sync your field definitions.** Terminology often varies between CRMs and marketing automation tools. You need to determine which terms your marketing automation tool uses to describe Leads, Accounts, Contacts, and Opportunities, and list them side by side so that you can make them sync.
- **Prep your CRM admin.** You need your CRM admin for at least a few hours. You may need him or her more depending on the complexities of your CRM system. Talk to your CRM admin and make sure that his or her time is available when you need it.
- **Get your sales team to buy in.** Discuss with your sales team the addition of new tools, and share the benefits and processes that will be changing. Training happens later, but the buy-in discussion should happen early on in the process.
- **Download your data sets.** You need to have a clean list of every prospect and every data point that you want to put into your marketing automation solution. I discuss cleaning up your database in Chapter 3.
- **Keep your vendor support information handy.** Share your marketing automation vendor's support information, including contact information and terms of service, with everyone involved in your CRM integration in case questions arise.

Some marketing automation tools have much better integration than others for specific CRMs. This connection can either remove frustrations or just create more.

Diagramming your campaigns and lead-flow paths

The goals of diagramming your marketing programs are to give you the best estimate of your true needs for CRM integration and to appropriately estimate the time and investment required to execute your lead nurturing programs.

Start with your full team and work together to diagram your programs. Some people prefer to do this on a whiteboard; others prefer to use a visual flow program such as Microsoft Visio to create a document. Figure 5-1 shows an outline of a campaign to help estimate the time required to build it. No matter which tool or approach you use, the following steps help guide you to a useful diagram of your program.

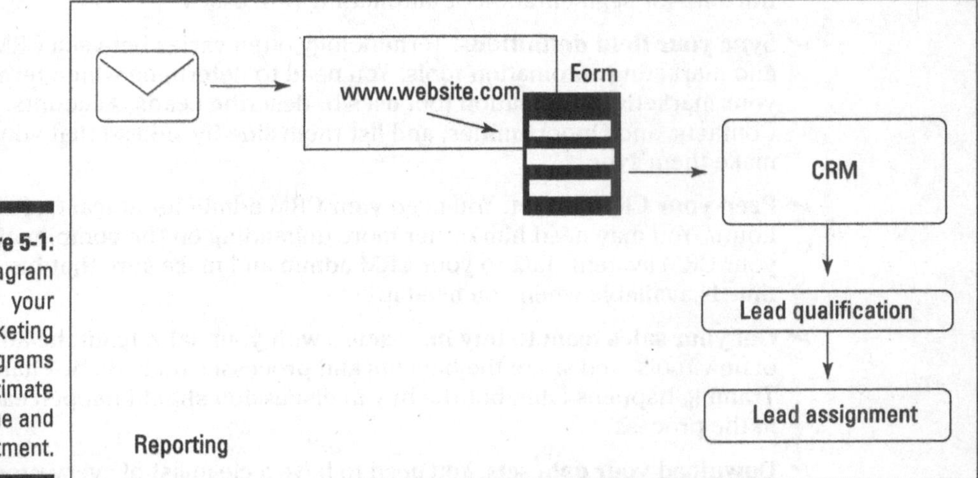

Figure 5-1: Diagram your marketing programs to estimate time and investment.

1. **List each campaign.**

   Begin by listing each campaign, breaking your campaigns down into groups if possible. You can start with the basics, such as inbound and outbound campaigns, or you can get more granular by listing lead-generation campaigns, lead-conversion campaigns, cold-lead campaigns, sales-support campaigns, and cross-selling campaigns. Most campaigns fit into one of these groups. If you have other groups, that's okay.

2. **Diagram all moving parts.**

   Diagram all the moving parts within each campaign. If it is an inbound campaign, begin with your search term or paid search ad. If it is an outbound campaign, begin with your list and how you obtain this list. From here, diagram each part of your campaign. Make sure to list every small detail, all the way down to each field on your lead capture form, and where that information goes in your CRM.

3. **Identify data flow.**

   Note how many different applications you are using and how the data is moving back and forth to and from each tool. Take note of issues you are currently dealing with and issues you are facing.

Cleaning Up Your Database

Cleaning up your database is a must to protect your sender score and sending reputation. Your *sender score* is a numeric grade that spam filters put on your IP address. The higher your score, the better your chances of getting your emails delivered to a person's email inbox. One of the reasons people obtain a lower score is that they send emails to bad email addresses or spam traps. If you have been building your database for years, you likely have a large number of both in your database.

While you're preparing your CRM system for marketing automation, it's a good exercise to clean your database so that your CRM integration starts out with a clean bill of health. You have two good ways to clean a database. One is by using tools to do it yourself; the other is by hiring someone to do it for you.

Using tools to clean up your database

You can easily access many tools for cleaning up your database through online services. The cost of your database cleanup will be a direct reflection of how large your database is and what, specifically, you need cleaned. For the purpose of protecting your sender score, you need to be concerned only with the validity of the email address, not all the information in a record.

Data brokers are another way to clean up your database. Companies such as Data.com, Dun & Bradstreet, and Equifax can help you to clean up your database in one fell swoop and help you augment your data at the same time, as shown in Figure 5-2.

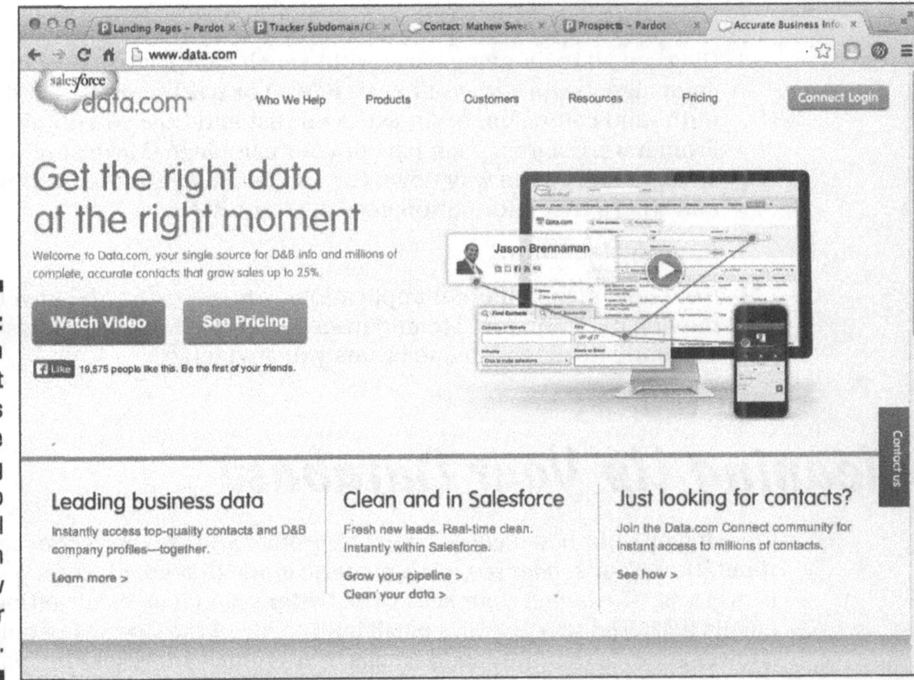

Figure 5-2: You can connect Data.com's database cleaning solution to run in real time on each new lead to your database.

Part of cleaning up your data involves verifying whether data is accurate. Two different types of data are used for verification:

- **Crowd-sourced data** is collected when people enter their own information into a public database. For example, people on the social media site LinkedIn create a profile and enter data about themselves.
- **Verified data** is collected by companies who are in the business of data collection. For example, Dun & Bradstreet is a company that collects data from a variety of sources, including credit reports, public documents, and questionnaires.

List-cleaning tools such as NetProspex, RingLead, and FreshAddress are also great tools for cleaning up your data set in real time moving forward. Verified data sources such as NetProspex routinely call each data point to verify that the information is correct. This type of tool can be a more expensive option than using a data broker, but it tends to have a higher reliability. Data cleaning tools can also be integrated into a marketing automation solution to clean and augment each new prospect record that comes into your database in real time.

Tools such as RingLead help you to better de-duplicate data coming into your database to ensure that you are connecting the right information to the correct record. This type of tool solves the problem of having the same lead in your database five times because that prospect used five different email addresses. This is very important if you have very complex data sets or have multiple email addresses on a single person.

Hiring someone to clean up your database

If you can't use an automated tool because of the size of your data or the specific nature of the data needed, you can find consultants or outsourced call centers who can clean your data for you as well as offer data augment services without the need for automated tools.

Hire a consultant with specific industry knowledge to help expedite the process of data collection, cleansing, and augmentation. Hiring a consultant who knows how to use your chosen marketing automation solution would be prudent. Choosing a consultant who is not familiar with your industry is okay if you have to compromise, but do your best to avoid consultants who lack a working knowledge of your marketing automation solution.

An outsourced call center is a more expensive option than a consultant, and it tends to take the most time. This option is generally the best option for companies that need to constantly augment and cleanse data as it comes in. A call center can be tied into the lead qualification stage and manually verify data before that data is passed on to the next stage. The call center can also obtain data via a phone call that cannot be obtained via online interactions.

Connecting CRM Data Fields to Your Marketing Automation Tool

CRM integration eventually involves connecting data and database fields between your CRM system, marketing automation tools, and marketing process. Before all that can happen, you first need to take a look at the big picture so that your connections make sense and so that you can guide the technical details toward your business goals. Here's how you should be thinking about your overall plan. (I explain all the details of each of the following bullets throughout this section.)

- **The early days:** Focus on planning and setting up the standard fields of your marketing automation tool using modules and existing data sources to assist you.
- **Majority of work:** Focus on creating custom fields in your marketing automation solution that map over to your CRM system. These are fields that you were using before marketing automation as well as fields you think of during integration.

- **Finishing touches:** Focus on uploading data and testing your integration. Without testing, you won't know whether your connection can run your marketing programs.

Connecting default fields to your marketing automation tool

Default fields are generally standard fields common to all CRM systems and marketing automation tools. Examples include

- First name
- Last name
- Phone number
- Other basic information

Default fields usually represent the bare minimum of information needed to identify a record. It's highly likely that your marketing automation tool needs a set of default fields to function properly, so you need to connect those fields to the same fields in your CRM system, or create them if your CRM system doesn't already have them.

Start by installing your module into your CRM system. (I tell you where to find your module earlier in this chapter, in "Mapping out your CRM integration.") The module will set up the standard fields that your marketing automation tool needs but which your CRM system does not currently have.

After your module is installed to your CRM, you need to go into your marketing automation tool to map your default fields together with your CRM fields. The fields in your CRM and marketing automation tool will have different names at this stage, as shown in Figure 5-3, because the name as it appears to your users is different from the Field ID used by your CRM.

Name	Field ID	salesforce.com Field Name	Type
Account Status	Account_Status	Current_Account_Status__c	Dropdown

Figure 5-3: Field names are different when installing a module to connect your CRM.

Depending on your marketing automation tool, you may also be able to set up other field parameters during module installation. If the fields you are connecting are drop-down boxes, multi-select boxes, number fields, date fields, or radio buttons, make sure that you also set up these parameters in both your marketing automation tool and your CRM. These field characteristics can require a significant amount of time to set up. More advanced marketing automation tools include features to help expedite this task.

Inserting custom fields into your marketing automation tool

You likely already have and use specific data points for segmentation, qualification, or lead assignment among all your marketing applications. Your new tool will come with a basic database, which needs to be expanded to include these custom data points. This means adding custom fields by using the upcoming steps.

Custom fields are fields that you need in addition to the ones that come standard with your CRM. They might be used in your CRM, or they might be used only by your marketing team, specifically for segmentation and reporting.

Here are some examples of custom fields:

- Technology used by prospect
- Product number
- Number of locations
- Any field which *you* added to your CRM

After you have created and named your fields, make sure to note the data type and parameters of the field. If you aren't sure of the needed parameters, ask your vendor. The parameters vary from vendor to vendor. Parameters dictate whether the information can be overwritten, used in email communications, or even automatically updated from third-party databases.

Own your own fields

Fields used only by the sales team do not need to be synced with your marketing automation tool. The same goes for marketing fields that don't need to be used by sales. The marketing-only fields follow the same process as that used for all custom fields, but they don't need to map to a CRM Field ID name.

Follow these steps to add a custom field:

1. **List all the custom fields you use in your CRM for lead assignment and lead qualification.**

   Work with your CRM admin to obtain this list. You also need to obtain a list of any other custom fields your marketing team uses for segmentation or lead attribution.

2. **Create the custom fields in your marketing automation tool.**

   Figure 5-4 shows the screen for setting up a custom field in the Pardot marketing automation tool. Each tool requires a different setup process, but the basic data you need to set up a custom field are

   - Name
   - Field ID from your CRM application
   - Type of field
   - Special conditions

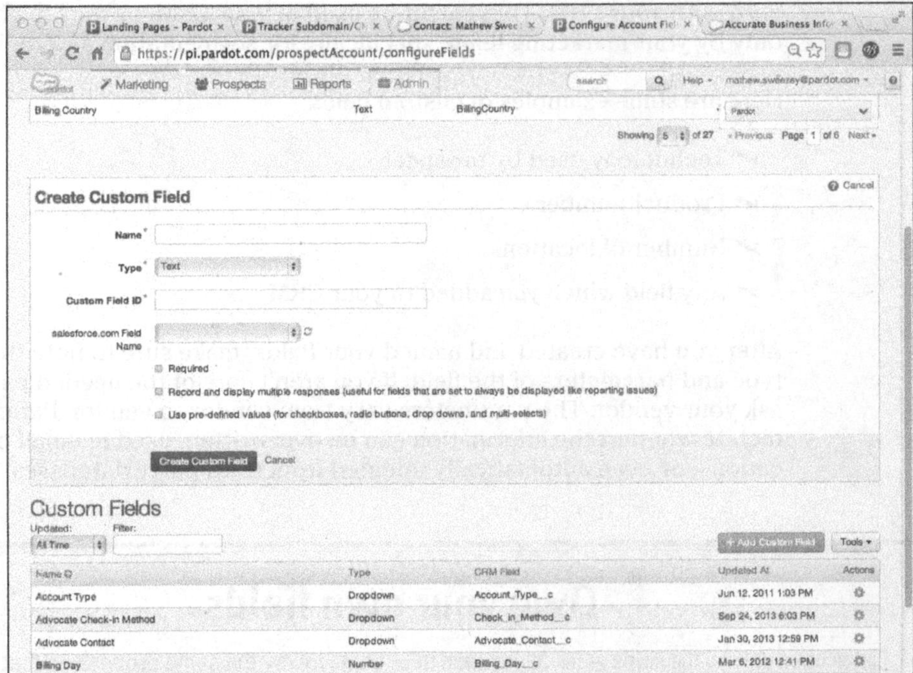

Figure 5-4: Creating a custom field in the Pardot marketing automation tool.

The Name, Field ID, and Type fields are fields you probably already have. You need to determine the special conditions for your field on your own. Special conditions might include

- Master vs. slave (which data set is the master record)
- Multiple responses requiring a record (Comment boxes are an example. A person might fill out multiple comments over time, and you should keep each comment. You have only one comment field in your forms, though, so make sure that you can keep multiple responses in a single data field in your CRM system.)
- Overwrite permissions (Overwriting things such as Phone number can be important.)

Your CRM system is likely to remain your database of record. When you're connecting custom fields, be sure that you are aware of which data set is to be the master record. You should always have the CRM tool be the master for most data needed for sales, and your marketing automation tool should be the master of data required for marketing reports.

Uploading your data sets into your marketing automation tool

Uploading your data sets into your marketing automation tool starts by collecting all your data and making sure that it is saved in a CSV file, as shown in Figure 5-5.

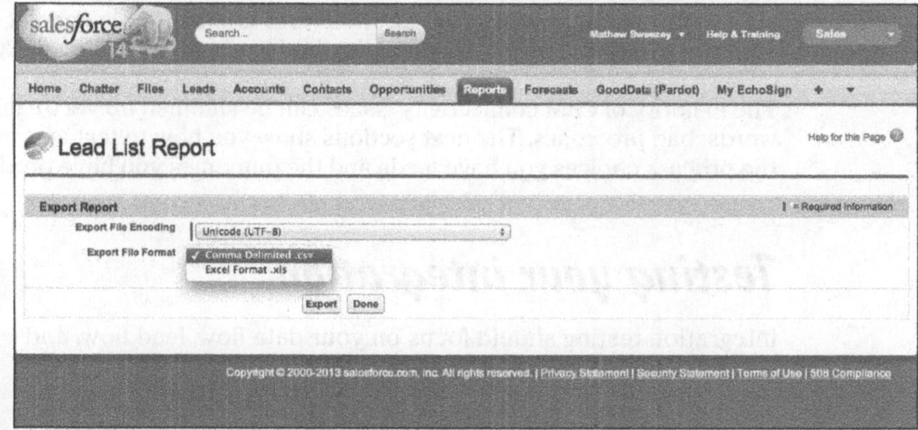

Figure 5-5: Export your data to a CSV file.

A *CSV file* is a spreadsheet file format that stands for comma-separated values. Most spreadsheet programs allow you to import and export using this file type.

After your data is in a CSV file, you can easily upload your data into the marketing automation tool. The time it takes to upload your data will depend on the size of your database. The larger your database, the longer the upload time. Most tools can pull over all data upon your initial startup; however, I advise against doing so because this is also the best time to clean up your data. (I discuss cleaning up your data in the previous section of this chapter.) Some tools require you to fully de-duplicate your database first, whereas others will handle de-duplication for you during the import process.

If your file size is very large and your tools support this feature, you can save time by using a file that contains only the minimum data, such as email addresses or CRM ID numbers. That way, you can import essential data more quickly and bring in the remaining information automatically over time. You need to ask your vendor which process you should use.

When you are uploading your data set, the tool will either ask you to visually map the data points to your new database or it will do them for you automatically. If your tool does this automatically, make sure that you understand the required information needed in the header of each column.

Testing and Troubleshooting Common CRM Issues

Testing and troubleshooting shouldn't take much time, but it's an important step. With testing, you'll know whether your connection is correct before running programs and potentially sending bad leads or confusing data to sales.

The majority of CRM connectivity issues can be summed up very easily in two words: bad processes. The next sections show you how to test and troubleshoot the process choices you have made and the outcomes you have produced.

Testing your integration

Integration testing should focus on your data flow, lead flow, and reporting. Follow these steps to test your integration:

1. **Create a dummy lead and campaign.**

   A *dummy lead* is a made-up prospect or customer that you add to your database as if it is a real record. A *dummy campaign* is a fictional marketing campaign. For a little fun, use a famous person's name and attributes in your dummy lead. Make sure that your dummy lead includes all data points, and include the word "test" in each field. If it is a preconfigured field, just remember what you selected. Attach your lead to your dummy campaign to allow you to test reporting in Step 4.

2. **Sync your dummy lead with your CRM to test your lead flow (see Figure 5-6).**

   Exactly how this is done depends on the application, but it should entail a Sync button that you can click.

   Your lead flow test is successful if your dummy lead is correctly assigned over to your CRM application after syncing your data.

3. **Test your data flow.**

   You need to test data flow in two directions. Make sure that all the data from your dummy lead is transferred to the new record in your CRM tool when completing Step 2. Then, create a new dummy lead in your CRM tool and repeat Step 2 by syncing the lead from your CRM tool back to your marketing automation system.

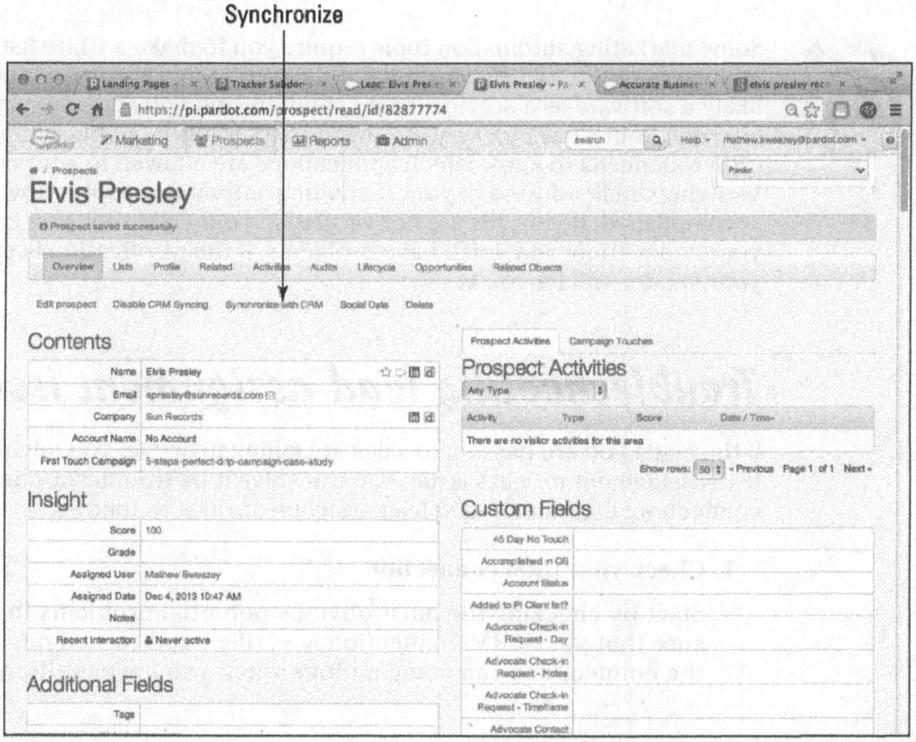

Synchronize

Figure 5-6: Syncing your leads usually entails clicking a Sync button.

Playing in the sandbox

Some applications allow you to test and play around with your tools in a background environment called a *sandbox*. A lot of tools include a sandbox environment for testing; however, the average user usually doesn't have these tools. This feature of a marketing automation solution usually comes only at the highest levels and is needed only by IT to test integrations before rolling out to a live instance of the CRM system. Remember that large companies may have CRM software with many installed instances. This situation is common for companies who operate various divisions. The purpose of the sandbox is to help mitigate any potential issues caused to the live CRM system by adding a new application to the currently running CRM system.

4. **Test your reporting.**

   Check your dummy campaign to see whether your reports are reading the information and your lead source report shows that your dummy lead has arrived. If you are not seeing the dummy lead in your reports, contact your vendor to see where you are going wrong.

Some marketing automation tools require you to make a white list of IP addresses of the tool. For instance, your marketing automation tool is most likely a software-as-a-service (SaaS) solution, and you access it via the Internet. Your CRM tool may also be an SaaS solution. If this is the case, your CRM tool needs to know which applications are allowed to access your data. Verifying the IP address of your marketing automation tool is how this is accomplished. If your IPs are not verified in your CRM tool, you can't finish your connection, and you'll have problems. If this verification is required, your vendor will let you know.

Troubleshooting lead-assignment issues

If the leads you are passing to sales are failing to arrive, you might have a lead-assignment process issue. You can solve it by troubleshooting your CRM connection, usernames, and lead-assignment rules as follows:

1. **Check your CRM connection.**

   Start by checking the most obvious potential problems first. Make sure that your CRM connection is verified and turned on. Many times, the connections can come undone when you have multiple people inside the application who aren't sure of what they are clicking on. The main reason for the connector to come undone is one of the following:

- IP addresses become unverified in your CRM system (a cause for concern only when your CRM requires verification of your marketing automation tool). This issue is easily solved by adding your IP addresses to your CRM whitelist.
- Someone accidentally clicks the wrong button in the marketing automation tool.

2. **Check your usernames.**

   If you complete step one and salespeople still aren't receiving leads, you should check your usernames. You might have lead assignment set up but haven't connected your users between the systems. When you create custom fields, you should create users in each system. Creating users in each system allows you to a pass a lead to a sales rep through the rep's CRM tool. If you didn't connect your leads when you set up your custom fields, your leads will be passed to your CRM tool without being assigned to the correct person.

3. **Check your lead-assignment rules.**

   If steps one and two fail to solve your lead-assignment issue, you are likely to find the reason to be your automation rules. Your lead-assignment rule might be too complex, which could cause a condition to remain unmet. This is usually the result of a complex "if/then" statement. ***Remember:*** The simpler your lead assignment, the better.

Troubleshooting data mapping issues

A data mapping issue can be tricky to notice. It is one of the more frequent issues companies have, and it derives mostly from a misunderstanding of how the marketing automation system and the CRM function together. You need to understand the relationship between the master and the slave data to ease any future issues with data mapping.

- *Master data* is a data record that is in control. For example, if you have a CRM field and a lead record with a person's first name, your marketing automation tool will also have a matching record of the same person and the same name. Both solutions are talking back and forth to each other, so they need to know which system can override which data points.
- *Slave data* is copied data. The slave data can never override the master data. For example, if your sales rep keys in a new name for the person in the CRM, that name will flow down to your marketing automation tool, but if the marketing team changes the name, the person's name will not be changed in the CRM.

Here's how you can troubleshoot your mapping issues, keeping in mind your master and slave data relationship:

- **Check the settings of the field.** When you check the settings in your marketing automation tool for your field, you will find the ability to control all the settings pertaining to how your tool passes and receives data. Figure 5-7 shows a field in Pardot's marketing automation tool as well as the settings for the custom field named CRM. Check to make sure that the field ID in your automation tool matches the field ID in your CRM for the field you are troubleshooting.

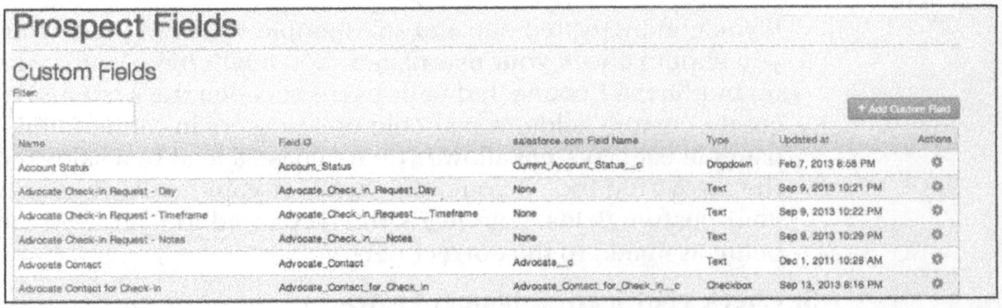

Prospect Fields

Custom Fields

Filter:

+ Add Custom Field

Name	Field ID	salesforce.com Field Name	Type	Updated at	Actions
Account Status	Account_Status	Current_Account_Status__c	Dropdown	Feb 7, 2013 8:58 PM	
Advocate Check-in Request - Day	Advocate_Check_in_Request_Day	None	Text	Sep 9, 2013 10:21 PM	
Advocate Check-in Request - Timeframe	Advocate_Check_in_Request___Timeframe	None	Text	Sep 9, 2013 10:22 PM	
Advocate Check-in Request - Notes	Advocate_Check_in___Notes	None	Text	Sep 9, 2013 10:29 PM	
Advocate Contact	Advocate_Contact	Advocate__c	Text	Dec 1, 2011 10:28 AM	
Advocate Contact for Check-in	Advocate_Contact_for_Check_in	Advocate_Contact_for_Check_in__c	Checkbox	Sep 13, 2013 8:16 PM	

Figure 5-7: Make sure that your field IDs match in the event of data issues.

- **Check your master and slave relationship.** Check to see which database is the master and which is the slave of the data. The master data table can write over other slave data points. The CRM should be the master of this data and should not be overwritten, and for good reason — most people put fake data in forms!

  A study from MarketingSherpa in 2008 showed that 65 percent of people give a fake phone number when asked for this information on a form. A lead's phone number in the CRM system is a great example of this. If your CRM has a correct phone number and it was not the master, the data could easily be overwritten with the false information. If the slave data is the phone number listed in your marketing automation tool, and a prospect gives a fake phone number, the information will change in the marketing automation tool, only to be changed back instantly by the CRM.

Your marketing automation tool should also be the master of all reporting fields used by marketing. This gives you the control to change your reporting fields and keeps sales from messing with your reports.

Chapter 6

Creating Segmented Lists

In This Chapter

- Exploring the types and uses of segmentation
- Implementing your first segmentations
- Creating advanced segmentations

A *segmentation* is a way to identify distinct groups of people and add them to separate lists in your marketing automation tool. A list can be filled with many segmentations. For example, your list may have a segmentation of VPs in New Jersey derived from an online form with a field asking for a job title. Anyone who fills in the title field with the title VP is added to the list segment.

Most marketing automation tools manage segmentations and lists in the same way, as follows:

- **The list is the physical list of people.** Think of the list as the result and the segmentation as the rule to putting people on the list.
- **The segmentation/automation is the set of parameters.** The segmentation dictates who, when, and how people are added to the list.

In marketing automation, segments become targets for marketing campaigns. Segmentations can be set up to run all the time or only once. It all depends on what you're trying to accomplish with each segmentation.

With marketing automation, you can segment on more data points than ever before. This chapter shows you how to choose your segments as well as how to use different types of segmentation strategies to make sure that you have the correct list of segments created for your automated marketing campaigns.

Understanding the Types of Segmentations

Segmentations tend to be dynamic when using marketing automation. However, there are actually three main types of segmentations. Knowing your goal for each list helps you to determine how to craft your segmentation correctly. Consider the following model when determining your goal:

- One-time use: Static segmentation
- Keeping track of a specific action: Semi-dynamic list
- List that needs to be regenerated every day: Fully dynamic list

The next sections explain static, semi-dynamic, and fully dynamic segmentations so that you can approach your segmentation strategy with all three options in mind.

Static segmentations and their use cases

Static segmentations are lists that are populated with names only once. For example, if you set up a static segmentation to find all leads who are VPs in New Jersey, your marketing automation system will find that list. But after a static list is generated, people will never be added to the list again. This is typically the only type of list that people are familiar with before using marketing automation. The most common uses for static lists are as follows:

- **One-off campaigns:** Campaigns you don't run on a regular basis.
- **Targeted sales support:** If you are supporting sales, and sales is asking for a specific email to go out, static lists are great to make quick work of the job.
- **Creating personas:** *Personas* are a very common segmentation of people based on demographic information. They are based on data points and need to be run only once. You can get very advanced with these and make them fully dynamic, but to start, use static segmentations to create your personas. I discuss personas in more detail a little later in this chapter.
- **Basic reporting:** Segmentation can easily help you see how many people have performed a combination of specific actions, which can be helpful in reporting.

Static campaigns are the lowest level of segmentations. As you look to increase your use of marketing automation, you should consider using static lists for the aforementioned specific purposes, as well as learn to use dynamic lists for your automated programs.

Semi-dynamic segmentation's role in programs

Semi-dynamic segmentations are lists that can add more people to, but not subtract people from, the list. For example, if you set up a semi-dynamic segmentation of VPs in New Jersey, your marketing automation system will find all the people who meet the criteria and add the new people who meet the same criteria every day. Because semi-dynamic segmentation does not allow for subtractions from the list, if someone changes a job title from VP to CMO in your database, it will not remove him or her from the list by the same automation that put that person on the list. Removing the person would require another semi-dynamic segmentation.

Some uses for semi-dynamic lists are as follows:

- **High-level segmentation on engagement:** For example, if you want to keep a list of everyone who's ever attended a specific webinar, a semi-dynamic list is a good choice because your follow-up marketing probably doesn't depend on whether those people attend another webinar in the future.
- **Segmenting on product interest:** A list of people who have shown interest in a specific product segment is a good example of a list that does not need the capability to remove people from it.

The advantage of semi-dynamic lists over fully dynamic lists is the speed at which they can run. Depending on your marketing automation tool, speed may be a large concern. Most semi-dynamic lists use less computing power and can work larger sets of data quicker. This means that your segmentations can run more times per day.

Fully dynamic segmentation's use cases

Fully dynamic segmentation means that a person can be added and removed from the list based on the same data point changing. For example, a fully dynamic list of prospects who have visited your website in the past 30 days is a list that will grow and shrink every day, based on visits to your website.

Case study with Beyond the Rack on email personalization using dynamic segmentation

Beyond the Rack, a private online shopping club, is dedicated to providing its customers with authentic designer merchandise at the lowest prices possible — sometimes up to 80 percent off retail. The company takes great care to learn about its members and their preferences so that they receive only the most relevant messages and exclusive offers.

Challenge

Beyond the Rack needed to send personalized messages to millions of customers—and fast! As a flash-sale retailer, it was incredibly important that the millions of messages reach customer inboxes quickly and provide dynamic content that was created using personalized information for each customer.

Solution

Beyond the Rack got straight to work, implementing dynamic email content to match daily offers to members' behaviors and geographic location. This dynamic content was critical to the success of Beyond the Rack's flash sale model. Also, the solution's scalability and speed helped support the company's double-digit growth, with up to 2 million personalized emails, sent twice daily.

Plus, Beyond the Rack implemented a responsive design strategy — creating smarter and more engaging email designs optimized for mobile devices. With an increasing number of shoppers accessing the company's emails via smart phones, this simple change created a huge lift in revenue.

Results

Beyond the Rack has proven the power of messages tailored to each customer. With personalization and responsive design techniques, the company achieved some phenomenal results, including the following:

- Annualized run rate representing tens of millions of dollars
- 18 percent increase in click-through
- 12–15 percent increase in revenue
- Decrease in unsubscribe requests
- Increase in open rates

Subtracting people from a campaign is called *suppression*. For example, marketers who want to subtract leads in an opportunity stage from their email blast often refer to the subtracted list as a suppression list. CRM data is a very common data field to use for suppressing leads.

Here are some good uses for fully dynamic lists:

- **Drip nurturing:** When setting up a nurture list, you should use a fully dynamic list. This allows you to add people to the list and to remove them after they no longer need to be nurtured. I discuss lead nurturing in Chapter 10.

- **Keeping up with lead stages:** Many companies break down their marketing cycle into stages. Fully dynamic lists segmented by the marketing cycle stage are always up-to-date with a clear picture of your lead funnel.
- **Estimating future lead flow:** If you are using a fully dynamic list to keep up with a segment of leads with a specific score, you can easily estimate future lead flows.
- **Marketing campaign execution:** When your campaign requires a conditional list of people and the list might be different from day to day, fully dynamic segmentations are a must.
- **Segmenting for personal touches:** Segmentation can be very useful when trying to find your most influential and most vocal fans. Setting up segmentations to find them and keep them together makes identifying people for case studies and testimonials very easy. When looking to set up a segmentation for vocal prospects, consider looking at lead score, social engagement metrics, and overall activity as key identifiers.
- **Segmenting for reporting:** Segmentation can be very helpful in reporting. By tailoring your report to a specific segment of people, you have a much more granular and specific report. For example, you could segment all prospects who ever engaged with a drip nurturing campaign and run a report to see whether they have a higher close rate than leads who do not.

Generating Your First List

Generating your lists is very easy and usually requires only a few clicks in your marketing automation system. Regardless of the actual steps involved in list setup in your specific marketing automation tools, the following sections show you a few important things to keep in mind when building your first list to make your list-building life easier.

Not all tools use the same controls on a list. Make sure that you know the answers to the following questions before you build your lists:

- Does your tool automatically de-duplicate upon sending an email? De-duplicating means that the tool recognizes when a person appears more than once in an email list and allows duplicates to receive only one email regardless of how many times someone may be on a list or a combination of lists. This feature is extremely helpful when you deal with multiple lists.
- What is your tool's key identifier for de-duplication? It will most likely be either an email address or a CRM ID field.
- Does your tool allow someone to be on the same list more than once?

Identifying your key data points for segmentation

The more data points you have for your segmentation, the more complicated it will become to manage your segmentation. This can mean bad lists, so make sure that you try to minimize the number of data points you are using for segmentation. The most common data points used in segmentation are the following:

- **Demographic data:** For example, name, zip, and company size.
- **Actions:** For example, downloads, clicks, and page views.
- **Behaviors:** These include lead score and last activity date.
- **CRM data:** For example, last sales activity, lead status, account status, and opportunity stage.

Developing a naming convention for segments

When you're just getting started, you might start off with only a few lists. You won't need a plan for naming your lists with so few, but over time, the number of lists you have will grow exponentially. A *naming convention* is a plan for naming your lists intuitively. Figure 6-1 shows a good naming convention and demonstrates how easy it can be to understand what each list is for. For example, Figure 6-1 shows "WN" being used as shorthand for "webinar" and "3P" standing for "third party."

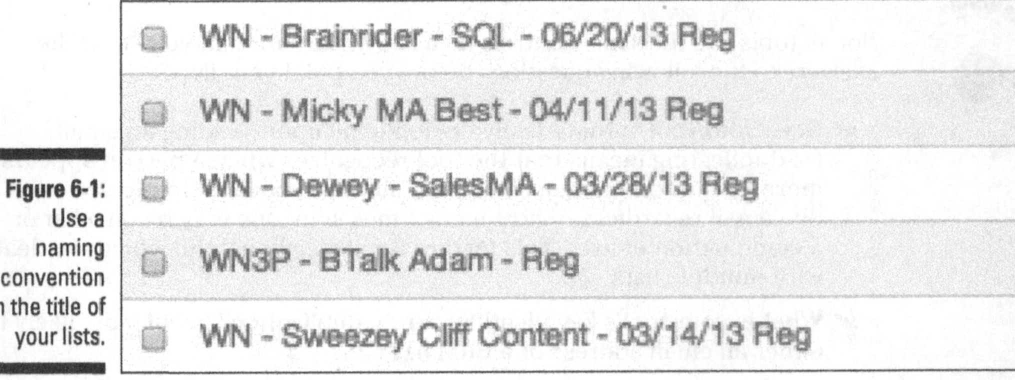

Figure 6-1: Use a naming convention in the title of your lists.

Knowing when to kill a list

Many lists have a finite life span. When they have run the course of their life, you need to delete them from your database. Deleting them helps keep your system clean and keeps the clutter out of your list views. Your lists are just ways to look at your data. Deleting a list doesn't delete your data or the prospects on the list. Only the list itse f is removed. So remember to keep your lists cleaned up so that you don't have to sort through hundreds of lists every day.

Naming conventions are especially useful when you have multiple people on your team who are all creating lists for different uses. Some good things to include in your naming convention are the following:

- Dates
- The department that uses the list
- Campaign name
- What the list is being used for
- Region that owns the list
- Person who created the list
- Any specific data to help you understand what the list is for

Adding people to your list

There are a lot of ways to add people to your segmentation lists, so I've included the most common ways in the following bullets:

- **Mining your database:** Many times, you'll need to make a list from people in your database. You already have the data, so you just need to find the people who meet your criteria.
- **Segmenting in real time:** Some marketing campaigns require real-time segmentation. For example, you may want to instantly segment someone who visits a web page into a campaign or list so that you can automatically initiate follow-up marketing campaigns.
- **Adding people manually:** Just because you have automation doesn't mean you'll always use it. For example, your salespeople may need to add people to a list manually. This situation usually happens when your sales team needs you to run a marketing campaign to a group the sales team identifies.

- **Removing from lists:** Sometimes when you add someone to one list, you need to simultaneously remove him or her from another list. Don't forget to add this action to your segmentations if a segmentation change makes a former segmentation obsolete.

Exploring the Many Uses of Segmentation

Every marketing campaign should be relevant to the person you're targeting. The good news is that targeting your message through segmentation is the fastest way to be relevant. That's because segmenting your database based on activity allows you to find core groups of people with similar levels of interest.

The next sections show you common uses of segmentation and explain how to make your segmentations as relevant as possible in the context of your segmentation.

Segmenting from email actions

Email actions are a segmentation most marketers are familiar with. Email opens, bounces, and clicks are the standard email actions used for segmentation. Learning to use, or not use, the following email actions will help you understand how to segment correctly from these actions and increase the accuracy of your segments.

- **Segmenting on email opens:** Email opens are a very bad segmentation to use in most cases. Email opens are a false positive. It is better to segment on other email activity. This has been used mostly because there were not better metrics to segment from. Now you have better ones, so leave this one on the shelf.
- **Segmenting on email bounces:** Segmenting your list on email bounces is very helpful for cleaning your database. Many times, a bounce on an email requires a manual effort to determine the validity of the email address. Bounces may also signal sales to work other leads in the account. Segment your email bounces into emails that hard bounce (which denotes a bad email address) and emails that soft bounce (which denotes an out-of-office response) four or more times. For more information about what to do with bounced emails, read *E-Mail Marketing For Dummies,* 2nd Edition, by John Arnold (John Wiley & Sons, Inc.).

- **Segmenting on email link clicks:** Segmenting on email link clicks is the best way to segment on email actions. A link click is a direct action that is very accurate, revealing a specific interest in the content the link points to. Depending on your type of email, segmenting on email clicks helps you
  - Segment leads by product interest
  - Segment leads by level of interest
  - Move leads into different campaigns

Segmenting from prospect actions

If your goal is to have a segment of people with a specific interest, you can easily accomplish this goal by segmenting based on one or more actions such as content downloads, pages visited, and emails clicked. Understanding and segmenting on multiple actions helps you understand your audience much better than segmenting based on only one action.

To segment from prospect actions, create one segment for product of interest and add people to that segment as many different ways as possible. For example, if you want to create a segment for people who are interested in your high level of service, you should add people to this segment based on search terms related to service, service links people click in your emails, and the service pages they visit on your website.

Segmenting from prospect inactivity

Inactivity can tell you as much about a person as the actions the person takes, because inactivity can give you insights into someone's behavior patterns. Learning how to correctly segment on the following behaviors is key to your future success with marketing automation:

- **Segmenting on time:** Create segments for inactivity time frames. Consider using segments such as
  - Date of last interaction
  - No action within the past 60 days
  - No marketing touch in past 60 days

- **Segmenting on lead score:** Scores should be calculated based on a combination of activity and inactivity. I discuss lead scoring in more detail in Chapter 12. Consider these segments:
  - Leads with no scores
  - Leads whose scores have gone up the most in the past 30 days
  - Leads with the highest score over a period of time
  - Leads whose scores have gone down in the past 60 days

Segmenting off of CRM data

Marketing automation makes it easy to access CRM data. Because CRM systems are usually central data repositories for a company, your marketing automation tool won't be the only system putting data into your CRM system. Any data that is in your CRM system can be used for segmentations by your marketing automation tool. Consider looking at data sets that are helpful for more targeted campaigns:

- Segmenting on last purchase
- Segmenting on total purchase history
- Segmenting on lead stage
- Segmenting on opportunity stage
- Segmenting on a specific sales rep's leads

Sales activity is also recorded in your CRM and can be used for segmentation. Segmenting on sales activity helps you pick up the slack when sales reps are too busy to reach all their leads.

Creating Personas for Personalization

A persona is a very effective way to segment your database. Personas are used to make sure your messages are as relevant as they can possibly be. Personas can be interest based as well as demographic based. There are two types of personas:

- **Interest-based persona:** This type of persona is based on actions people take, not just who they are. These may include the following actions:
  - Page views (Number of or specific)
  - Length of time on site

   - Frequency of visits
   - White paper download
   - Lead score

- **Demographic-based persona:** A demographic persona is based on information about a person. This data usually lives in your CRM. Examples of these data points are

   - Job title
   - Company size
   - Location
   - Region
   - Existing client

The next sections explain how you can use personas to make your list segmentation decisions more relevant to the people you're marketing to. I also explain how to use personas to activate inactive leads in your existing database.

One person can easily have multiple personas. For example, a lead who is a VP can also be a decision maker and a lead in the early stage of a buying cycle. Every persona changes how you market to a person. I suggest starting off using buyer-stage personas. So you market to people based on where they are in the buying cycle instead of basing your marketing on their job title. If you want to use them both, run a few campaigns first so that you can see whether the additional work is worth the effort.

Creating demographic personas

Demographic-based personas help you create automated campaigns relevant to a data point such as a job title. To create your demographic-based personas, look at past deals that have closed and ask sales to help you determine how many people are part of the decision-making process on average. Do your best to determine common characteristics between people such as job title, company size, and so on. Try to do your best to keep this list to only three roles in the buying cycle.

- **Decision maker:** This is the person who has the final say. Usually this person signs contracts and is involved with only a very small part of the buyer's journey and sales cycle. The decision maker is easy to identify by job title when you're creating a behavioral segmentation. You can also identify this person by specific content engagements, such as which white paper she read or which blog post she found helpful. This assumes, of course, that you have content tailored to such a person.

- **Information gatherer:** This is usually a lower-level person on the team. This person is tasked with getting all the information for the team to then review and decide. The information gatherer is usually a main point of contact, but he can't make any decisions.
- **Champion:** The champion can hold any job title in the organization. This person is a fan of your technology, company, or employees. This is your inside person who is fighting for you. Identifying champions is very hard by job title because they can be anyone. They are much easier to identify by their level of activity and engagement within the company. Your true champions are likely to be very active on social media and to frequent your blog.

After creating your demographic personas, create your segmentation rules to build your lists by persona. You should start with a list for each persona. For example, if you have three personas, you have three lists. This should leave you with three specific lists.

Creating interest-based personas

To create interest-based personas, you need to use a combination of segmentation and lead-scoring methodology. (I explain the details of lead scoring in Chapter 12.)

Use segmentation to track where someone is in his or her buyer's journey and then use a score to measure the level of interest. Interest-based personas should be broken down into three levels (the following score ranges are based on a 100-point scoring model):

- **Leads with low scores:** 0–30
- **Leads with mid-range scores:** 31–75
- **Leads with high scores:** 76–100

Identifying existing personas in your database

You might not have enough information to create personas when you first set up your marketing automation system. Do the following to identify personas in a database with limited behavioral information:

- **If you have a cold database, do some testing:** You won't know the interest-based persona of people in your database if they have no engagement. Set up special campaigns created to test different types of messages and content tailored to people at each stage. This will help you identify people's personas based on their engagement.

- **Go fishing:** Because people typically engage with emails that are relevant to their interests, you can send a series of emails with content targeted to a variety of interests. The people who engage in each type of content can be grouped into personas based on the content.
- **Use what you have:** If you have data on the demographic persona of each person, start there. After you get people to engage, you can then switch to interest-based personas.

There are no "silver bullets." If you think that you can have a 100 percent engagement by using a perfect segmentation and a perfect piece of content, you'll find out differently. You will have much better engagement rates, but you can never hit perfect because you cannot control all the other factors surrounding a person's engagement. You are just stacking the odds in your favor for when all conditions are right.

Reaching out again to old leads

Segmenting your database by persona allows you to reach out with marketing campaigns and identify leads. If you create your segmentations and nurturing programs correctly, reaching out to leads happens consistently without your having to lift a finger, and it helps you to generate more leads from your existing database. Figure 6-2 shows an automation rule for finding the leads and placing them on your nurturing campaign, with an automation rule identifying sales-ready leads and passing them to sales.

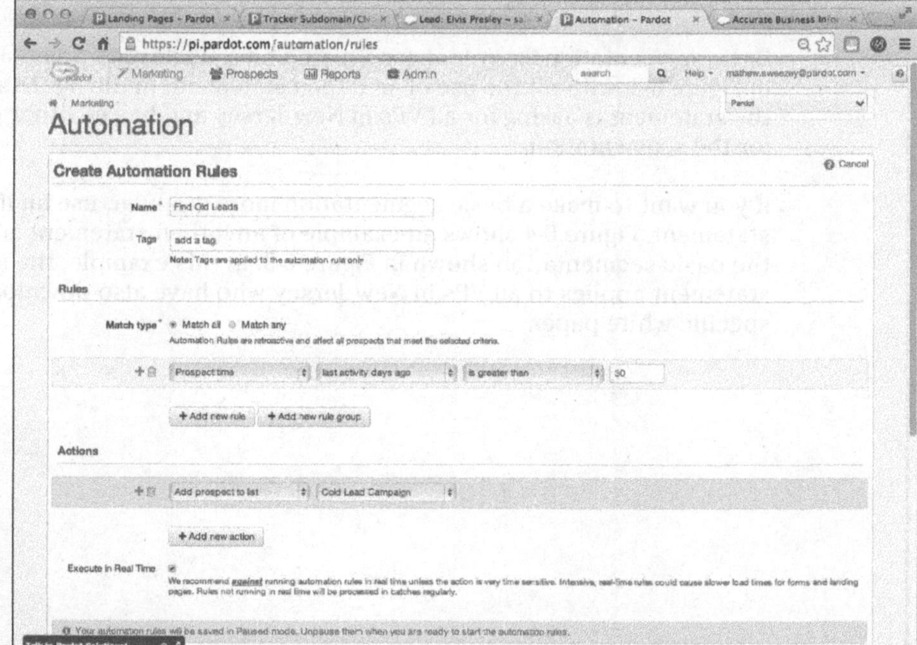

Figure 6-2: Use automation to find and reach out to old leads.

Use a single nurturing campaign to stay in front of leads you identify in your database. You can get more granular over time by breaking your campaign into many targeted campaigns for each buyer stage and persona, but a single campaign will suffice as a starting point.

Creating Advanced Segmentations

After you have the basics of segmentation down, you'll quickly move into more advanced segmentations. Segmentations are automations. So understanding the key parts to advanced automations helps you to better manage your list and segmentations.

Each tool runs automations in a different way, so make sure that you are fully versed on how and where you create your segmentations and automations. Many tools can do them in the same place, but not all tools allow for this.

Understanding if-then statements

An *if-then statement* is an advanced rule that you can use to segment based on a true or false condition. For example, you can program your software to look at data in your database and apply the following if-then statement:

> ***If*** <condition> is true,
>
> ***then*** do <action>

Basic segmentations may look for a match on a single data point, as shown in Figure 6-3, without the use of an if-then statement. In the figure, notice how the statement is asking for all VPs in New Jersey and has no other conditions for the segmentation.

If you want to make a basic segmentation more granular, use an if-then statement. Figure 6-4 shows an example of an if-then statement added to the basic segmentation shown in Figure 6-3. In this example, the if-then statement applies to all VPs in New Jersey who have also downloaded a specific white paper.

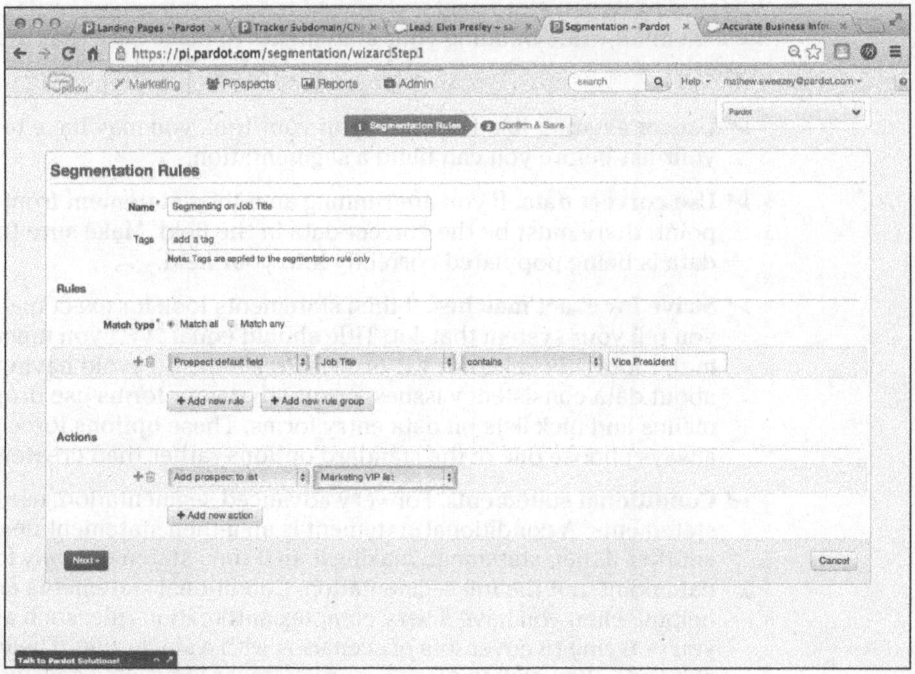

Figure 6-3: Basic segmentations often match a single data point.

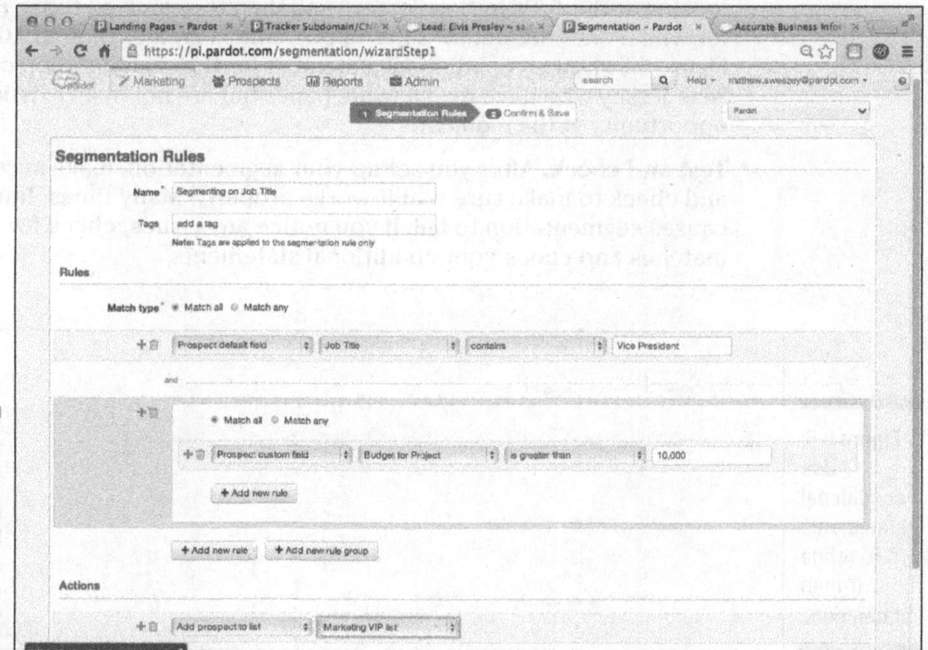

Figure 6-4: Use an if-then statement for more granular segmentation.

When using if-then statements, you need to know a few basic rules. Keep these in mind while building your statements to make sure that they work properly:

- **Use an existing list.** Depending on your tool, you may have to set up your list before you can build a segmentation.
- **Use correct data.** If you are running an if-then statement from a data point, there must be the correct data in the field. Make sure that your data is being populated correctly into your field.
- **Strive for exact matches.** If-then statements look for exact matches. If you tell your system that Job Title should equal "VP," you must have "VP" in the Job Title field, not V.P. or Vice President. To avoid having to worry about data consistency issues, ensure that your forms use drop-down menus and pick lists on data entry forms. These options force people to always choose one of the standard options rather than create their own.
- **Conditional statements.** For very advanced segmentation, use conditional statements. A conditional statement is an if-then statement nested within another if-then statement, making it an if-then statement only for that data point, not the full segmentation. Conditional statements are very helpful when you have a very complex automation rule, such as when you're trying to cover lots of scenarios with a single rule. The conditional elements allow you to place a more granular focus on a specific part of the automation rule. So, for example, the statement might first call for looking at the "VPs in New Jersey" and then to search all those records for which ones are not in "sales opportunities greater than $10,000." Figure 6-5 shows a conditional statement for the segmentation of VPs in New Jersey who have read a white paper but are not in an existing sales opportunity at the moment.
- **Test and check.** After you set up your segmentation, make sure to test it and check to make sure that it works properly. Many times, human error causes segmentation to fail. If you notice any issues, check for exact matches and check your conditional statements.

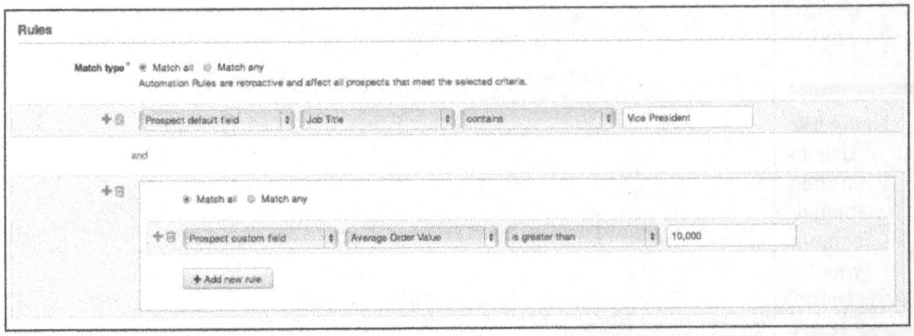

Figure 6-5: Use conditional statements to refine if-then statements.

The importance of minimizing the complexity of advanced segmentations

Advanced segmentations can become unwieldy very quickly. When you start using multiple if-then statements in a single segmentation, you run a high risk of human error. Human error is the number-one reason that segmentation fails. So use the following advice to minimize your complexities and keep you sane:

- **Minimize your risk of failure.** When running very complex if-then statements, you need to monitor a number of rules based on the data in numerous different fields. Changing your database or a field in your database causes your segmentation to either work improperly or fail completely. Fixing these errors is easy. Finding which field to fix is more of a problem.
- **Give yourself a hand.** Use automations and related segmentations to help you, not to do everything for you. Some segmentations require a manual step or attention by a person. Overcomplicating your segmentation only wastes more of your time.
- **Remove issues with turnover.** You probably aren't staying where you are at your company forever, and neither is everyone else at your company. If you and your team make complex rules, consider the difficulty for the next team in managing those rules when you leave. Using simple segmentations minimizes the risk of having to start over from scratch.

Chapter 7

Sending Leads to Sales

In This Chapter

- Involving sales in key decisions
- Turning on sales-enablement functions
- Running campaigns for sales

Marketing automation is not just a tool for marketers, it's a tool for sales as well. Failing to realize this will cause you to run into many issues with salespeople misunderstanding what is being passed to them and misunderstanding how to use the new technology you've invested in. Without proper explanation, sales staff won't understand how to use the information received from marketing correctly, and that leads to salespeople who won't buy in to your new processes. Remember that it's all about generating more revenue, and both sides of the team have the same goal.

You should include sales in all steps of investigation, implementation, and refinement of your marketing automation tool. Give salespeople a voice because you need them to believe in many of these ideas for you to be successful.

This chapter explains how to turn on sales-enablement functionality in your marketing automation system. I also tell you how to align your sales and marketing teams and run your first campaigns for your salespeople.

Aligning Sales and Marketing Teams

Sales and marketing can easily find themselves at odds with each other. Sales can say that the leads being passed aren't any good, and marketing can say that sales isn't closing the leads that marketing passes over. It's a very common struggle within most organizations. Getting both teams aligned and on the same page can happen very easily with the proper technology.

In the next sections, I show you how to involve sales in your marketing automation decisions so that you can align your sales and marketing teams and reduce friction between the two departments.

Working with sales to define fields in your CRM system

The main objective of connecting your marketing automation tool to your CRM is to allow data to flow freely back and forth between sales and marketing. Identifying your key data points on each record before you begin implementation helps you to make sure that you are selecting the correct tool and properly integrating your two tools. Start by defining with sales which fields are required for a lead to be marketing qualified. Marketing-qualified leads are ones that have met all marketing criteria to be considered a lead and are then passed to sales. These fields will be the first fields you need to integrate. The fields you use for segmenting your list will be the second set of fields you need to list. Overlap is likely here, and that is okay. You don't integrate fields twice. Continue this process with each CRM object you use.

Fields you don't use for segmentation and that are not required by sales for a lead to be qualified don't need to be integrated. Fields you don't currently have but that will be required for advanced automations generally are automatically set up when you install your marketing automation tool into your CRM.

Some good examples are fields such as the following:

- Prospect score
- Campaign of origin
- Marketing touch points affecting the lead
- Last time on website
- Last campaign engaged with

Agreeing on sales-ready lead definitions and time frames

If you have a problem with communication between marketing and sales, it's usually a mismatch in definitions. For example, to sales, a lead may mean a person ready to buy. But to a marketer, a lead may mean someone who has an interest. Marketing automation gives you the ability to merge these definitions for a more cohesive team. The three main definitions you need to work on with your team are

- **Sales-ready score:** This score is the minimum threshold that a lead has to meet to get passed to sales. Both sales and marketing have to agree on a score at which a lead gets passed on. Having a minimum threshold is easy to measure and implement with marketing automation, and it removes the frustration stemming from a host of reasons that a lead may have been passed to sales.

- **Service-level agreement:** Sales and marketing teams sometimes disagree over how much time is given to a sales representative to allow him or her to respond to a new lead after it has been passed on sales. The two-way communication between your CRM and your marketing automation tool will provide you the ability to track and automate an agreed-upon time frame and align on the actions to take when this time frame has passed.
- **Sales-ready lead:** A *sales-ready lead* is a lead that is ready to make a purchase decision or have a conversation with a sales representative. Many actions can be signs of a sales-ready lead, but without the context of other actions, they are not enough on their own to accurately qualify a lead as sales ready. Marketing automation gives you the ability to combine all sales-ready actions across all channels so that you have insight into the true sales readiness of a lead based on the entire context of your marketing program. Tools within your marketing automation solution such as lead scoring and lead tracking provide you with the data points to determine when a lead becomes sales ready. The automation part of your solution helps you to nurture the nonsales-ready leads up to that point and hand off the truly sales-ready leads to your sales team in real time.

Identifying the important data points of a lead, contact, account, and opportunity

Engaging sales to create common definitions for all aspects of the lead life cycle is key to a successful integration. Engaging with sales to have sales staff help create the following definitions will foster buy-in to the concept and help them understand what is being passed to them and why.

- **Lead:** Define the information, activity, and score required for a person to become a lead.
- **Contact:** Define when a lead is converted to a contact. This includes what processes need to happen and by whom, and whether the lead needs to be tied to an account or an opportunity at this stage.
- **Marketing Qualified Led (MQL):** Define when a lead is passed to sales, which includes defining what information is required by marketing to be attached to the record.

- **Sales-Qualified Lead (SQL):** Define the process of sales accepting marketing-qualified leads. This is usually called a *Service-Level Agreement* (SLA). The SLA should define how long sales has to respond to accept a marketing lead and the process for accepting and declining a lead. When the MQL lead is accepted, it becomes an SQL.
- **Opportunity:** Define when a lead or account is created into an opportunity. This should be qualified by a buying timeline and marked on the record.

Collaborating with sales

You can run many types of sales support campaigns, but you should never run one without collaborating with sales in the following ways:

- **Define goals together.** You need to sit down with the head of your sales team and define goals for your campaigns. Defining goals helps to get cooperation with each idea as well as a clear idea of what the campaigns are supposed to help with.
- **Obtain acceptance on ideas.** Your ideas need to be bought into by the sales team. You might need to attend sales meetings to present your ideas, or do this via an email. I suggest meeting in person so that sales staff can ask you questions. I promise you that they will have lots of questions.
- **Create a test group.** Set up a test group if you have a tough crowd. The test group is the first to use the campaign and then share their results. A test group can be a great asset if your team is reluctant to change.
- **Set a report date.** You must have a defined end of your campaigns. Having an end allows you to obtain feedback. If sales doesn't want your campaigns to stop, you don't have to, but putting a defined date down on paper gives you a predetermined date for reevaluation. It also allows you to push off sales' comments until that date.

Asking sales for content suggestions

Your salespeople may have a lot of good ideas. Remember that they are on the front lines; they get a lot of information and generally keep their ears pretty close to the action. They know what other companies are using, they see campaigns others are using, and they know what's working and what isn't. Asking them for content suggestions is a great idea; however, you need some structure around this process. Here are ways to create that structure:

- **Use a form.** You have a marketing automation tool that can make forms. You can use your form tool within your marketing automation tool to create a place where sales can give you feedback. This is an outside-the-box use of your new form-building tool, located within your marketing automation tool. Your form should have only a few fields. You might use a drop-down list for campaign type, such as email, white paper, and so on, and you should have a free text field in which sales staff can type an idea. Your form can also send an auto responder back out to the sales rep saying "Thank You."

- **Make it clear that not all ideas will fly.** Have a dialogue with people about your idea-creation process. They need to know that not all ideas make it to a full campaign. If you are not clear on this, many reps will think you don't like their ideas. This may well be the case, but you need them on your side to keep giving you ideas and to help push these campaigns. Playing a bit of politics helps keep the relationship between the two departments at its best.
- **Put a bounty out.** Another great way to get feedback on content ideas is to put a bounty on other companies' collateral. You can use any prize you want, but incentivize your salespeople to find other companies' content and send it to you. This approach eliminates their subjective input and just gets you what's happening out there in your marketplace.
- **Sit in on sales meetings.** This is the other best way to get content ideas. Your salespeople can voice their issues with deals and describe where they are stuck. Creating content to help them get around these issues is a big win for you — and them. Just listening to their meetings can be a great source of information.

Copying your best salespeople

Because any email communication you will be sending in a sales support campaign will appear to come from a salesperson, you need to make sure that they look as though they came from a salesperson. Many marketers cringe when they think about the emails their salespeople send; their salespeople, however, usually know a thing or two about what they are writing. Learning to take tips from your best salespeople will greatly increase engagement with your emails.

- **Ask for their best email.** Every sales rep has his or her "best email." I was in sales for years and I can still remember my best ones. They are the ones I'd use the most often, and they were usually tailored to a specific point in the buying process and were easily changed. The latter two points give you two big wins. Sales will give you the best messaging for a particular point in the buying cycle, as well as give you a template, which works very well with dynamic text. Figure 7-1 gives a good example of a great sales email, which is set up to be able to just drop in names and other information.

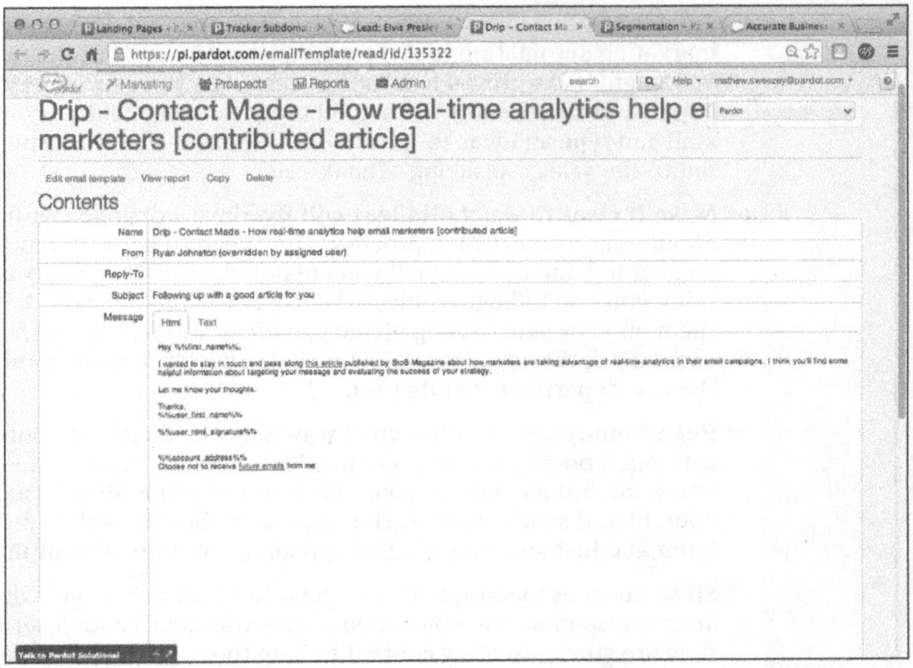

Figure 7-1: Creating a dynamic email template can be very easy.

- **Find out their cadence.** Cadence is something every sales rep has as well. Each rep has a process for when they call, how often they call, and when they do different types of touch points. Having a process is systematic and makes keeping up with a lot of leads much easier. Your best sales reps will have figured out a very effective cadence for your marketplace. They know how often is too often to reach out, and how soon is too soon to reach out.

  When I was selling, my cadence was 2-5-12-30. I called, left a voice message, and then waited two days. I then followed up via email and then waited five more days. I finally placed my last call, left my last voice message, and sent my last email after 12 days. After 30 days, I reached back out to the prospect if I had no sign of engagement during that time. I promise that your sales team does something very similar.

- **Speak their language.** Despite any bad grammar, bad formatting, and careless mistakes your salespeople make on a daily basis, this is what makes them salespeople, not marketers. Speak in their vernacular, and write as they would — maybe not *exactly* as they would, but similar. Notice how they write an email and how they speak about topics. Pick up some of these tricks and it will make your emails more believable and increase your engagement.

  Note that I'm not saying to have bad formatting, but rather to have none. Personal emails are what most salespeople send when they are communicating with a person, and these are short, with no formatting. Salespeople get into trouble when they try to format emails or make emails not look handwritten.

Turning on Sales Enablement Functionality

Turning on sales enablement is the last part of your implementation between your marketing automation tool and your CRM. The reason to save this part for last is that everything else has to be done first before you can leverage any of the features for sales. Getting your sales-enablement tools set up also is likely to require you to have very solid understanding of your tool because you are now the expert in your office, so be prepared.

Some salespeople like to try new tools but others will never use them, so make sure that you share the potential impact with your salespeople. The impact to the sales organization is often so large that salespeople who sell with marketing automation won't sell without it again. They often become the champions for marketing automation when they move to a new company that is not using it.

You shouldn't activate sales enablement without introducing these features to your salespeople. You should take the following three important steps just before or immediately after you turn everything on:

1. **Have a "town hall" meeting.**

   Get all your salespeople together and go over the changes they are about to see in the CRM application. Let them know that they do not have to change but that they can leverage these new tools to sell more. Show the CRM screen with the new features turned on and explain what each feature is supposed to do.

2. **Demonstrate the process of the lead flow.**

   During your town hall meeting, show a prospect record. Create a dialogue based on a salesperson who got a lead, saw the lead go cold, reconnected after getting a lead activity notification from a drip campaign, and then generated the closed ROI. Make sure that your demonstration shows salespeople how they now have visibility into all actions of leads, automatic nurturing, and instant reporting.

3. **Conduct a training class.**

   Set up a short training class online or in person. Most companies use either video tutorials or live trainings in a classroom setting. Getting your team trained saves you countless questions and hours of frustration.

You don't need to have sales enablement functionality turned on to get your own marketing value out of your tool after you integrate your CRM system with your marketing automation tool. However, enabling sales functionality doesn't take any meaningful amount of time, and the value for sales is huge. So it really doesn't make any sense to leave it turned off.

You also don't have to turn on all sales enablement technologies right away. Many marketing automation tools have various levels of sales support. Most tools have three levels: sales notifications, daily emails, and campaigns. They all work independently of each other, so I suggest starting with one and moving toward another later on. Start with daily emails and then move to more frequent notifications, followed by sales campaigns.

Supporting Campaigns for Your Sales Team

Marketing automation can lend a huge hand when you're crafting campaigns to support your sales team. If you can get sales support campaigns down, you can greatly shorten your sales cycle and increase your salespeople's close rates very easily.

Building automated campaigns for cold sales leads

The first campaign you should build for sales after turning on sales enablement should be designed to catch and nurture the leads that sales can't reach through the selling process. These leads usually fall through the cracks and are never heard from again. Many articles that cover sales effectiveness reference a statistic that says these unreachable leads will buy from someone over the next 24 months. If you aren't communicating with these leads somehow, it's unlikely they will buy from your salesperson.

Creating this campaign requires you to first identify a few key fields for segmenting your campaign. I suggest looking at two fields. One is a lead stage and the other is the lead's last activity date:

- **Lead Stage:** The *lead stage* is the prospect's place in the sales process. For example, a lead could be in the assigned stage or the accepted stage depending on whether the lead is assigned to a sales rep or assigned and also accepted by the rep. If you don't currently use a lead stage, you need to change that situation so that you can create a campaign to catch cold leads. The field is filled in by a sales rep manually, or you can use CRM automations to change it for you.

- **Last Activity Date:** Last Activity Date is a custom field already in use by your CRM tool or a default field added by your marketing automation tool during integration. This field displays the last activity date of the lead in question, helping you gauge that lead's last interactions with any of your marketing activities.

After you have the aforementioned two fields set up, use them to create your campaign by assigning the campaign to a condition. For example, if the lead has not had activity within 10 days, and the lead is in the assigned lead stage, your lead has been assigned but the sales rep hasn't accepted or started working the lead. To keep the lead warm, your marketing automation system can now add the cold lead to your cold lead nurturing campaign.

The other big win is the fact that any activity the lead shows will go directly to the sales rep because the lead has already been assigned. That way, marketing is helping sales to stay in front of leads, and sales is helping marketing get more value out of the leads they created.

Using lead assignments to drive leads to the sales team

Lead assignment rules allow you to pass sales-ready leads to sales in real time. You should be thinking about when to pass on a lead, and how to do so. Here are the most common scenarios and how to accomplish them:

- **One person owns the relationship and sells multiple products.** When your sales team is relationship-based with a large book of products, you don't need to do much work on lead assignment. Your leads are already assigned to your rep, and your rep gets updates on when his or her leads are engaging with the campaign.

  Figure 7-2 shows a lead-notification tool that shows your reps in real time who is engaging with the campaign. Because you don't need to reassign the lead, you need only to set up an automation to let your sales reps know when a certain level of sales readiness has been reached. Your CRM tool can accomplish this for you if you choose to have it do so. CRM tools have the capability to create custom list views. So if you have your lead score synced with your CRM tool, your sales team can have a list of leads with a score over "*X*." This allows the team to just check this list for any new leads.

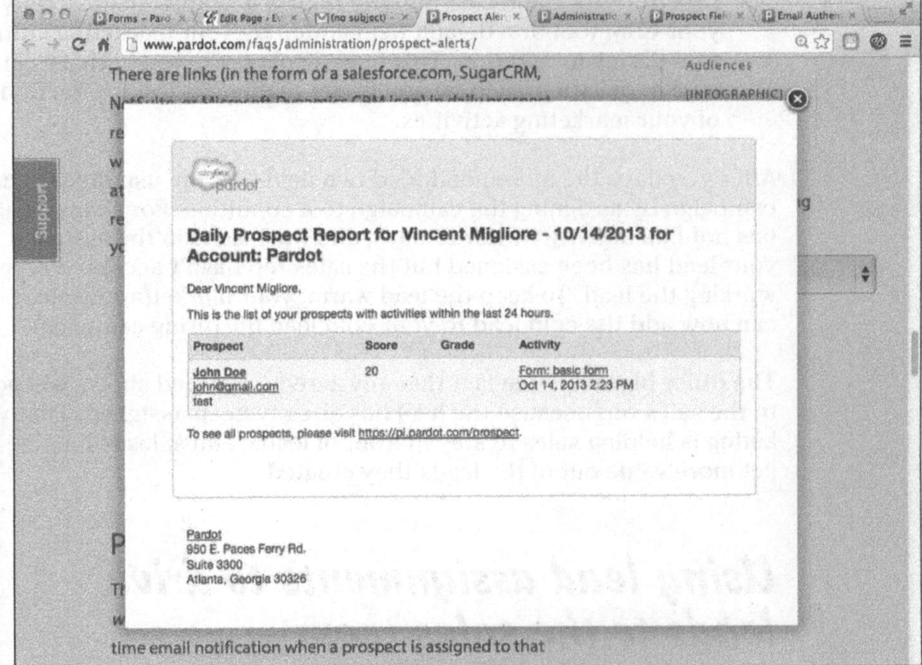

Figure 7-2: Use lead assignment rules to show campaign engagement to your reps.

- **Sales reps sell one product line.** When you have a sales team on which each sales rep sells only a single product, and you have multiple products, driving leads to the correct salesperson on the team can be tricky. A lot of your lead assignment will depend on your CRM setup at this point. Whether you use duplicate lead records or a single lead record will also determine the complexity of your lead assignment at this point. Consult your vendor to get further information on how to accomplish this scenario because your tool will determine how it can be done.

If your emails are being sent from a salesperson automatically, email replies will go back to that salesperson as well. Keep this fact in mind, because if you have an automated campaign sending emails out on a sales rep's behalf and a person replies, the sales rep needs to know where that email reply came from. This situation should be covered in your training.

Never give your salespeople access to execute marketing campaigns on their own. Many salespeople want to send email blasts to their leads. Again, don't let them do this — it's a bad idea for many reasons, with the biggest one being that you're now moving into one-to-one marketing methods with your marketing automation tool. Mass email blasting damages the relationships you're building and can greatly damage your company's reputation as well. Your marketing automation tool is very powerful, and you run the risk of wasting all your efforts if you give control to sales. If salespeople do need to run campaigns, give them a place to submit the campaign they want, and you can run it for them.

Impacting sales with lead notifications

Salespeople love to have data on their prospects and they love to be notified when prospect data changes. The more data they have, the better decisions they can make when they engage. Any notification you plan to set up for your salespeople needs to be communicated after integrating your CRM system. One of the most common is the lead activity reports included in your CRM tool after integration, as shown in Figure 7-3.

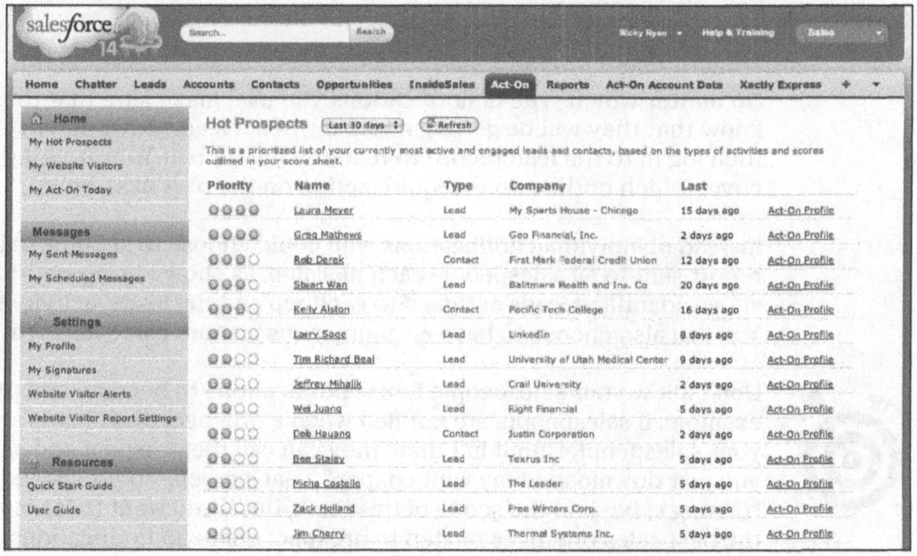

Figure 7-3: Lead activity reports should be communicated to sales.

Logging your lead history into your CRM system allows sales to use one tool for all prospect data and notifications. Each tool has a different way of notifying salespeople. Some tools use notification tools within a CRM application; other tools use desktop notifications outside the CRM application, as shown in Figure 7-4.

Figure 7-4: You can use desktop notifications in place of CRM notifications.

No matter which type of notifications you use, make sure that the sales reps know that they will be getting notified when a lead shows activity. They can then log in to the lead record to read the full report. Your training should cover which notifications require action on the part of sales.

Instead of individual notifications, you could choose to set up a daily summary report sent to all salespeople each morning, as shown in Figure 7-5. A summary shows identified leads assigned to each rep and the leads' activity that day. You can also choose to have all anonymous visitors listed and sent to sales.

Don't allow your salespeople to use notifications to become creepy. For example, if salespeople are notified when a prospect downloads a white paper, your salespeople shouldn't think they can call the prospect and say, "I know you just downloaded my white paper." That's creepy to prospects. Anticreepy training is beyond the scope of this book, but if you want to learn more about the best sales practices related to prospect data and notifications, go to `http://vimeo.com/64080251` and take the training session titled "Social Selling, How Not to be Creepy."

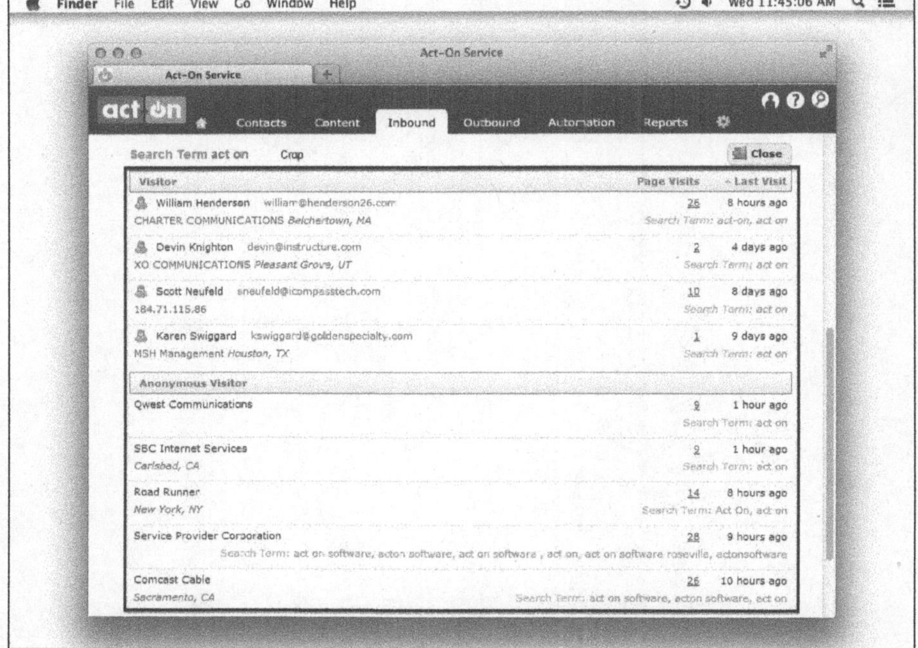

Figure 7-5: Use daily reports to summarize data from multiple notifications.

Catching leads who fall through the cracks

When leads are passed on to sales, they will have to meet some basic level of qualification. Leads are also a time-sensitive item. Harvard Business Review, in an article titled "The Short Life of Online Sales Leads," by James B. Oldroyd, Kristina McElheran, and David Elkington, researched this issue and found that a company is seven times more likely to qualify a lead and engage in a conversation with the lead if the company responds to a customer engagement within an hour of receiving the inquiry. Being able to use automation to ensure fast sales assignment and fast follow-up is a huge business driver in any modern business.

Good leads buy from someone eventually, and if it's not from you, it's from your competition. So it's important to ensure that sales is following up on leads on a timely basis to help keep leads from falling through the cracks.

One of the biggest values of marketing automation is the capability to align the sales teams by creating joint programs to catch these leads before they fall through the cracks. When the marketing automation and CRM tools are connected, marketing can create programs to recapture a lead if there is no activity from sales, and sales can create programs to request marketing programs when they are unable to get in contact with a lead. These programs can automatically bring the lead back to the marketing team and put the lead on a drip program right away, keeping your company in front of the lead.

Part III

Running Automation Campaigns

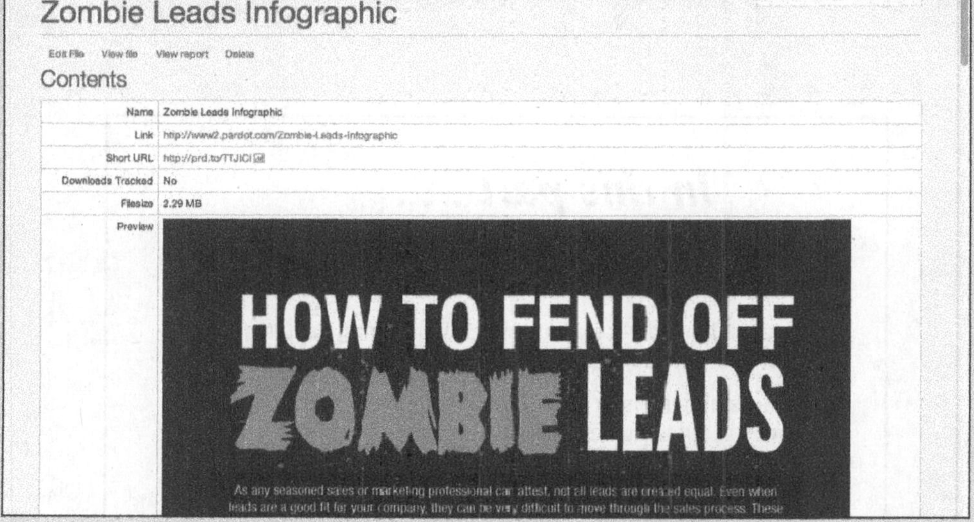

Visit www.dummies.com/extras/marketingvirtualization to read more on how to create the perfect email follow-up for an automated campaign.

In this part . . .

- Get to know how content marketing plays a key role in marketing automation, and learn how to create this content.
- Find out how to get started with drip nurturing campaigns and how to create campaigns that will convert prospects.
- Understand the new best practices for forms and landing pages in automated campaigns.
- Discover the new world of personal emails and how to use them in an automated fashion.

Chapter 8

Content Marketing and Its Place in Marketing Automation

In This Chapter

- Developing content for the buyer's journey (a.k.a. the funnel)
- Gleaning new insights about content
- Tying video and webinars into automation

When you have a marketing automation engine, you need to fuel it. Content is the fuel for all modern marketing, especially if you use a marketing automation tool. Marketing automation helps you derive insight from content that you never had before. It tells you where a prospect is in the buying cycle, which content is getting stale, which content is most influential to a closed deal, and much more.

These insights are obtainable only if you understand the new relationship between content and marketing automation. In this chapter, you find out how to create content specifically to be used with your marketing automation tool, when to use short-form versus long-form content, and how to prove the value of content marketing through your marketing automation tool.

New Content for a New Tool

To maximize the use of your marketing automation tool, first you must understand people and their relationship to content. Automation is great *only* if you are sending the correct content to the correct people. To build a basic understanding of how to get it right, you need to realize that people engage with two types of content:

- **Problem-solving content in the buyer's funnel:** Within the buyer's journey, or funnel, people look for content to help them solve a problem. This means that you need to make sure to send the correct content at the correct time.

- **Content for professional development or entertainment.** This is content that is consumed on a daily basis and is not a signal of a buying process. Most people consume the same amount of professional development and/or entertainment on a daily basis. The blogs you read every day, or the Twitter followers you listen to daily, are good examples of this content.

When designing content, you need to set goals for your content as it relates to your lead life cycle. Follow these pointers to help make sure that the goals for your content match up to its relationship to the lead life cycle.

- **Early-stage leads:** Early-stage leads don't need to hear from your sales team. They don't need to be prompted for a demo and don't want to read your press release. When crafting content to attract early-stage leads, consider creating content to help leads be better at their jobs. Your goal for early-stage content should be to build a relationship, not sell. Jay Baer (@jaybaer) said it best: "Helping is the new selling." Some good forms of content for early stage leads are
    - Blog posts focused on how to identify a problem
    - How-to articles
    - Short video clips
- **Mid-stage cycle leads:** Leads that are in the middle of a buyer's journey generally have a problem, or pain point, but not a way to solve it. Generally, buyers in this stage also do not have the budget, authority, or timeline to purchase. Content for leads in the middle of the buyer's journey should help explain options to solve their issue.

  You also need to show substantial social proof, that is, show how others have benefitted from your solution. This proof can be in the form of an interview with a person who is a client, or a testimonial letter. This information helps prospects see how others solved a problem by using you. The goal for this content should be to help people identify the way to solve their pain as well as to get their team to buy in. Social proof provides validation from outside your company. Some good forms of content for mid-stage leads are
    - Blog posts focused on how to solve the pain points
    - Webinars featuring client success stories
    - Case studies
- **Late-stage leads:** Leads later in a buyer's journey have already agreed on how to solve their problem and are looking at vendors. They are in the process of making a short list of vendors to vet. Your goal should be to get on the short list. Some good forms of content for late-stage leads are

    - Blog posts comparing you with other vendors
    - Buyers' guides
    - Sample RFPs (Requests for Proposals are typically used by large enterprise companies looking to evaluate vendors. They consist of spreadsheets of standard questions to be asked of all vendors as a screening round before demonstrations are set up.)

- **Sales leads:** Leads in the salespeople's hands still need content. The sales team usually sends it, but you need to create it. Some good forms of content for sales leads are
    - Blog posts on achievements
    - Case studies (can be the same ones used for mid-stage leads)
    - One-page sales sheets

When advertising on Google AdWords, test different advertisements for the same piece of content. You might find that the same piece of content can work at different stages in the lead life cycle, so make sure to test this possibility. Craft your advertisements specifically to a single stage in the lead life cycle to increase your odds of engagement and extend the life of the piece of content.

Blogging and its place in your automation strategy

Blogging is usually the first type of content most companies create. It is low cost, low effort to create, and it's effective. Blogging online is easy, but it's a difficult way to drive traffic in the short term. Blogging is a long-term strategy that needs to be correctly understood so that its benefits can be maximized. Also, a blog isn't something people are going to read during the buying cycle. So you need to understand that blogging is for audience building, which in turn builds your funnel. But it is very different from the content you need to create for the buyer's journey. Here are some tips to keep in mind when writing for your blog and tying it into your marketing automation solution:

- **Evergreen posts:** Posts that have a very long life span should be given more attention than shorter, time-sensitive posts. Evergreen posts should be well researched and heavily optimized for SEO. These posts pay dividends long into the future. Also, use these posts to advertise your content. Figure 8-1 shows a blog post with the source of research to drive downloads of the content.

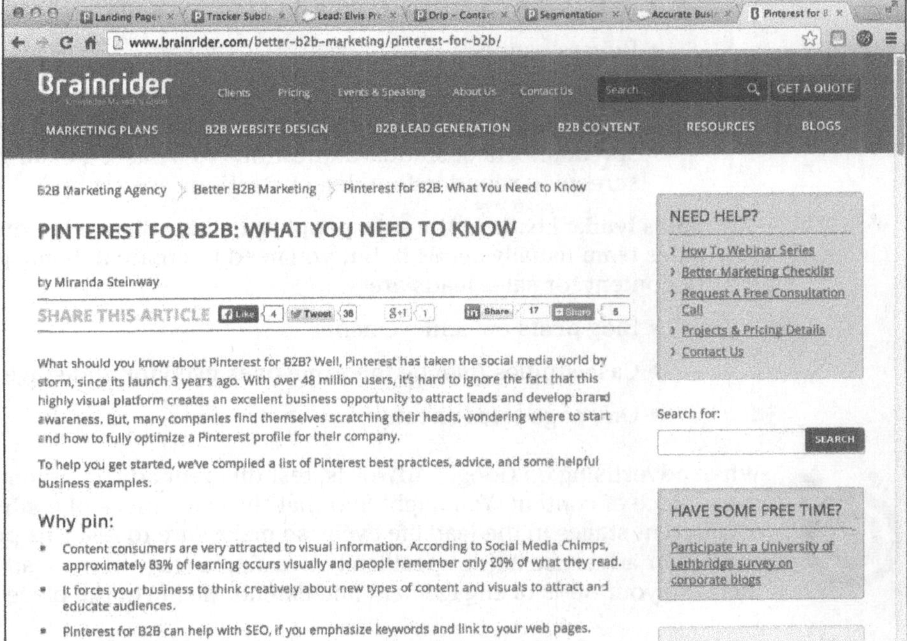

Figure 8-1: Evergreen blog post supporting content downloads.

- **Breaking news posts:** Breaking news posts are generally quick-hit posts. They are very timely and have short life spans. They drive a lot of traffic in a short time period. When writing breaking news pieces, make sure to work appropriate content into the body of the article. The goal is for your breaking news to be shared and conversational, thus driving people back to the post and seeing your content.
- **Thought leadership:** Your blog is your soap box. Use it wisely and effectively. With 2 million blog posts going up every day, the amount of content you have to compete against is huge. Keep focused on your goal of being the brightest mind in your industry and you can gain the thought-leadership spot. If you fill your blog with reposts of other people's thoughts and ideas, you are going to get traffic but won't be considered a thought leader. If people consider you a thought leader, they are more likely to engage with and share your content.
- **Being noticed:** Many times, you have tactical goals. They might not be lead-generation goals but rather visibility goals. Maybe you need to get on the radar of analysts. When your goal is to get noticed, consider creating content specifically for analysts. Interview them, do research that they will find interesting, or propose a question for them.

- **Readership:** For your blog to be read, it has to be seen. Don't just wait for it to be found; to drive readership, you also need to promote it. When you have evergreen posts, you can use them in lead-nurturing campaigns and even as social engagements. Think about advertising posts on Facebook ads, Twitter, and LinkedIn. Consider promoting a post just as you do a piece of content in these advertisements, not your blog's name. Driving people to your blog gives them a reason to come and helps them to find more of your content.

Some blog platforms have sidebar callout features. The features are just advertising spots on the side of your blog. Use these features to advertise content offers as well. These are good places to show a video, the cover of a white paper, or an impressive statistic. Think of these as mini billboards used to generate a click to download the content. These also are easy to change so that you are always promoting your most important content regardless of which post someone is reading. These are a great place to use dynamic content populated from your marketing automation solution.

Six people in content marketing to follow on Twitter

Content marketing is a world unto itself. It takes a lot of work and planning along with great execution to have an awesome content strategy. Whether you're new or a veteran content marketer, make sure that you're following the best people to learn from. Here is a short list of some of the best minds in content marketing:

- **Joe Pulizzi (@joepuizzi):** Joe is the head of the Content Marketing Institute.
- **Nolin Lechur (@nolin):** Nolin is cofounder of Brainrider, a boutique marketing firm specializing in content marketing.
- **Jay Baer (@jaybaer):** Jay is the founder of Convince and Convert and author of *Youtility* (Penguin Group, 2013).
- **Wistia (@wistia):** Wistia is a video hosting company that teaches you how to do video content — and teaches it better than anyone else.
- **Ann Handley (@marketingprofs):** Ann is cofounder of Clickz, Chief Content Officer at Marketingprofs, and author of *Content Rules* (John Wiley & Sons, Inc., 2012).
- **Joe Chernov (@jchernov):** Joe received the 2012 Content Marketer of the Year award (awarded by Content Marketing Institute) and is Chief Marketing Officer at Kinvey.

Knowing when to use short-form content

Short-form content is a shortened version of a full document. A good example is a blog post created from a full white paper or industry report. The report is the long-form content, whereas the post is the short-form content. If you break the report up into sections and make each section a separate piece, this would be considered short form as well.

When using short-form content, the best place to use it is in outbound marketing efforts. Because of its length, short-form content is easy to engage with and easy to create, thereby allowing you to generate a lot of email content from very few long-form pieces of content. Use it for

- Lead nurturing
- Email marketing

Knowing when to use long-form content

Long-form content is a full version of a document. A good example is an ebook, a white paper, or a long industry article. The report is the long-form content, whereas the post is the short-form content. You typically use long-form content for inbound traffic. It is promoted via paid search and SEO and is found by buyers doing research.

Site visitors are more likely to engage with long-form content than short-form content when you require them to fill out a form. The consumer finds more value in a larger document and is more likely to fill out a form in return for your content. Use long-form content for

- Paid search
- SEM lead generation
- SEO lead generation
- Social lead generation

Creating content for lead nurturing

The number-one complaint I have heard from people getting started with marketing automation is that they don't have enough time to create content. This is also the number-one reason that I have seen companies delay their adoption of marketing automation. However, the real issue is that they are thinking about content in the wrong way. When you are building content for lead nurturing, it is very easy. Take a look at some easy examples of content for nurturing programs:

- **Short form:** The opposite of long is short. Short-form content should be easily digested within five minutes. In a recent research report I conducted, only 1.7 percent of respondents said that they prefer content over five pages long. To create short-form content, you can break down long-form content or create it from scratch. The content should consist of specific ideas that can then link to bigger pieces of content if the person wants to read more.
- **Blog posts:** You don't have to write them! Two million new blog posts go up each day. If you want to be considered a thought leader, you should also consider helping people find information, not just creating it yourself. Other people's blogs are a great way to do this. Send emails with links to other blog articles by industry experts. You are sending a link to the blogs, not putting the blog content into your email.

  Being a thought leader doesn't always mean that the thought belongs to you. Raising awareness of good thinking is also a way to become a thought leader. If you use this technique, make sure to let readers know why you are sharing the ideas. Tell them the reason that a post is great, for example, and what they should try to learn from it.
- **Videos:** Video content is currently one of the most engaging forms of content. You can create videos quickly, easily, and with little expense. If you have not done videos before, I suggest going to Wistia.com (@wistia) to find out how to do video well. Wistia.com also shows you how to shoot video with anything from your iPhone to a production camera. My first video was shot on a Sony HandyCam with a microphone from a computer attached to it. You don't have to put the video in your email, and it is not advisable to try to embed video in email. Instead, take a screen shot and make the image a link to your video. Or just use a hyperlink to the video.
- **Testimonials:** These are a super great form of content as well. They are key to lead nurturing because they show social proof. Social proof is something all buyers are looking for before they set up demos with your company. I suggest having testimonials in different content forms. Consider having a few videos, a few interviews hosted on your blog, or a few case studies. A testimonial can consist of only one item, such as a single quote. Don't try to overproduce these elements at this stage. It is more important to have just one quote from four companies than to have one single case study with lots of quotes in it.
- **Short research:** Proprietary research is a must. There are 294 billion emails sent every day. For your emails to be engaged with, they have to be fresh and relevant. The easiest way to ensure that they are fresh is to create new research. Research is interesting in lots of ways and can provide

you with tons of value. Consider using SurveyMonkey or LinkedIn to conduct short surveys. You can pay for survey submissions for about $3 each. Remember that you need just one metric, so don't go overboard with your research.

Observations are a form of research, too. One of my best and most productive research projects was to chart the adoption of best practices for the marketing industry. I did the research by observing 150 websites and checking the basic items such as their forms, emails, and website. This was all observation based, but it told a very compelling and powerful story. So don't always think that you need to hire someone for research or that it's outside your means.

- **Survey:** Send a survey to your prospects. This is a great form of content. You are asking for their input, which is not a typical form of engagement; it is, however, highly effective. You can survey their biggest pain points, their thoughts, or their opinions on how your company can improve.
- **Infographics:** The current golden child of many marketers, infographics have become a must for any company. If you don't have the means to create them, find your local design school and pay a cheap artist. I've paid $200 dollars per infographic and driven tons of engagement through it. The infographic is a visual depiction of data. It's usually fun and uses graphics to showcase the data. Graphics are used frequently to take mundane topics and make them fun through good graphical layouts. Make sure that you have fresh data and then worry about making it pretty. This is where you can use your survey data or your research to drive increased engagement.
- **Webinars:** Conducting webinars is another great way to drive engagement in a nurturing program. ReadyTalk (@readytalk), a webinar-hosting company, suggests that hosting a webinar recording on your website can increase the life span of your efforts and increase your lead count. In a recent survey I conducted, I found that only 16 percent of consumers preferred to watch a webinar live. The largest majority said it didn't matter whether it was live or recorded. So consider putting links to your webinars in your nurturing programs.

Managing Your Content

After you have content, it's time to learn to manage it. Tracking your content — knowing who is engaging with it and where it is being engaged with — helps you figure out how to present it better the next time. Marketing automation makes content management very different from how it used to be.

Hosting content in your marketing automation tool

Your marketing automation tool has a content repository, which is where you can upload content. The purpose of hosting your content here is to track it. When you host your content in your marketing automation tool, it records every person interacting with your content and allows you to run segmentations and automation based on content engagement. The content to host in your marketing automation tool is as follows:

- White papers
- Sales collateral
- Image files needed for email templates
- PDF files
- Ebooks
- Case studies

Content you should *not* host in your marketing automation tool is the following:

- Blog posts (These remain in your blogging platform.)
- Videos (These are stored in your video-hosting solution.)
- Webinars (These are stored in your video-hosting solution.)

When you host your content in your marketing automation tool, it gives your content a new URL. See Figure 8-2 to see the URL of the white paper I uploaded. You use this URL to promote your content. This is the URL that you will use in social media, as a hyperlink on your blog, and for your AdWords campaigns.

When you host content in outside sources, such as video files, make sure to understand how your solution deals with tracking these. The reason you usually don't want to host these files inside your marketing automation tool is their file size. Generally, you have a limit on the amount of content you can host in your solution. A single video sometimes can eat up your entire storage space, so using an outside hosting solution for videos is recommended. Using outside hosting also gives you many other advantages that I cover when I talk more about videos later in this chapter.

Figure 8-2: The URL I use for promoting content via my marketing automation tool.

Easy ways to track your distributed content

When you have a third party send out content for you, or your content is hosted on another site, you're distributing content. Sending distributed content is very common if you ever put on list rental email campaigns or engage in comarketing with your partners. In these cases, you need to be familiar with ways to track your engagement when your assets live off your website. Uploading a sales presentation into an online tool like SlideShare and posting videos to YouTube are both good examples of assets living off your website. If you learn to utilize your marketing automation URLs and custom redirect URLs, you'll always be able to track your assets. Here are some methods for tracking distributed content:

- **Given URL:** Your given URL is the URL you are given by a tool or program. This is the URL your marketing automation tool gives you when it hosts your asset. Figure 8-3 shows the given URL of a white paper I loaded into my marketing automation tool.
- **Redirects:** A redirect is a URL that allows you to track a person back to another location. Figure 8-4 shows a redirect URL being set up to go to a YouTube-hosted video. Using a custom redirect is great when you are doing a comarketing campaign and using assets hosted on other sites.

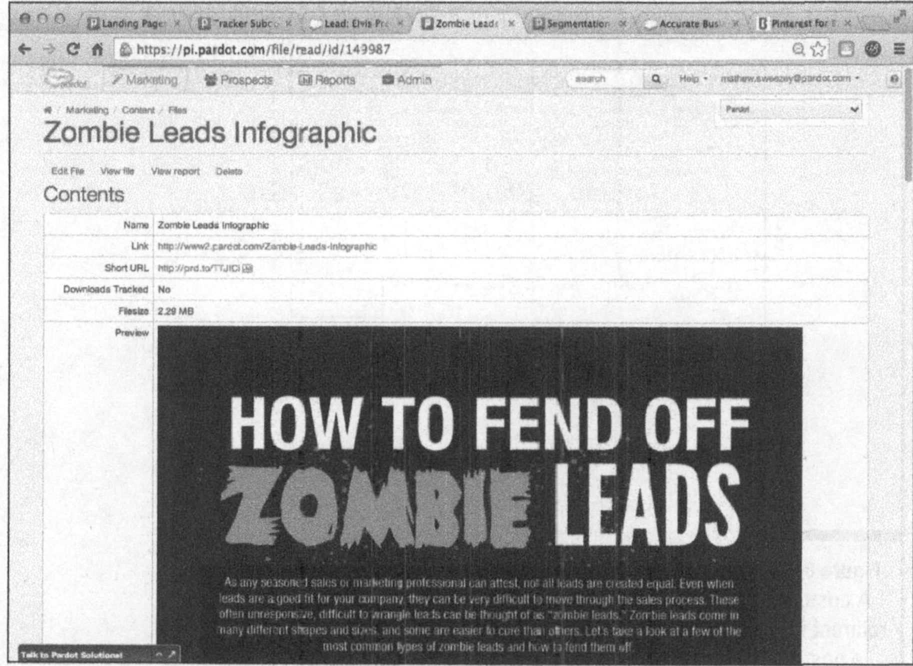

Figure 8-3: The given URL of a recently uploaded white paper.

- **Master campaign.** If your campaigns include many different content pieces and assets, you might want to create a master campaign, which allows you to tie a lot of assets together to track the full campaign much more easily. Creating a report is something you do for any campaign you run on your own site; however, you should go to this trouble only if it is a large campaign. To do this for every small comarketing piece might be overload. Having a master campaign makes your life a lot easier when trying to digest the effects of a full six-month marketing campaign that uses many microsites and assets.
- **Automatic redirects.** If you want to protect content that you're not hosting, you can do so. Your forms or landing pages can automatically redirect a person to another web URL after the person completes the form. You can easily set up a redirect on your form or landing page; how to do it depends on your tool. Having a redirect allows you to have your lead capture form on your site while driving people automatically to other third-party sites so that you can track the action.

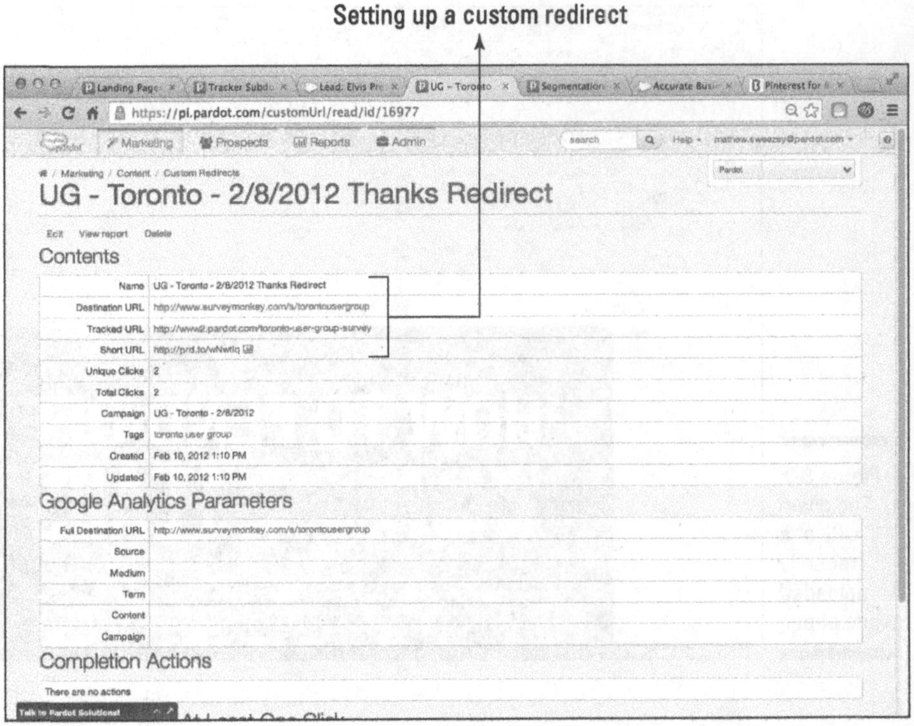

Setting up a custom redirect

Figure 8-4: A custom redirect for a hosted video.

Creating new content reports

If you've followed the suggestions in this chapter for tracking your content, the guesswork is now gone: You know exactly which content is getting engaged with, by whom, and when. This is the biggest difference you will notice about your content between pre- and post-marketing automation. Before marketing automation, you knew whether people filled out a form to download your content. Post-marketing automation, you know when they actually read it, watch it, or share it.

Here are a few basic reports to consider creating after you have this visibility:

- **Engagement/time report:** Now that you can track every person who engaged with your content, you need to be able to look at the data and determine whether your content is trending up or down. Some content will have timelines, but other content (such as evergreen content) won't. Make sure that you can export a CSV file of your content engagement and can see a trendline of engagement. If you notice that your content has declining engagement, look at the content and the distribution. Have you reduced the distribution of the content? Or is the content in need of an update?

- **Influence report:** Much of your content can now be tracked to see what influence it has. An influence report helps you see whether your content is helping to move people through the funnel. This is also easily seen in a stage-based report. A proper stage-based report will show the last content engaged in by a lead moved to the next stage. Both of these reports will help you identify which content to send to people and at which time. This allows you to easily build an automated program to send the correct content at the correct time.

Tying Webinars and Video to Your Automation

We have been trained to love video. It's the status quo, so jump on board. The average American reads only one book per year and watches 40 hours of television each week. Learning how to engage consumers where they want to engage is key for the future of your marketing.

The two most popular media are webinars and hosted videos. Both are very engaging and can be directly tied into your marketing automation tool to give you deeper insights into how people are consuming your content, how to improve your content, and how well it is driving revenue for your organization. In this section, I show you how to tie webinars and hosted videos into your marketing automation tool.

Understanding webinars for automation

Along with all forms of video, webinars have become one of marketers' greatest lead-generation tools. If you have been on the hosting side of a webinar, you can understand the difficulties of trying to engage with an audience you can't see. Webinars can increase their effectiveness when tied together with a marketing automation tool. Here are a few tips to keep in mind to get more out of both your webinar and your marketing automation tool when they are tied together:

- **Integrate your tools:** Integrate your webinar platform with your marketing automation tool. Doing so removes the need to import and export your lists. It also allows you to score leads based on their engagement with the webinar, in turn allowing you to easily segment attendees and score prospects on webinar engagement.

- **When using slides, make them fun:** A webinar is a visual and auditory experience. If you are neglecting either part of this experience, it could be boring. If it's boring, you hurt your future webinar attendance. Have fun with your slide deck presentation so that your audience wants to look at it. If you don't have design skills, buy prebuilt slide templates through Themeforest. Figure 8-5 shows some of the great designs you can buy instantly.

  Learn to use the Master Slide feature in PowerPoint. This feature allows you to easily edit a slide deck template. Customize a basic PowerPoint prebuilt template to create your own in seconds.

- **Use polls:** If your webinar tool allows for polls, use them. They help you engage with your audience. Also, other webinar tools, such as ReadyTalk, allow you to score leads based on engagement with polls, as shown in Figure 8-6.
- **Replay:** Make sure that you host your webinar so that others can watch it later. Anita Wehnert from ReadyTalk says the company has seen pre-recorded webinars drive 47 percent more leads over time than the webinar did the day it aired. Make sure to protect your recording with a lead capture form. For more details on lead capture forms, check out Chapter 9.

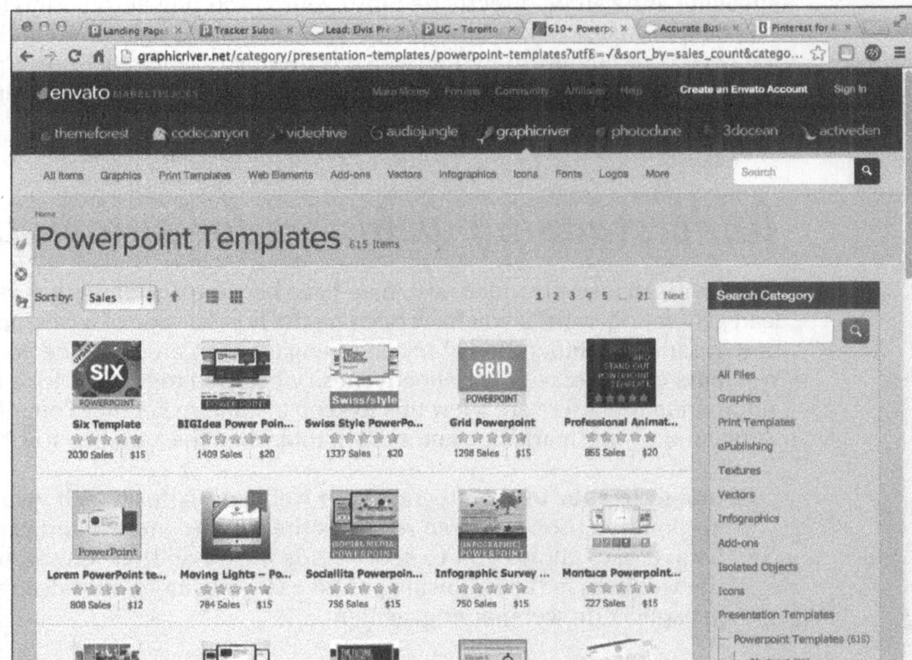

Figure 8-5: Themeforest PowerPoint designs.

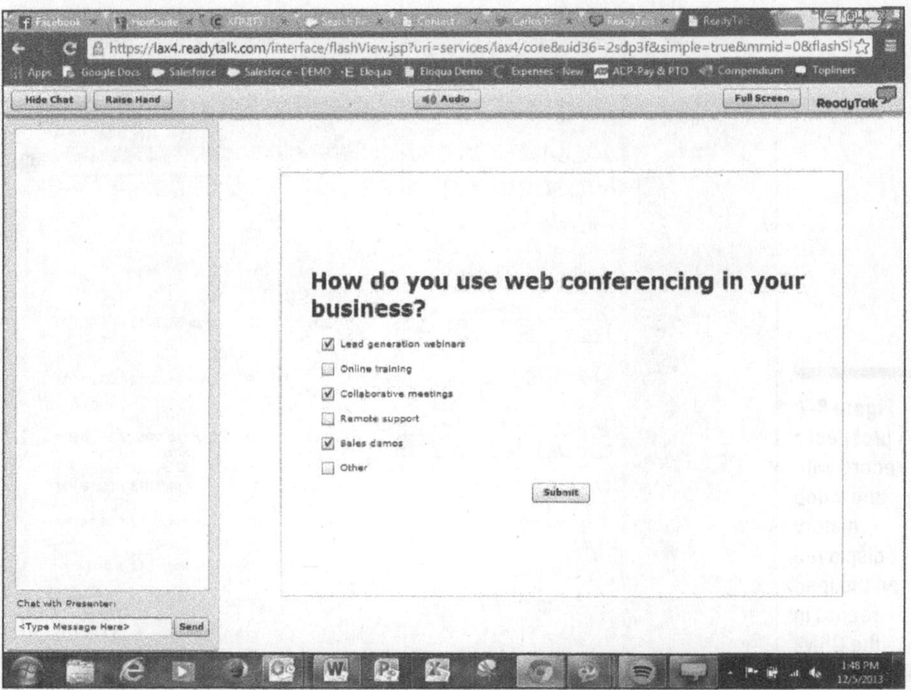

Figure 8-6: A poll in use in a webinar.

Before you run any webinar, always have a dry run. Failure to get everyone together to go over which buttons to hit and when, perform a sound check, and double-check other aspects of the process *will* result in a flawed webinar. You can resolve all issues with webinars by making sure that everyone knows what to do and when to do it.

The world of video and automation

Webinars are a type of video; they are performed live and then hosted later on to continue to drive engagement. Video is an extremely powerful tool when combined with automation. Automation allows you to capture email addresses from your videos, track a prospect's engagement with the video, and even serve up different videos based on the prospect's lead score. Here are a few keys to integrating video into your automation tool:

- **Host your videos:** You need to first host your videos with a video-hosting tool. Most of these tools integrate into a marketing automation tool. These tools allow you to track exactly which prospects watch which videos, and even how much of each video they watch. Figure 8-7 shows an example of a prospect record and the amount of the video the prospect watched.

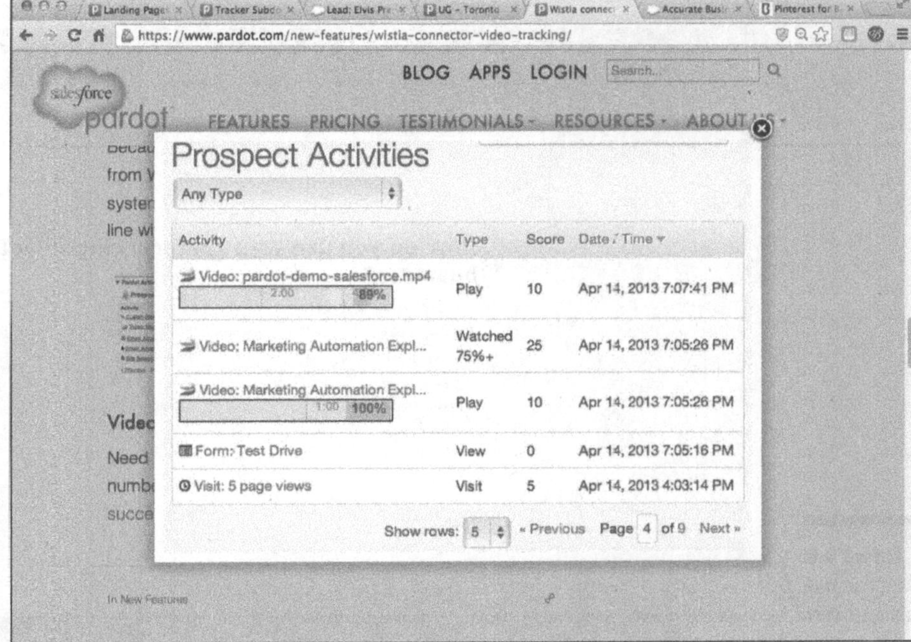

Figure 8-7: A prospect's record with the video history displayed on the lead record in the CRM.

- **Integrate your calls to action.** Calls to action are usually buttons that get people to take an action, such as Sign Up, Download, or Register. Your calls to action need to be tied to your marketing automation tool, which is easy to do if your video tool is connected to your marketing automation tool. If they aren't connected, just use a traceable URL or a form embedded in your video. Figure 8-8 shows a video with an email call to action used to capture email addresses to add people to nurturing programs.

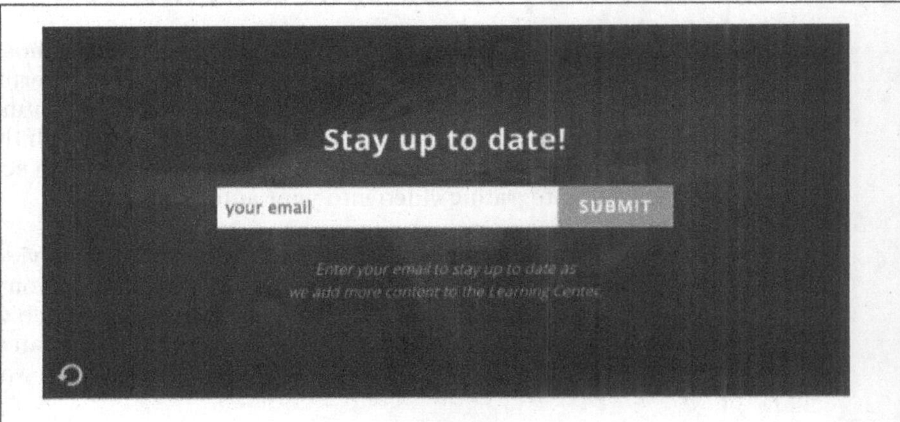

Figure 8-8: A video call to action from the Wisita video player.

- **Dynamic actions for more engagement:** Earlier in this chapter, I mention using dynamic call outs and dynamic automations. Consider taking your video to the next level by suggesting other videos for people to watch when they are done watching one. You can easily use your marketing automation tool's dynamic functionality to display different video suggestions based on a person's lead score. Figure 8-9 shows an example of this. When prospects have a score of 0–10, they are shown video number 1; when their score is 11–35, they are shown video 2; and leads with a score of 36+ are shown video 3.

Default Content
The default content is shown when the viewer is not a prospect or when no variations match.
Add to list if they
Download
Static
Semi-dynamic
Variations
Variations are based on the value of field: Score
Variations are checked in the order they are configured below.
The first variation that matches will display.
Variation A Remove Variation
Show when "Score" is greater than 50
Variation B Remove Variation
Show when "Score" is greater than 75
OVERCOME
THE S FFECT

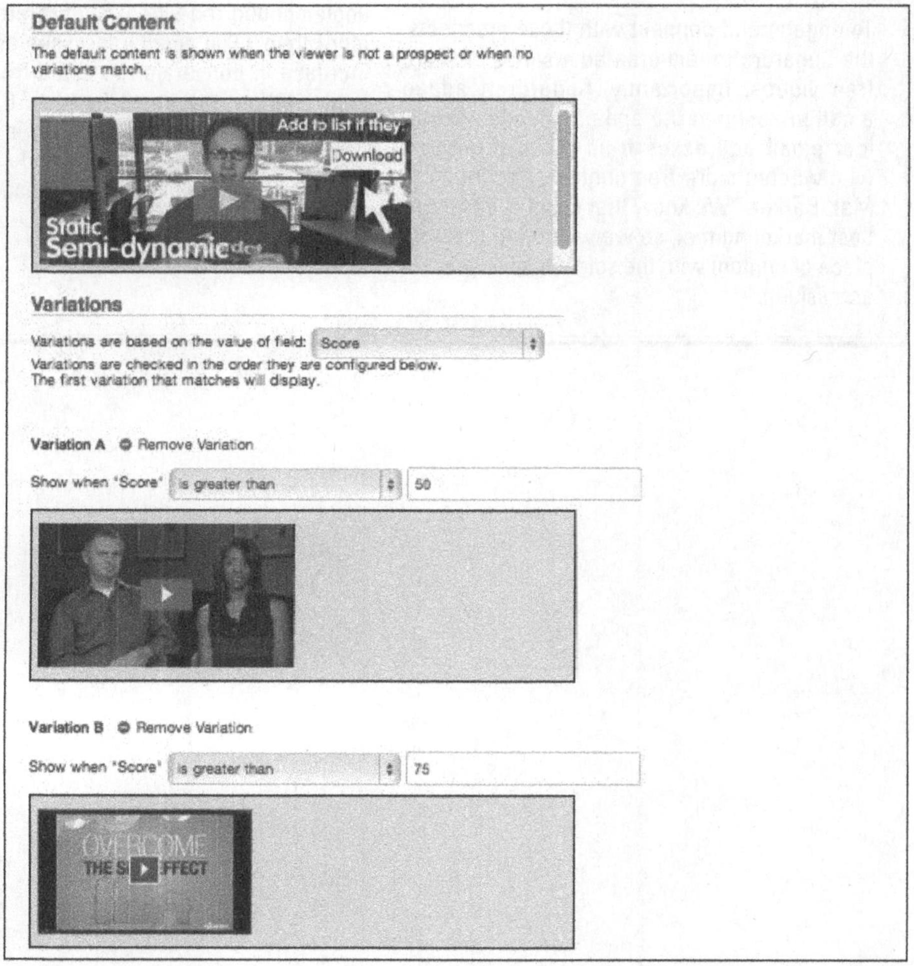

Figure 8-9: A dynamic call to action promoting a video to watch.

A case study for using video for marketing

The Paul Bradford Sugarcraft School offers online classes and instruction in cake decorating. Many visitors come to the Sugarcraft site and immediately purchase the courses. However, lots more visitors are interested in the content but are not yet ready to commit to a paid membership.

To engage and connect with these prospects, the Sugarcraft team created a series of short, free videos. Importantly, Sugarcraft added a call to action at the end of the video to collect email addresses from those prospects who wanted more free content. According to Matt Barker, "We know that email is by far our best marketing tool, so we wanted to create a piece of content with the sole aim of new email acquisition."

This call to action at the end of the video gives the Sugarcraft team an opportunity to engage with prospects who are not quite ready to convert to paid customers. Prospects are added to an email list to receive regular updates and new videos, which helps Sugarcraft stay in touch with these leads. In the first month after implementing the video, Sugarcraft collected more than 7,000 email addresses and saw an increase in conversion to email from 3.4 percent (without the email form) to 8.2 percent (with the email form). The team is hoping to build out its free video series and continue to use email marketing to convert these prospects into paid members.

Chapter 9

Creating Forms and Landing Pages

In This Chapter

- Creating and publishing forms
- Building landing pages
- Avoiding common mistakes

Aside from email, forms and landing pages are the most common use of HTML in a marketing department. It also can be one of the most technically demanding projects in a marketer's day if she has to create the forms, deploy them, and manage the hosting of these pages. Forms usually require IT to create the fields and place them online. Landing pages usually require IT to help create and launch these online microsites as well.

Marketing automation solutions have created a very easy way to create, deploy, and manage these key marketing assets. In this chapter, I show you how to think about forms in a new way, how to create forms that convert more leads, and how to work with landing pages that are easy to create.

Publishing Forms

After your marketing automation system is loaded with a full database, your email templates, and your content, you should build your first form and publish your form to your website or a landing page.

Building your first form should not take a significant amount of time unless you like messing with CSS or HTML. I suggest that you refrain from coding when building your first forms and instead stick to the form builder in your marketing automation tool.

Connecting forms into your existing marketing workflows can be time consuming, usually because you are trying to upload a form to a website, connect the fields to your CRM, or figure out how to respond to all queries. The following sections help you focus on building the forms correctly to help minimize the time required to get your forms up and running.

Identifying your questions

Choose the questions you want to ask in your form. Asking a lot of questions isn't necessary if your marketing automation system is set up to collect behavioral data on prospects. So consider omitting the following fields from your forms because you will get it from your behavioral tracking:

- **How Did You Hear about Us?:** Your marketing automation tool will tell you.
- **Job Title:** You can easily get this information from a third-party source.
- **Phone Number:** Marketing Sherpa states that 65 percent of people lie when asked this question.
- **Company:** You'll get the prospect's email, which has his company name in it.
- **Last Name:** You don't need the prospect's last name to email her.
- **Company Size:** Consider using data augmentation to help with this.

Placing fields in your forms

Select the fields that map to your questions. For example, if you need "First Name," select "first name" from your data points. You need to have all your custom fields set up before this step. This setup should involve only a simple drag-and-drop process at this point if you set up the fields beforehand.

When placing the fields in your form, start with the most logical ones first. These are usually Name and Email, with custom questions following. Custom questions are those outside the standard Name, Address, and Contact information.

Developing form look and feel

Many solutions let you control the look and feel of your form, either by controlling the CSS and HTML or by giving you a WYSIWYG editor to control the form styling. Some solutions let you create forms that automatically take on the look and feel of your website when placed on your site.

Setting form automations

You might be able to set up automations on your form submissions, or you might have to set up a campaign that's attached to your form. Standard automations accompanying a form submission are as follows:

- Auto-responder email
- Score change
- Segmentation
- Lead assignment
- Campaign attribution

Placing lead capture forms on your website

You have two ways to place live forms on your website:

- **Marketing automation hosted placement:** Your marketing automation tool can host both your form and landing page. This placement is usually set up during the process of building your landing page or form. The benefit of this option is that you can publish your form instantly after you are finished building it, and no other steps are required to get your form live and online.
- **Live website placement:** If you want your form on your own hosted website, you need to copy the HTML code for your form using your marketing automation tool and paste the code into your website (see Figures 9-1 and 9-2). The code for your form is usually provided to you after you have built your form. Where and how you can copy the HTML code for your form depends on your tool.

Some applications don't allow you to place the form on your own website, requiring instead that it be built on a landing page and hosted in your marketing automation tool. Make sure to spend time educating yourself so that you know what your tool supports.

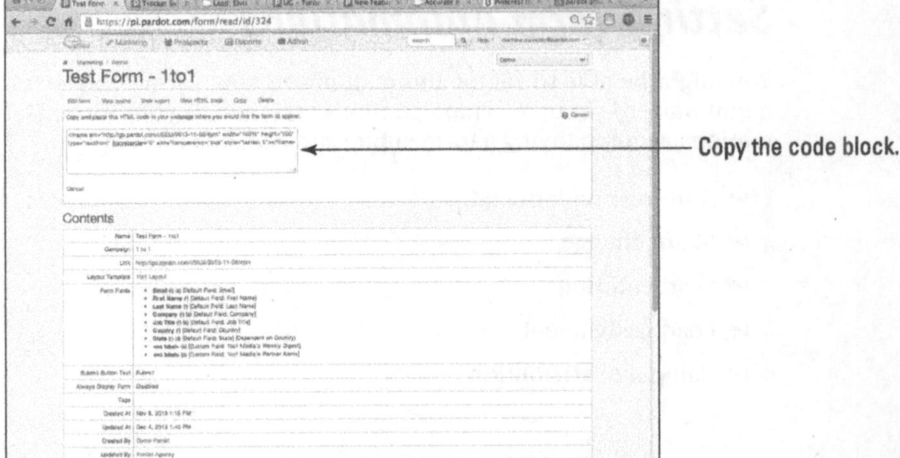

Figure 9-1: This block of HTML code is what you copy and paste to your landing page or website.

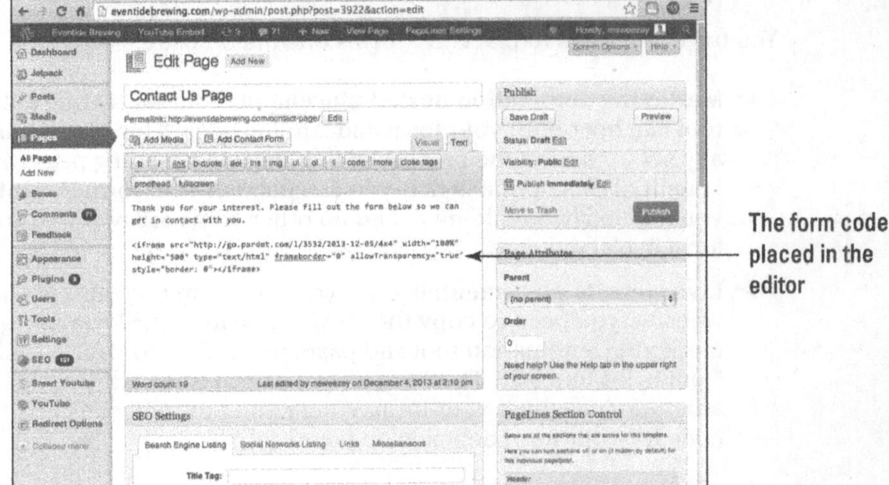

Figure 9-2: Place the form code into the HTML editor of a page (a WordPress site, in this case).

Knowing the importance of short forms with inbound marketing

The more questions you ask, the lower your engagement rates will be. In its report "The Science of Lead Generation," HubSpot looked at 40,000 landing pages and determined that the more fields you ask people to fill out, the lower your engagement rates. The HubSpot study suggests that each question you have beyond three decreases your engagement rates. The engagement rates were at about 30 percent at only three questions and down to 10 percent by eight questions.

So keep your forms short. You can use progressive profiling to help you get the information you need. *Progressive profiling* is a technology provided by almost all marketing automation tools and allows your forms to ask different questions based on what your database knows about a person. Your form can change each time a person is asked to fill it out.

The form using progressive profiling asks a limited set of questions each time, allowing you to increase your engagement rates by capturing a lot of information over many interactions. You must utilize progressive profiling as much as you can because it helps you to keep your forms short and increases your engagement rates.

Publishing Your First Landing Page

If you choose to build a basic landing page within your marketing automation tool, simply follow the instructions in your tool. Most applications walk you through a series of fool-proof steps. This is the best approach for most people, but issues sometimes arise with building a landing page in a marketing automation tool:

- **Limited functionality:** Depending on your tool, your landing page creation and functionality may not be as robust as your current website solution.
- **Limited SEO control:** Some companies have very heavy SEO needs and optimize their landing pages for inbound marketing. Your marketing automation tool may not be able to meet certain special needs.

You should investigate your marketing automation's landing page tool to see whether these issues might arise. Many landing page tools don't have limitations in these areas. If your marketing automation tool's landing page builder is not up to par for your needs, you should consider the following options for building your landing page.

All the following options will still work with the rest of your marketing efforts, and having to use one of them should not deter you from choosing a marketing automation solution. Just understand that some additional amount of work is required.

- **Build it from scratch:** When building your landing page from scratch, you need to use your tools and incorporate a form from your marketing automation tool. This is the best option for those who have an existing website with landing pages and don't want to re-create them in a marketing automation tool, or those companies that have such complex requirements that their marketing automation tool does not suffice.
- **Upload an HTML template.** When you upload HTML, you can easily copy the look of your web page by simply copying the raw HTML file. Right-click the page you want to mimic and then copy the page source. You can then paste the source code into a raw HTML editor and save the file. This process is not fool-proof, though, and will probably get you only 90 percent of the way to a fully functional page.
- **Use your content management system (CMS) to build a landing page.** For the most customizable option, use your CMS. Your CMS gives you the greatest control and is already set up to look like the rest of the pages in your website. The capability to build a landing page is not available with all marketing automation tools, but a majority of them include this feature.

  Most marketing automation tools allow you to have special pages added to your website. Adding pages is easy and maintains all automation options for your future campaigns. You create the landing page in your CMS and then post the URL into your marketing automation tool, making sure that it recognizes the URL as a landing page.

Avoiding landing page mistakes

Creating forms and landing pages is easy, but you want to watch out for common mistakes when publishing your landing page. For example, when you use a lead capture form, make sure that it's capturing the leads correctly. Test your form as soon as the page goes live to see that it works as you intend.

Verify that your landing page renders correctly. Also, WYSIWYG editors are not 100 percent perfect, so you should check your live landing page for correct rendering in all browsers. When you check the form submission feature of your landing page, make sure that the page is being tracked on your lead records: Create a dummy lead and visit your landing page.

You should also verify that the text on your form clearly explains what will happen when the user fills out the form, as shown in Figure 9-3.

Your competition is going to get their hands on your content regardless of what you do to try to stop them, so don't try to create ways to stop them. You'll just create barriers for the people you care about reaching. So when someone in your organization complains that a form is too easy or that the competition is going to get your great information, assure the worrier that the competition already has it!

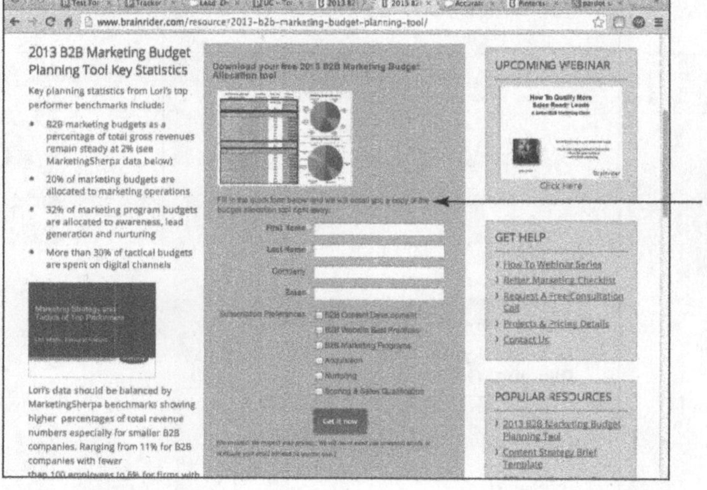

Describe what will happen when the form is filled out.

Figure 9-3: Clearly describe what will happen when your form is filled out and submitted.

Building a Best-of-Breed Landing Page

The landing page is a key tool in any online marketing campaign. Usually it is used as a conversion point and is attached to an advertisement. The advertisement goes through a paid search campaign, a banner ad, or an email. The prospect is then driven to a special place where he can receive the offer. Usually, the prospect fills out a form on the landing page. Landing page theory is very basic; however, applying this theory in modern times can get a bit complicated.

Optimizing for a single goal

The main thing you need to know about landing page theory is the idea of optimizing the page to achieve a single goal. Take a look at two different landing pages. Figure 9-4 shows a landing page that is not optimized for a single goal. Notice how many actions a person can take on this page. The top alone has a lot of links. This is BAD. If you have taken all this time to set up a campaign and have paid to get someone to this page, you have a goal, and you should optimize this page for that goal.

In 2005, a University of Minnesota study titled "Three options are optimal when conducting multiple-choice items" was concerned with the concept of how people make decisions when given options. The study found that the fewer options you give people, the easier it is for them to make a decision. This is where the idea of optimizing a landing page for a single goal comes into play. Figure 9-5 shows a landing page that has only one option on the page. You can convert on the form or leave the page.

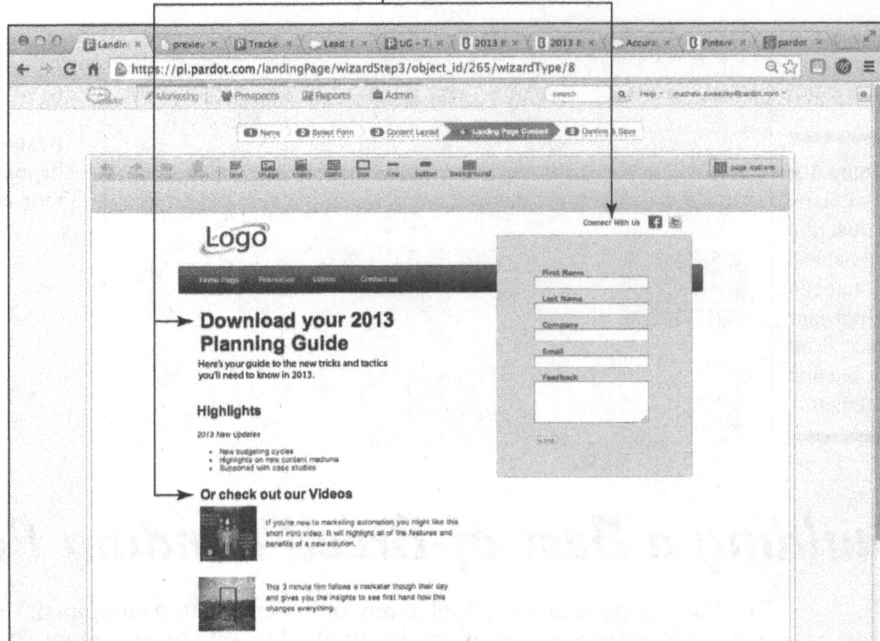

Figure 9-4: A landing page with multiple links is not an optimized page.

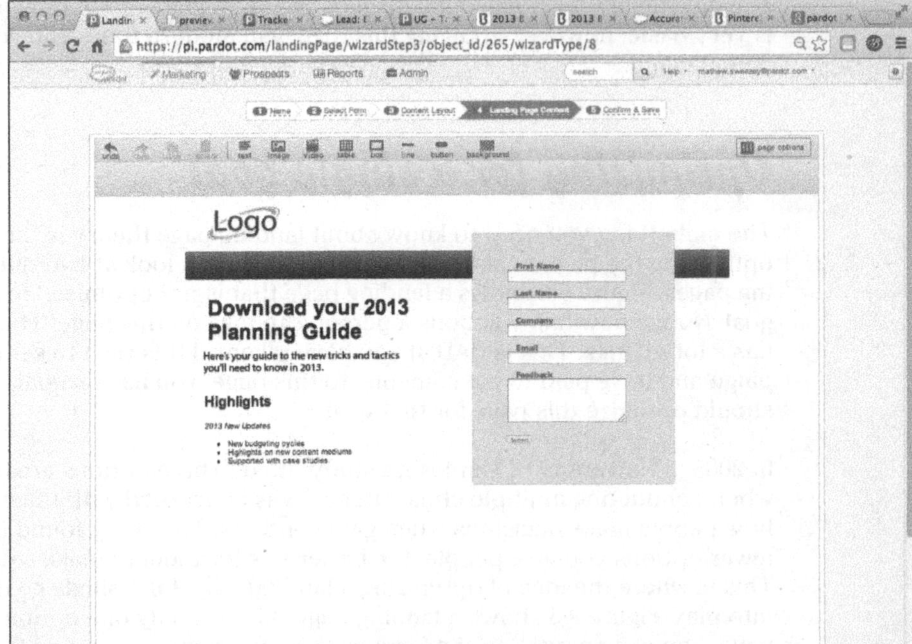

Figure 9-5: An optimized landing page with a simple choice.

Using dynamic content to increase conversions

The concept of optimizing for a single goal is great, but you also need to understand the concept of relevance. If you're successfully driving lots of people to a single landing page, how do you make it relevant to each person with only a single call to action?

The answer is, you don't; that is, you use dynamic content to make the single landing page different for each person. *Dynamic content* is a feature that reads a variable pertaining to each visiting prospect and changes the offer based on this variable. You have a few different ways to create dynamic content, as follows:

- **Embedding dynamic content blocks:** The dynamic content block is something your marketing automation tool may have. If you have this advanced feature, you can take your landing pages and website to a new level. Using dynamic content will be the same for landing pages and your website. Here are a few things you need to know before adding dynamic content to your landing page:
  - *Data point:* You need to have a data point that you want to use to change your content. This data point is the trigger to show different content. Good data points to use are lead score, job title, or stage in the buying cycle.
  - *Content created:* You need to have your different content pieces created; your dynamic content will render the correct piece of content based on the data point you choose. For example, if a VP shows up to your landing page, the page will show a different piece of content than it would to a manager.
  - *Content blocks and automations:* You set these elements up in your marketing automation tool. If your tool allows for the creation of dynamic content blocks, your vendor can walk you through the steps of setting up these blocks. Make sure that your automation rules are based on the same data point to ensure consistent results.

  Figure 9-6 shows a dynamic content block on a landing page, which is based on the lead score as the data point. Notice how the content being shown is tailored to the early stage of the buying cycle. Figure 9-7 shows the same landing page with a dynamic content block running off of lead score as the data point. This time, the content shown is tailored to someone with a higher score. This is the power of using dynamic content, making your content relevant to someone at all times.

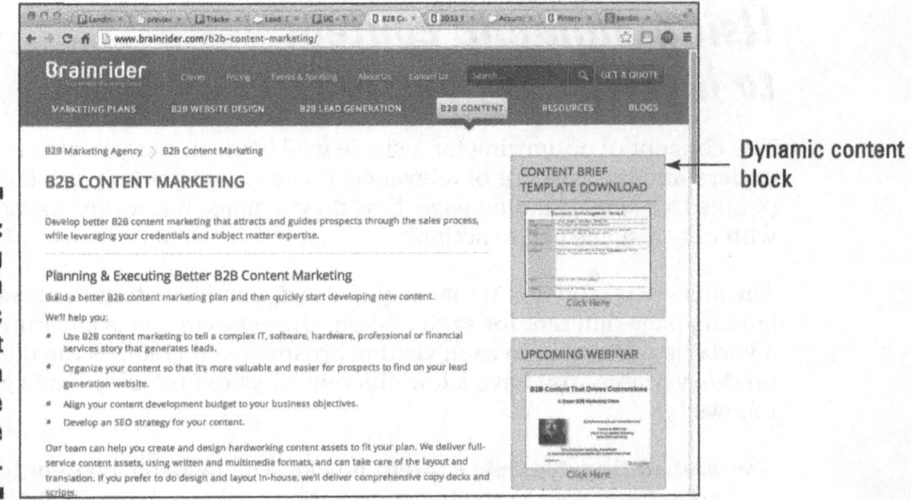

Figure 9-6: A landing page with dynamic content being driven off of the lead score data point.

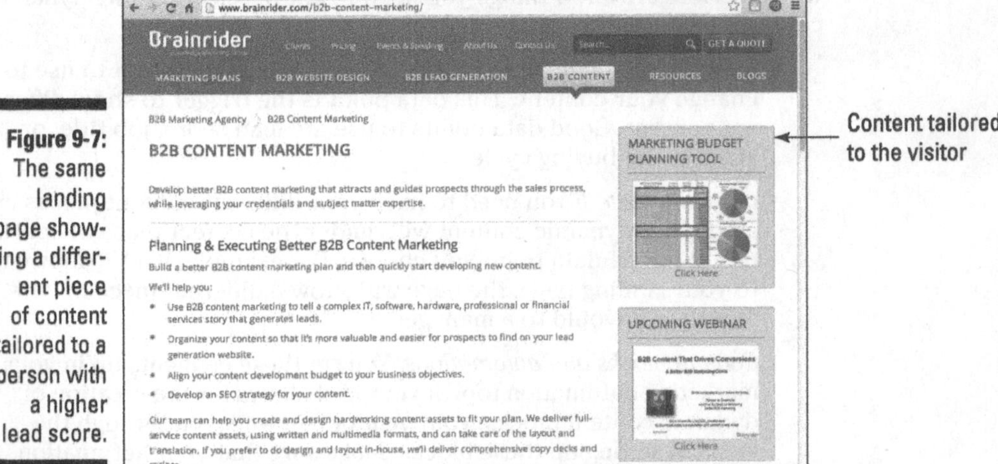

Figure 9-7: The same landing page showing a different piece of content tailored to a person with a higher lead score.

- **Using a dynamic CMS:** Your marketing automation tool might not be capable of offering dynamic content. This feature is currently found only in the higher-end tools or as an expensive add-on to your existing marketing automation tool. Despite this, you still might be able to get the effect of dynamic content through functionality in your CMS. Some CRMs offer plug-ins to create your landing pages and use dynamic messaging. The WordPress CMS system is a good example of a CMS that offers plug-ins to help accomplish some dynamic actions.

A *plug-in* is a basic tool that you can add to your CMS to get more out of it. Plug-ins are usually built by other people who use WordPress, and they're offered for free or at very little cost. Be aware that plug-ins offer a wide variety of functions and more are being added daily, so make sure to check on what's available. Consider each one's strengths and limitations. Some plug-ins can track users and suggest content for them; others can help you create content to ensure that yours is always fresh. Do note that a plug-in specific to your CMS might not connect to your marketing automation tool — because it is a feature of your CMS, not your marketing automation tool.

The more advanced you are looking to get with dynamic content, the higher the likely cost to your organization because of the level of technology required by fully automated and highly customized dynamic content.

Video embedded for increased engagement

I tell you about working with video as content in Chapter 8, but you can also use it specifically to drive higher conversions. To create more advanced video, make sure that you have a few basic options with your video-hosting tool:

- **Auto play:** This option allows your video to begin playing the moment someone lands on a page. This is not a super-advanced option, but it's a feature that you will need to test for more advanced tactics. Having auto play allows you to remove the need for a person to click a button, thereby getting a prospect deeper into your content, faster. Auto play can help increase engagement by reducing the number of steps required to engage with your content.
- **In-video call to action:** I tell you about embedding a call to action in video in Chapter 8. Make sure that your video-hosting solution has this feature if you want to use video to drive higher prospect engagement.

There are three basic levels of video embedding to increase your engagement rates: basic, advanced, and expert:

- **Basic:** To drive increased engagement rates with embedded video, start by simply testing auto play on your video. As soon as someone lands on your landing page, the video begins to play. The idea here is instead of requiring people to read about what they are about to download, you show them with a video. The video should be above your form so that visitors can fill out the form at any time. Figure 9-8 shows a landing page with the basic auto play feature and form.

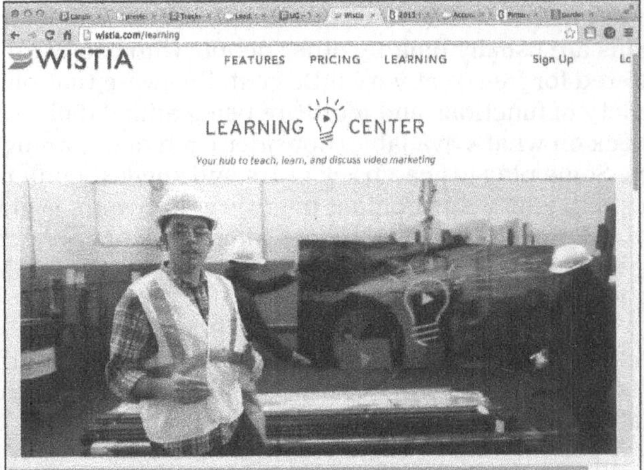

Figure 9-8: A landing page with an embedded video set to auto play, and a form.

- **Advanced:** To have visitors step into a more advanced landing page experience with video, consider combining video calls to action with auto play. Figure 9-9 shows a landing page using these techniques. Notice that the page has no form. The conversion point is an in-video call to action, which means that the video will stop after a set amount of time and prompt the watcher to fill in her email address. This is a more advanced option because you need to combine your video-hosting solution and your marketing automation tool.

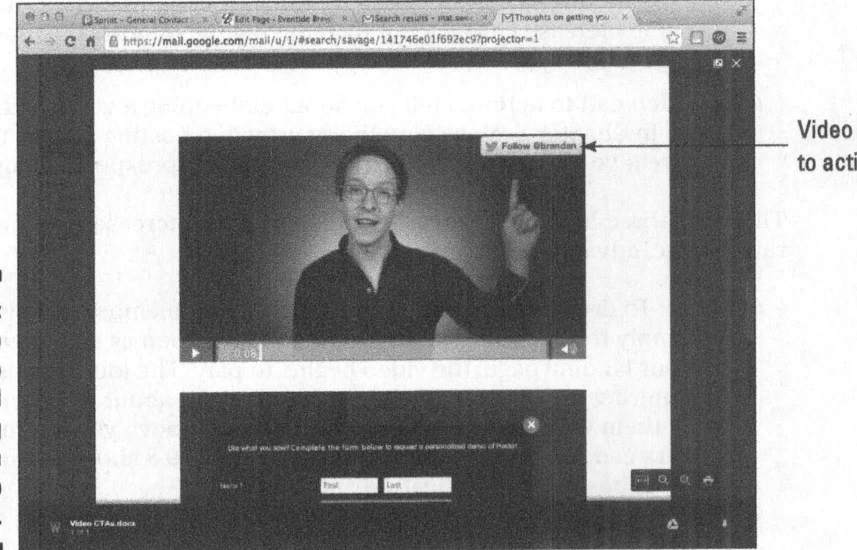

Figure 9-9: An auto play video embedded on a landing page with a video call to action.

- **Expert:** This level uses the most advanced option offered by most technologies and is something for you to consider when you're looking to drive maximum engagement or test new techniques. This level combines dynamic content, video, and in-video calls to action and works as follows:
  - **Set up your dynamic content:** Your dynamic content is in video form. Depending on your data point, a video tailored to the visitor pops up on the landing page.
  - **Use a form to protect the video:** You may want to protect your video rather than play it automatically. This means that the form has to be completed before the video plays. Different marketing automation tools have this feature, so ask your vendor how to accomplish this. Consider just asking for the prospect's email address on this form.
  - **In-video call to action:** If you ask only for an email address, you might need more information. With an in-video call to action, you can have your video ask for a different piece of information after a set period of time. This approach allows you to gain more information as the video plays.

Microsite landing pages

Another way to look at a landing page is as an experience in itself. Some marketing automation vendors allow for the creation of microsite. A *microsite* is a small website that sits outside your company's main website. Microsites are very popular for events, new products, or other offerings. If your marketing automation tool does not have a microsite feature, it likely has a landing page feature. The purpose of the microsite is to create a highly customized experience on a very specific topic. Here are some ways you can build a custom experience outside your website:

- **Microsites:** Microsites are a great way to give people a custom experience around a central idea without distracting them with other information. In fact, this is the purpose of the microsite. As with a landing page, you should optimize it for a single goal, such as announcing an event. Salesforce.com does a great job with this with its Dreamforce microsite (see Figure 9-10). Dreamforce is a single website dedicated to an event. It does not talk about the software, only the event. If your marketing automation tool allows for microsites, use them; they are very powerful and functional.

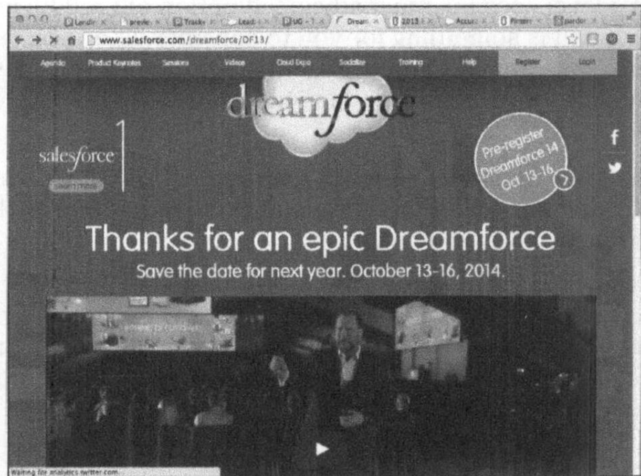

Figure 9-10: Salesforce.com's Dreamforce microsite.

- **Tying landing pages together:** If your marketing automation tool does not support true microsites, you can still provide a similar experience, with just a bit more work being involved. If you can create a landing page in your marketing automation tool, you can connect a few of them by linking them with hyperlinks or by automations. Figure 9-11 shows conceptually how this may look. Here is more detail on how to connect landing pages:
  - *Using hyperlinks:* To connect landing pages using hyperlinks, you first need to create your landing pages. Next, on each page, create your navigation to another page. Simply use the URL of the other landing page and you have connected them.
  - *Using automations:* If you want to try something more advanced, you can connect sites with automations. For example, when someone completes a form, he should be directed to another page. You create this redirect in the automation section of your marketing automation tool, and you can easily direct people to where you want them to go without any effort on their part.

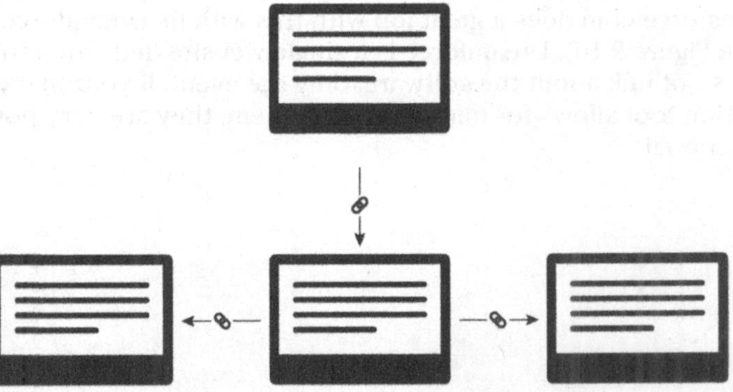

Figure 9-11: A diagram of how many landing pages can be tied together to create a micro site.

- **Using another tool:** If your marketing automation solution does not allow for stringing landing pages together, you may want to consider a tool such as ion interactive (see Figure 9-12). A specific tool such as ion interactive allows you to build a microsite with dynamic features. Tools made specifically to build microsites are great because for the marketer who isn't tech savvy, microsites are usually easier to set up than using your CMS, and the result can be much more robust than a landing page created in a marketing automation tool. Such tools also can be integrated into your marketing automation tool very easily.

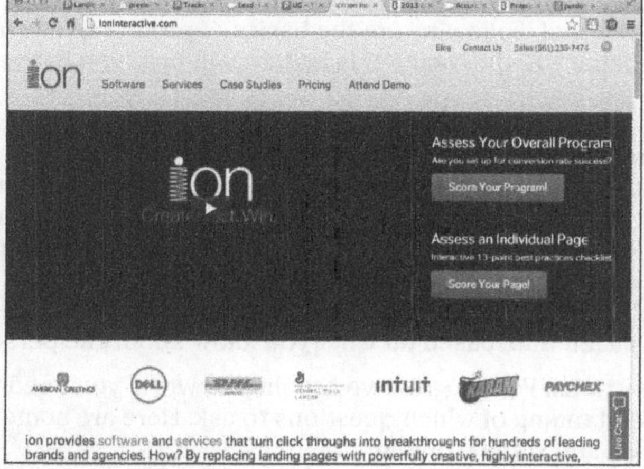

Figure 9-12: The ion interactive tool can create microsites.

You can connect any website to your marketing automation tool as long as you can place JavaScript on the page. When building microsites outside your marketing automation tool, remember to add your tracking code to them so that you can track a prospect's engagement with microsites. I cover how to attach JavaScript to a web page in Chapter 4.

Adding Advanced Forms to Your Campaigns

As discussed earlier in this chapter, forms are a part of your landing pages; however, you can easily increase the engagement of a landing page just by optimizing your forms. The following sections present some easy ways to increase landing page engagement by optimizing your forms.

Pondering progressive profiling

Progressive profiling is an amazing topic. Seth Godin first conceived it in his book *Permission Marketing* (Simon & Shuster, 1999). The technology, however, is only now reaching the mainstream in the marketing world. *Progressive profiling* is a form's capability to recognize an individual and ask only questions he hasn't already been asked.

Not every marketing automation tool has progressive profiling. All such tools will have this feature some day, but currently it is reserved for the more advanced tools. It also may require different levels of expertise to set up, depending on the tool. Following are the basics of progressive profiling to help you determine whether using this feature will help you increase your conversion rates:

- **Shorter forms:** Shorter forms have higher engagement rates. This is a basic fact that does not need much research to back it up. The question becomes, how do you know which questions to ask? Or how do you ask those questions? You can answer these questions by using progressive profiling on your forms or landing pages. Each time a person comes to your landing page, she is asked a few questions, and they are different questions each time based on what you know about the person.
- **Good questions:** For progressive profiling to work, you need to have a firm understanding of which questions to ask. Here are some good questions to ask and some to avoid:
    - *First name:* This is the first question you should ask. You never need last name until you pass the lead to sales. Remember that you don't use the last name in any communication.
    - *Email address:* Requesting an email address is the only question you MUST ask. Usually you can use a data augmentation tool to fill in all the blanks based on a single field.
    - *Special questions:* If there are questions whose answers you can't get from a data vendor and that you can't infer from a prospect's web page visits or content engagement, you need to ask these. Consider not making them mandatory (see the next item in this list for why).
    - *Bad questions:* A bad question asks for information that people don't want to provide, such as their phone number. People also dislike any question that you make mandatory. If you *require* a field to be filled out, people will lie. ***Remember:*** Bad data only hurts your marketing efforts.

Your progressive profiling will look different to each prospect but will give you the best odds at having people fill out your form. Figure 9-13 shows a progressive profiling form in action.

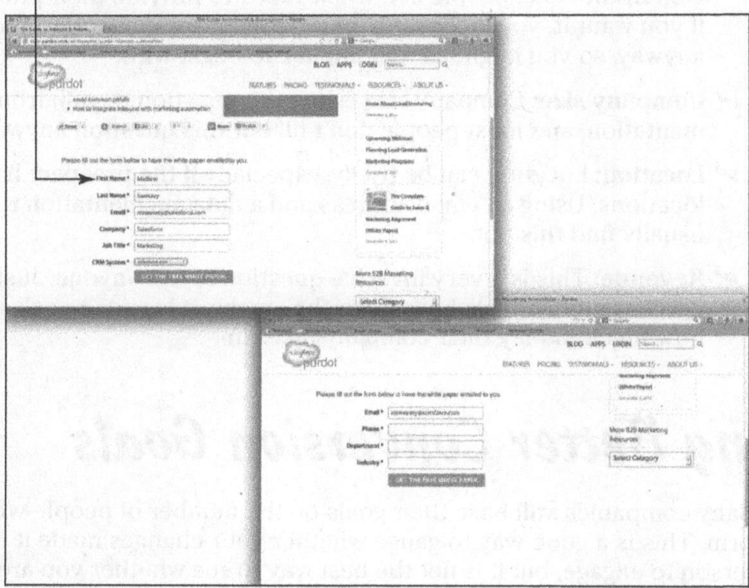

Figure 9-13: A form using progressive profiling over the course of multiple interactions.

Data augmentation and its place in forms

Data augmentation is a key factor when you want to increase your engagement rates. *Data augmentation* is the capability for a third-party software to fill in the blanks with your data set. The key point here is that if you can buy the information from a third party, you have no reason to ask people for it. So if you were thinking of having a question such as company size on your form, you might be better off leaving this question out and getting the information from a third party. The fewer questions you ask of people, the more likely they are to engage. After they fill out the form, you can then augment their record from third-party data sources to fill in the missing blanks, which gets you the information you need and increases engagement rates at the same time. Here are some data points for which I suggest using data augmentation:

- **Last name:** This information is most likely in a prospect's email address and can easily be gained from data augmentation.
- **Company name:** Likewise, this information is usually contained in the prospect's email address and is easily provided by a data augmentation tool. Also, keep in mind that very large companies are highly unlikely to give you their company name when trying to remain covert.

- **Phone number.** A recent study from MarketingSherpa found that 65 percent of the time, people lied when asked to provide their phone number. If you want it, you'll probably have to get it by some other means anyway, so you might as well not ask to begin with.
- **Company size:** Company size is an easy question to gain from data augmentation, and most people don't fill out this question anyway.
- **Location:** Location can be tricky, especially if the prospect has multiple locations. Using an email address and a data augmentation tool, you can usually find this out.
- **Revenue:** This is a very invasive question to ask anyone. Just as you don't ask individuals how much they make, it is rude to ask someone how much money their company takes in.

Creating Better Conversion Goals

Many companies still base their goals on the number of people who fill out a form. This is a good way to gauge whether your changes made it easier for a person to engage, but it is not the best way to see whether you are converting the correct prospects. This section covers a few topics that you need to understand to take your form conversions to the next level.

Quality vs. quantity

Creating more quality rather than quantity is the basis of why you got marketing automation in the first place. You want better leads, not just more of them. This idea goes hand in hand with forms and landing pages. If you judge yourself on the number of conversions you have, you're seeing only half the picture. Read on for a few tips to help you ensure that you're getting quality, not just quantity.

Your conversion rate is a leading indicator of possible future outcomes. It shows you what is possible in the future. If 100 people convert on your form, this indicates that you may have more quality leads in the future; however, it does not measure the quality of those leads — just the possibility of them. You should also measure the number of those 100 who closed as opportunities. This is a lagging indicator, which means that you can see it only after the fact. Consider looking at your form in two ways: initial conversions and percentage of total opportunities created. For each form, go back and evaluate your form based on how many of those leads were converted to sales. Some marketing automation tools contain this information as a built-in report.

Be prepared for the big dip

If you are refining your forms for better quality and less quantity, you'll see a dip in the number of leads that come in. This is a standard effect that almost all companies implementing marketing automation will see. I've included this topic in the chapter because when you get into more advanced forms and landing pages, this dip becomes more apparent.

Following are some tips to help you prepare for the inevitable dip:

- **Prep stakeholders:** You should set expectations about the big dip with sales and upper management before you implement marketing automation. If you are being measured only on the quantity of leads, your numbers will go down for a period of time. Make sure to let stakeholders know why so that they don't think you are doing a bad job.
- **Don't panic:** If you panic during these improvements, you'll likely not do a lot of them, which can mean staying in the back of the pack. The biggest piece of advice I can give you is to remember that the elements you change can all be changed back to where they were. If you find out that your idea wasn't that great, just revert back to your old form. All marketing automation tools save your old forms, so you can easily just swap them in and out.
- **Prove your value:** To prove that the dip in the quantity of leads was worthwhile, make sure that you can look at the number of sales generated by the fewer leads. The number of sales is the only way you can demonstrate that your tactic was worthwhile, so make sure that you have set up reports to track your sales from it. This capability is standard with some tools; others require you to set it up. Make sure that you know which kind of tool you have.

Chapter 10

Sending Emails and Nurture Campaigns

In This Chapter

- Getting started with nurturing
- Building effective nurturing emails
- Copy writing with a purpose
- Effective calls to action

Lead nurturing* refers to the automated process of taking a person from one step to the next automatically. This process generally involves marketing to people from the time they are leads with a basic interest to the time they are ready for a sales conversation or a purchase decision. Lead nurturing may also be referred to as drip marketing, drip nurturing, and drip emails, but they are all basically the same.

Lead nurturing is the single greatest revenue-generating source of marketing automation. You are likely to see more of a lift from well-built lead nurturing campaigns than from any other feature in your marketing automation tool. Gartner reports that companies using lead tracking and lead nurturing have seen an increase in sales-ready leads by more than 451 percent.

This chapter shows you how to build lead-nurturing campaigns and associated emails in your marketing automation system.

Getting Up to Speed on Nurturing

On average, email marketing engagement rates are in the single digits, which goes to show the importance of relevance. With mass email sending, it is very hard to be relevant to everyone with a single message. Nurturing solves this problem by giving marketers the ability to have 100-percent personalized campaigns for every person in their database. This personalization is the main reason that nurturing has become the hottest topic in marketing, and it's the number-one reason that people adopt marketing automation.

Nurturing is, however, a very different method of communication than anything you've used before, so the next sections explain how to use it correctly.

Mass email sending vs. email nurturing

Nurturing is an email technique using a marketing automation tool. Before running a nurturing campaign sending a lot of emails, you need to understand the high-level differences between email marketing and email nurturing. Here's a breakdown of those differences:

- **Email is one to many; nurturing is one to one.** Mass emails, regardless of your segmentation, are not one-to-one communications. A mass email consists of one email sent to many people, which means that its message is not relevant to many of them. Nurturing, on the other hand, is a one-to-one communication method.
- **New email templates are a must for nurturing.** Because nurturing is one to one, you need to create completely new email templates that will appear to be one-to-one communication. I discuss building the templates later in this chapter, in "Setting Up Nurturing Email Templates."
- **Nurturing uses automated execution.** With email marketing, you have to create a list and send an email to the list. With marketing automation, you create many emails that are sent out automatically based on an automation program you have set up. So you are no longer the one hitting the Send button because everything is automated.
- **Nurturing gives your leads more visibility.** With mass email sending, you generally can see only opens, bounces, and clicks. With marketing automation, you can follow each lead to a website and identify sales-ready leads from there. With more visibility, you don't weigh email opens and clicks as heavily as you do website page views.
- **You create personalization with nurturing.** With mass email sending, you send one email to thousands of people, typically with a generic subject line and copy. With marketing automation and lead nurturing, you send one email to one person, thousands of times, with much more personalized subject lines based on your new visibility and automations.

Nurturing use cases

Nurturing is an amazing communication vehicle. Even though nurturing campaigns are primarily used for moving leads through the sales funnel, nurturing has other benefits if you use it correctly. Table 10-1 shows the main use cases for lead nurturing and the benefits you should expect.

Table 10-1 Nurturing Use Cases

Main Objectives	Use Cases	Description
Generating more leads	Net new lead campaigns	These campaigns take leads from an online action and work them into a sales-ready state.
	Pre- and post-event follow-up	Take some time back and automate pre- and post-event follow-up. This also helps to ensure that your follow-ups happen and that you generate more leads from your events.
	Upselling	If you have current clients and want to try to upsell them on other solutions, nurturing makes this easy to market to them and identify when they are ready for sales to call them.
	Cross-selling	Cross-selling other solutions to your existing client base can be difficult with cold calling. Nurturing removes the legwork and allows you to focus on creating compelling campaigns, not just hitting the Send button.
	Staying "top of mind"	If you have a very long sales cycle and need to stay in front of someone for a long time, nurturing fits this bill perfectly.
Reviving cold leads	Wake-the-dead nurturing	Not every lead is sales ready when it comes in, and many leads go cold over time. Forrester Research estimates that the best-of-breed companies convert 1 percent of all of their leads into sales. After leads have gone cold, revive them with a special nurturing program.

(continued)

Table 10-1 *(continued)*

Main Objectives	***Use Cases***	***Description***
Sales support	Managing churn rates	It's much less costly to keep a client than to get a new one. Use nurturing to stay in front of your clients to keep them happy and help mitigate your churn rates.
	Dead-deal nurturing program	Many deals die in the opportunity stage for many reasons. These deals are not lost, just stalled. Using nurturing to help sales staff stay in front of these leads frees their time to focus on closing still-active deals.
	Competitive lead-nurturing program	When your sales team is responsible for hunting new leads, these programs help them to stay in front of people using a competitive technology, allowing them to cover more ground while staying in front of leads who may take a long time to convert into an opportunity.
	Lost-deal nurturing program	When salespeople lose a deal, they have already invested a lot of effort and built a solid rapport with the client. Many times, this rapport can be leveraged into reopening conversations toward the end of a contract. Use nurturing to remove this task from salespeople and automate it to free up their time.

Getting Started with Nurturing

All nurturing programs have a few standard pieces to them. They all start with a goal, have email templates, lapses of time between emails, content to develop for the emails, and ways to get people on and off the program. This section gives you the basics of each of these elements so that you have a solid foundation on which to build great nurturing programs.

Defining your nurturing program's goal

Begin your nurturing campaign by creating a very clearly defined goal. Nurturing programs are made to accomplish one goal at a time. Here are some tips for crafting your goals:

- **Get specific.** The more specific you can be with your goal, the better your campaign will be. For example, if your goal is to create more marketing-qualified (MQL) leads, it is not specific enough. You need to have your program specific to a persona, interest, place in the buying stage, or something else more specific. From there, you can have a much more relevant conversation and generate more MQLs.
- **Know your next steps.** Since your goals and timeline are specific, you need to know your next steps. Many nurturing programs tie together to build a full campaign. So consider having small goals that lead to next steps, which might be another nurturing program. It is much easier to move someone one step at a time than through all steps simultaneously.
- **Account for all interactions.** Nurturing isn't happening in a bubble, so remember to take all web interactions into account to determine which nurturing program you should have someone on. I suggest using a lead score to help you determine where someone is in the buyer's journey; then map your nurturing programs to specific score ranges.

Adding people to nurturing campaigns

You can place people on your nurturing campaigns using various methods. The way in which you add someone to a nurturing program depends on your overall campaign. In the easiest terms possible, you can think about adding leads to a nurturing campaign in two different ways: automated and manual.

- **Automated:** In an automated campaign, people are added dynamically; no one has to click a button. When you want to have a fully automated program and automatically identify a person who needs to be nurtured, this is the type of campaign to use. These campaigns are harder to set up and are not for all types of campaigns. Most marketing campaigns can be set up in this fashion; however, I suggest manual campaigns for your sales support nurturing campaigns. Figure 10-1 shows an automated program adding people to a nurturing program.
- **Manual:** A manual campaign requires a button to be clicked or some other manual action to add someone to the nurturing campaign. Use this type of campaign when you want a human interaction to add someone to a campaign. You will want a human interaction when you have a multitude of factors and many different scenarios, or when sales leads are involved and you want to give the sales team full control over who is added, and when. Figure 10-2 shows a nurturing campaign that has a static/manual option to add leads to it. Notice that this option is inside the CRM tool.

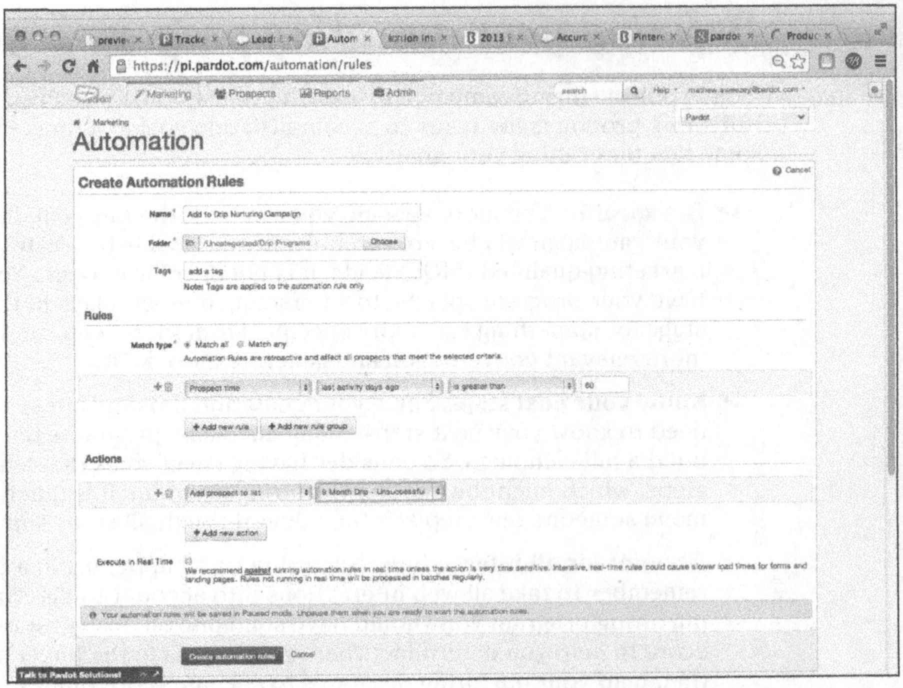

Figure 10-1: An automated rule adds leads to a nurturing program.

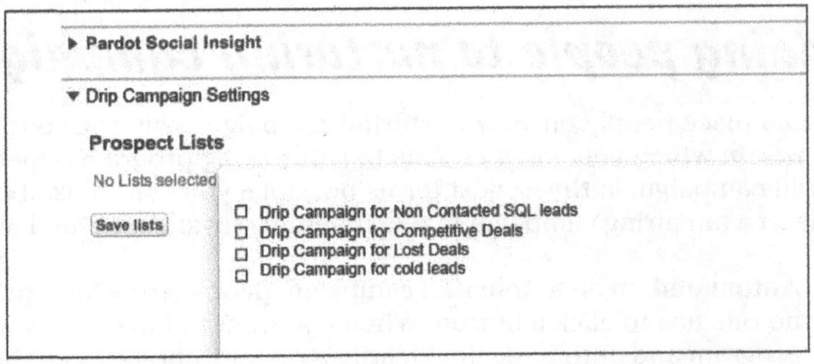

Figure 10-2: A manual option to add leads to a nurturing campaign from inside the CRM tool.

Branching out in your nurturing programs

In nurturing programs, you need to be able to take people through different scenarios based on their behavior within the program. One way to provide the various scenarios is by creating different campaigns and linking them together; another way is to branch your nurturing track. *Branching* means to have different paths within a single nurturing campaign. This approach allows you to have a single screen managing very complex nurturing paths, rather than having to manage many different nurturing tracks tied together. Many of the same campaigns can be executed with either approach; branching just makes it much easier to manage.

Your tool dictates the level of branching you can accomplish — *if* you can accomplish it at all. To find out whether your marketing automation tool can branch programs, ask your vendor. Here are some helpful tips for how to correctly use branching when building your nurturing programs:

- **Main line:** Have a main line of your nurturing program. The main line (see Figure 10-3 for an example) is the core of your nurturing program. It is the work horse. Branches should be broken off of the main line. A branch may or may not lead back to the main line, depending on your campaign.
- **Branch lines:** The branch lines of your nurturing program are for very specific and granular actions. These are the times when you want to take just one person down a very personalized experience based on very specific actions. Figure 10-4 shows the branch line in a nurturing program.

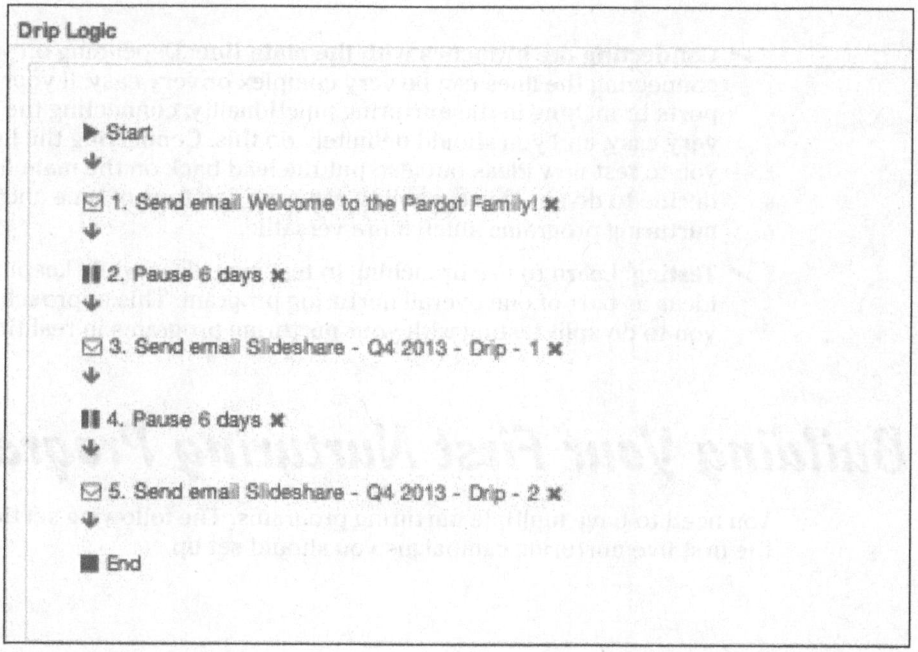

Drip Logic

▶ Start

1. Send email Welcome to the Pardot Family!

2. Pause 6 days

3. Send email Slideshare - Q4 2013 - Drip - 1

4. Pause 6 days

5. Send email Slideshare - Q4 2013 - Drip - 2

End

Figure 10-3: The main line is the core branch in a nurturing program.

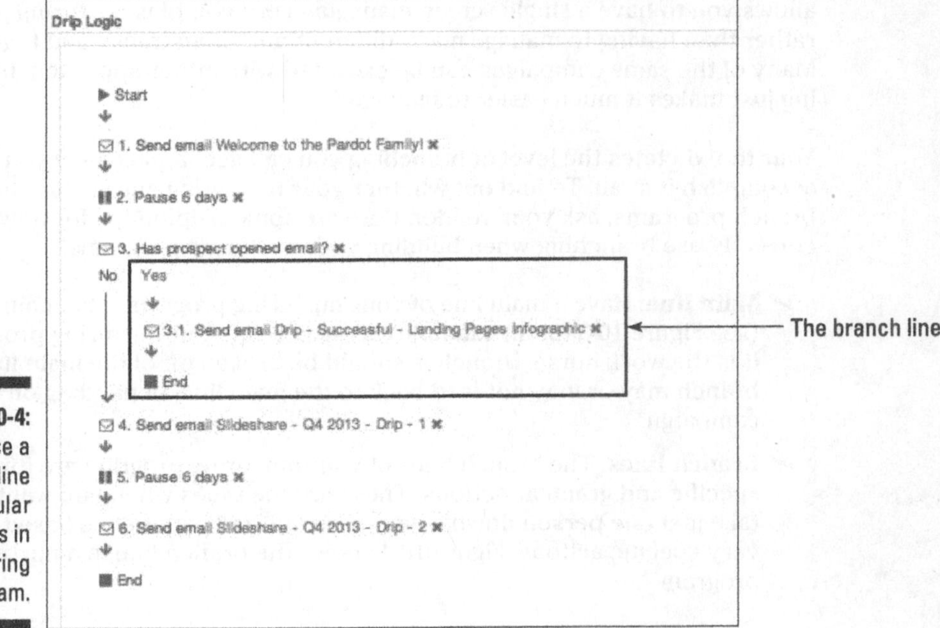

Figure 10-4: Use a branch line for granular actions in a nurturing program.

- **Connecting the branches with the main line:** Depending on your tool, connecting the lines can be very complex or very easy. If your tool supports branching in the nurturing functionality, connecting the lines is very easy, and you should definitely do this. Connecting the lines allows you to test new ideas but also put the lead back on the main line if you decide to do so. This capability can save you tons of time and make your nurturing programs much more versatile.
- **Testing:** Learn to use branching to test new ideas while keeping those ideas as part of one overall nurturing program. This approach allows you to do split testing with your nurturing programs in real time.

Building Your First Nurturing Programs

You need to have multiple nurturing programs. The following sections explain the first five nurturing campaigns you should set up.

Case Study: How VMware built a better lead-nurturing program

VMware is a global leader in virtualization and cloud infrastructure solutions. The company has been market leader for a number of years; however, new market entrants, including Microsoft, resulted in a more competitive marketplace. The challenge for VMware was to use lead nurturing to maintain its position and accurately portray its differences, helping the company to combat new competition in its marketplace.

The Problem

Because VMware is a target-driven organization, it expects the marketing team to provide a high volume of leads to the inside sales team. The company wanted to move away from one-off email "blasts" and focus on longer-term nurturing campaigns, but it needed to avoid a slowdown in qualified leads.

Campaign Objectives

VMware wanted to use a global SMB campaign to deliver qualified leads and quick-win conversions.

The Approach

The original campaign consisted of a series of one-off email sends to attract form submissions. Of the six emails supplied, four had identical call to action (CTA) text and focused strongly on the product. To create a more intelligent campaign and improve the user experience, the company took these actions:

- It divided the content into three stages, Awareness, Interest, and Consideration, and categorized the content as either high or low value. Having three different stages allowed contacts to either fast-track through the journey or gather more information as they went. Prospects could choose the speed of their journey, and if they showed interest in a topic, they received more valuable content sooner.
- Critically, the campaign included an additional email at the beginning. This email offered a free piece of educational content, creating a relationship rather than a transaction. This first contact made VMware a thought leader that provided information of interest to prospects without asking for a detailed form submission.
- The company included resends of emails, and although the content of the emails was identical, the subject line differed in tone and style to appeal to people who had not previously reacted. The alternative subject line was a simple, cost-effective tactic that attracted significant extra opens, clicks, and form submissions.

Results

Email metrics gave the first sign that the campaign was successful, with open rates and click rates reaching more than 40 and 6.5 percent, respectively. Further analysis identified what worked well or less well and tracked closed-loop revenue impact.

The nurture program phase created more than $48 million in new prospects. Having a closed loop enabled reporting by campaign element and activity type.

The true benefit of VMWare's nurturing campaign was the knowledge the company gained about the value of long-term, intelligent campaigns. Nurturing has now become a priority.

Building net new lead nurturing campaigns

The purpose of a net new lead nurturing program is to take a new lead from her first engagement to being a sales-ready lead. When building your first net new lead nurturing program, use the following checklist to make sure that you have everything you need to create a great program:

- **Content:** You should have both long-form and short-form content ready to go. Some great ideas to use in this program are as follows:
  - Blog posts from industry veterans
  - Links to articles in popular magazines
  - Industry studies put out by other people
  - Your own blog articles
  - Links to great videos related to a lead's interest
- **Templates:** Have your email templates ready to go. I discuss creating templates for lead-nurturing emails later in this chapter.
- **Segmentation:** How will you add people to the program? For inbound campaigns, I suggest using a segmentation on your form or content. That way, when someone fills out a form, he is added to this campaign. You might also choose to have special content, to which you can add a segmentation/automation rule as well. For outbound campaigns, you can put people directly on your program. Or you can use a semi-dynamic rule to have them added automatically. I discuss creating semi-dynamic segmentations in Chapter 6.

Building a sales lead-nurturing campaign

You can empower sales reps with nurturing programs to help them be more effective with their time. Here are some items to consider before you create these specific nurturing programs:

- **Segmentation/automation:** You need to set up a way for sales to put the leads into the drip program in the CRM tool. I suggest making this a manual effort at first. Consider adding a field to your CRM, which your salespeople can check. Some marketing automation tools have a solution for this situation.
- **Content:** Your content should always appear to be coming from the salesperson, so use links to existing content. Great content for the sales team to share includes
  - Articles they found while doing research

  - Blogs they like to follow (Sharing the blog is just as good as sharing a post. Also, the blog is an evergreen item, whereas a post might become dated quickly.)
  - An invitation to watch a webinar you have coming up
  - An invitation to check out your resource library
- **Templates:** Get some of the emails that salespeople are currently sending out, and use those emails to help you craft emails that mimic their best practices. This approach can save you a lot of time in creating new emails for your sales-nurturing programs. It also encourages sales to buy in to the program.
- **Dynamic signatures:** All emails to a lead should appear to come from a lead's sales rep. A dynamic signature is a standard feature in marketing automation tools, so make sure you are using it. This feature allows your nurturing emails to appear to be sent by their sales rep. Using this feature is usually as simple as clicking a button.
- **No branching needed:** Sales lead-nurturing programs should mimic the follow-up cadence of your sales team. These programs do not need to branch; they are very effective with just a main nurturing line. You can therefore create these more quickly than traditional nurturing campaigns.
- **Add phone calls:** With a few marketing automation solutions, you can also add tasks for your sales team, such as to drop a phone call in between emails. This way, your emails appear to be coming from a real person.

Building a cold lead-nurturing campaign

Cold leads are a standard part of a marketer's world. With the pressure to generate more leads, marketers generate a lot of leads, and only a few make it to sales-ready status in a short time frame. The rest of the leads should be viewed as sales-ready in the future. Nurturing those leads using the following checklist helps you make sure that they turn into sales-ready leads in the future:

- **Segmentation/automation:** These nurturing programs usually have a trigger of time, or length of inactivity, before they are added to this campaign. It's good practice to have leads who make it all the way through your net new nurturing campaign added to the cold lead program. Use semi-dynamic segmentation, or an automation rule (each term refers to the same thing; it just depends on what your vendor calls it). Consider these behaviors as triggers to add someone to this campaign:
  - *Lack of activity:* Lack of activity is a good sign that a lead is cold. Lack of activity might include no website visits over a period of time; no interactions after finishing the net new nurturing program; or someone having manually marked the lead as cold. All these are good indications that you need to approach the lead differently.

- *Lead status:* If the lead was passed on to sales, using the Lead Status field in your CRM tool is a great way to gauge whether the lead is cold. If you run a fully dynamic segmentation based on the Lead Status field, you can pull leads who never made it to a phone call with your reps back from sales.

- **Content:** Learn to mix up short- and long-form content for these campaigns. There is no silver bullet, and because the leads are cold, use this campaign for testing a lot of new ideas with content. Many times, great content turns a cold lead around.
- **Signature on emails:** The emails should come from the last person the prospect had engagement with, either from sales or marketing. Either way, keep the signature consistent when possible. The only time the signature should change is when the prospect's main contact changes within the company. For example, if your lead becomes a closed deal, the signature should no longer come from the salesperson if the customer's main contact is now another person within the company.
- **Templates:** Mix these up as well. Try HTML with Rich Text. Testing a combination of Rich Text emails and HTML emails helps you to see which ones work better, and in what cases.

Building a cross-selling nurturing campaign

If you sell multiple products, cross-selling with lead nurturing comes in handy. The goal here is to have short campaigns promoting other products that help salespeople know whom to call. Here are some things to keep in mind:

- **Keep it short:** These campaigns should be very short and highly targeted. The more you email about products a person isn't interested in, the more frustrated the person becomes with you.
- **Don't use branching:** If you have engagement because the lead is already a client, I suggest having sales place a call.
- **Leverage tasks:** Leverage your nurturing program's capability to schedule tasks in your CRM for sales. That way, when an action does happen, you schedule a task for a sales call. This approach helps you build your rapport much better than through an email.
- **Put the right signature on emails:** The signature should come from the person who owns the relationship, even if the rep will not be selling the solution. Introducing another rep via email hurts the rapport you already have.

Figure 10-5 shows an actual cross-sell campaign.

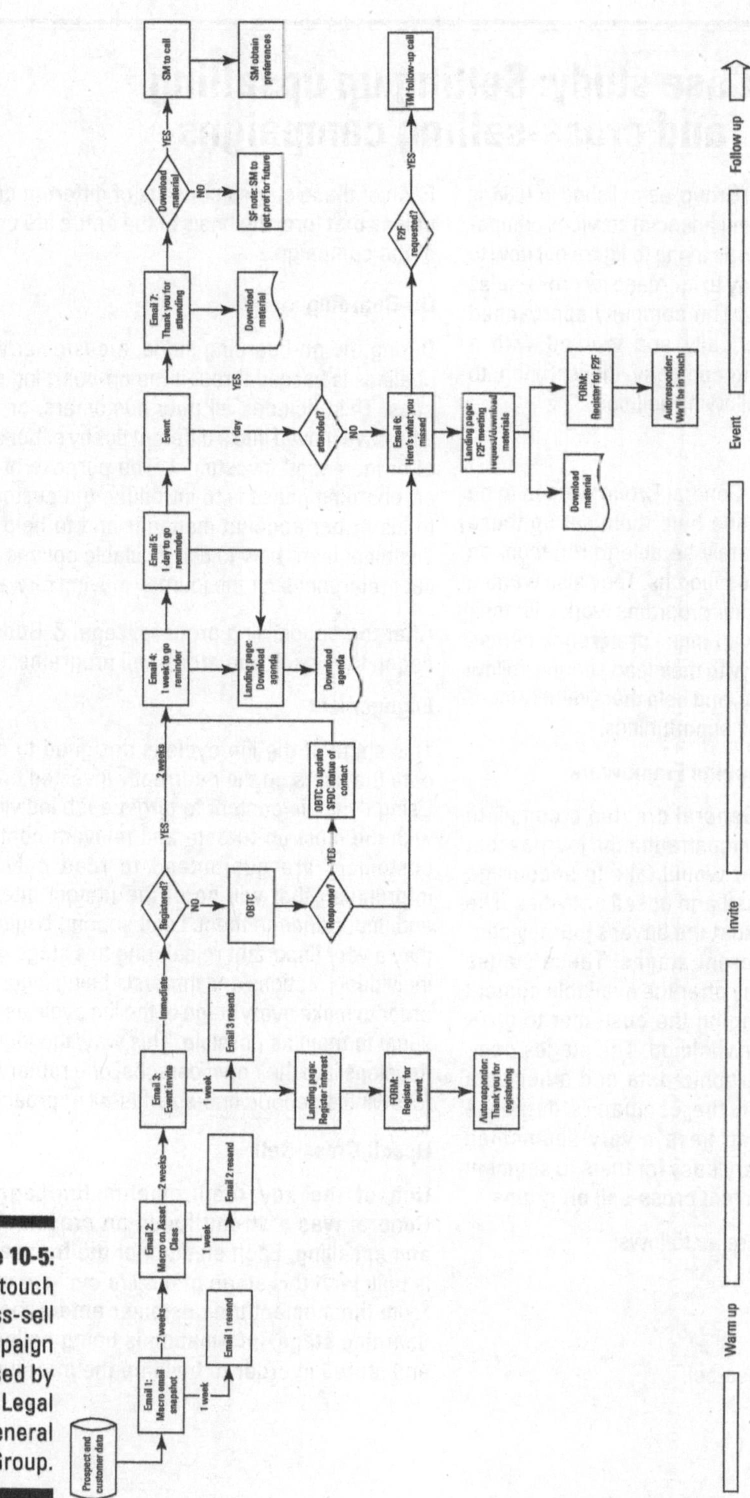

Figure 10-5: A multitouch cross-sell campaign used by the Legal & General Group.

Case study: Setting up upselling and cross-selling campaigns

The Legal & General Group, established in 1836, is one of the UK's leading financial services companies. The company was trying to figure out how to better use technology to increase its cross-sales and upsales efforts. The company approached nurturing very tactically and worked with a UK-based consulting company, CleverTouch, to come up with the following solution.

Goals

Staff at the Legal & General Group wanted to be able to have someone help them set up these programs but ultimately be able to run them on their own within three months. They also wanted to be able to have their programs work with their existing CRM, have an email preference center, be reuseable, work with their lead scoring, follow existing routing rules, and help them identify more upsell and cross-sell opportunities.

Cross-Selling Campaign Framework

To start, Legal & General created a complete buyer's journey demonstrating the journey that an existing investor would take to encourage growth via cross-sell and upsell activities. The company decided that the buyer's journey consisted of four different stages. These stages helped the company offer the available content gradually, encouraging the customer to grow without being overwhelmed. The stages combined with demographic data and other data already existing in the company's database allowed the staff to have a very segmented list. This made it very easy for them to segment people into the correct cross-sell programs.

The three stages are as follows:

1. On-boarding
2. Engagement
3. Upsell and cross-sell

Each of these stages consists of different campaigns that form the basis of the entire life cycle of the campaign.

On-Boarding

During the on-boarding stage, a customer who qualifies is passed through the on-boarding process. This includes all new customers, or any who have moved into a different tier by either lack of or increased investment. The purpose of the on-boarding phase is to introduce the customer to his or her account manager and to help the customer learn how to use available options and set preferences for the journey moving forward.

After the onboarding process, Legal & General began the upsell and cross-sell programs.

Engagement

This stage of the life cycle is designed to educate the users on their currently invested funds. Using dynamic content to target each individual with the most up-to-date and relevant content, customers are guaranteed to read only the information that will be of the utmost interest and importance to them. Lead scoring begins to play a very important role during this stage, with individuals' actions and interests being logged in order to make every stage of the life cycle as personal to them as possible. This way, the journey develops into their own personal one rather than following a generic one-size-fits-all approach.

Upsell/Cross-Sell

One of the key requirements for Legal & General was a strong focus on cross-selling and upselling. Each element of the framework is built with this stage of the life cycle in mind. From the moment the customer enters the on-boarding stage, information is being collected and stored in order to build up the information that will form the content contained within the upsell and cross-sell phase, whether the campaign centers around a particular fund that may be of interest or an event program designed to bring face-to-face elements into the equation.

In this phase, lead scoring indicates when a contact is engaged enough to be passed on to the sales stage, where the outcome of that stage determines what happens next for that particular customer.

Continuing Professional Development (CPD) Program

Alongside the ongoing marketing communications, those who have opted in can also participate in a monthly drip campaign focused entirely around CPD-eligible content. The company offers its customers knowledge and development throughout the life cycle of this campaign.

Summary

The Legal & General framework focuses on the individual's interests, requirements, and activities. Using a combination of lead scoring and dynamic content, each stage delivers a personal experience, always with the added offering of a comprehensive preference center that personalizes the customers' journeys.

The CPD program gives customers the added value of knowledge sharing and shows the individual that Legal & General cares about its clients' continuing development. The result is a very personal relationship that's precisely defined by the needs, interests, and requirements of each person, never by a collective.

Nurturing leads who are using competitive solutions

One of the most effective sales support campaigns is a campaign to nurture leads who are using a competitive solution. For example, a sales rep may be working a lead who can't buy today because she is stuck in a two-year contract with another vendor. Your sales rep still wants to build rapport over those two years, but he wants to minimize the effort in doing so because he has to close deals this year to make his quota. A nurturing campaign is a great way to help with this situation. You can follow three steps to set up this type of campaign:

1. **Set up the segmentation by creating a custom field in the CRM or using a preexisting field.**

   Some tools allow you to set up segmentation without CRM manipulation. All you really need is a data point to read so that you know when someone should be added to this campaign. I suggest looking at the lead status and the field where you mark the tool being used if it's not yours.

2. **Create the drip nurturing campaign.**

   You should craft your drip nurturing campaign for "competitive solutions" with sales support. The sales team will know the cadence of the emails, what to say, and what pain point the person is likely to have if using that solution. All these aspects are very important.

3. **Train your salespeople on the campaign.**

   Before you launch any campaign, make sure to train your sales team on how to add people to the campaign, what the campaign does, and what they can expect to see as a result.

I strongly suggest using this campaign if your industry uses contracts and you have competition. This campaign helps to remove the burden on sales to follow up every month and lets them focus on closing more business. Of all the campaigns I've created for my sales team, this is their favorite by far.

Setting Up Nurturing Email Templates

Nurturing emails are very different from mass emails. Remember that a nurturing campaign works as a one-to-one medium, whereas email blasting is a one-to-many medium. To increase your engagement rates, you must start with the understanding of the one-to-one campaign. In this section, I break down the parts of an email and teach you how to create emails that engage prospects.

Bringing in your first email template

If you have been doing email marketing for a while and you have a few email templates that you want to use for marketing automation, you can import them into your tool using the following steps as a guide. If you are brand new to email marketing and marketing automation, skip ahead to the next section, where I show you how to build assets in your tool from scratch.

To import an email template into your marketing automation tool, follow these steps:

1. **Open the email template source code in your former email tool.**

   You can easily open the source code by accessing the raw HTML, which you can find in your WYSIWYG editor's options. There should be a button to click that opens the full HTML code.

   Figure 10-6 shows the raw HTML code you are looking for.

Open the HTML file to select and copy the code.

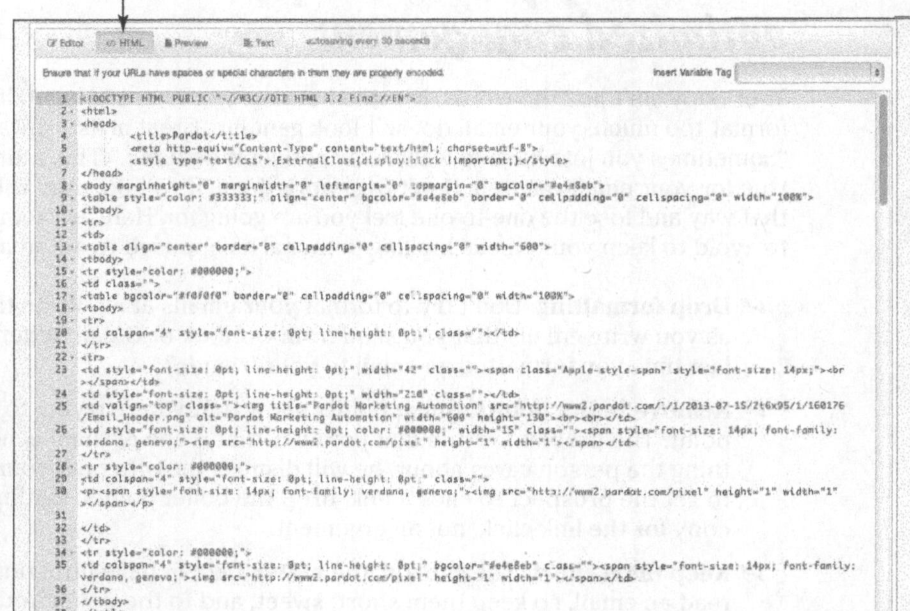

Figure 10-6: Copy the raw HTML file inside your email application.

2. **In the HTML file, select all the HTML and click Copy.**
3. **Open your marketing automation tool, locate your email section, and open a new email template.**

   The location of this section varies depending on your tool.
4. **In the new email template, access the raw HTML editor (not the WYSIWYG editor) and then paste the raw HTML from Step 1 into the HTML editor.**

After your HTML file is uploaded, you need to save your HTML code and check the WYSIWYG editor for errors. Errors are usually caused by image files or by URLs that have changed. If you have image files hosted in your old email tool, you need to host them in your new marketing automation solution as well. Some tools use a template system that allows you to reuse the same HTML file many times.

When naming your email files, use a naming convention. Consider naming drip emails differently from email blasts to make them easier to manage.

Formatting your email for optimized engagement

Your copy isn't just the words. It's also how the words are laid out. If you format too much, your email doesn't look genuine. Great artists always say, "Sometimes you just have to walk away and let it be done." This attitude holds true for your emails as well. Don't overwork them. If you do, they will look that way and lose the one-to-one feel you are going for. Here are some things to avoid to keep your emails looking personal as opposed to automated.

- **Drop formatting.** Don't try to format your emails at all. Write them just as you write emails that you send from Outlook or Gmail. When was the last time you formatted an email to your friends?
- **Remove bullet points.** Bullet points show that you're trying to make a point. The problem with bullet points is that if one of them is not something the person cares about, he will dismiss the others. If your goal is to get the prospect to click a link, drop the bullet points. Optimize your copy for the link click, not an argument.
- **Keep them short.** The shorter, the better. People have little time to read an email, so keep them short, sweet, and to the point. You'll easily increase engagements this way.
- **Scratch salutations.** Don't use salutations. They are way too formal, and nobody uses them unless they are sending a formal communication. Nurturing emails should appear to be sent manually, not automatically, and a salutation can work against that impression.
- **Remove heavy signature blocks.** Signature blocks take the person's eye away from the hyperlink. Optimize for the link click. The prospect already knows who the email is from because it is in your email address.

To see an example of a great one-to-one email, check out Figure 10-7.

Hey %%first_name%%,

I wanted to stay in touch and pass along this article published by BtoB Magazine about how marketers are taking advantage of real-time analytics in their email campaigns. I think you'll find some helpful information about targeting your message and evaluating the success of your strategy.

Let me know your thoughts.

Thanks,
%%user_first_name%%

%%user_html_signature%%

%%account_address%%
Choose not to receive future emails from me

Figure 10-7: A great example of a one-to-one email.

Copy Writing for Email Nurturing

To craft good copy and increase the odds of engagement, consider the tone and format of your copy. The copy inside a nurturing email is very different from copy in a newsletter or an email blast. Compare Figures 10-8 through 10-10 and notice the fundamental differences in the copy and layout.

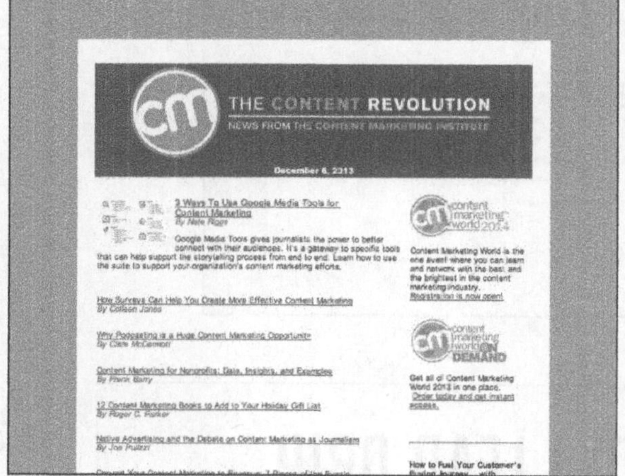

Figure 10-8: An email used for email newsletters contains a lot of information.

The email newsletter (see Figure 10-8) was designed to mimic a publication such as one that an actual news agency might send out, and to be informational, too. This was great when email sending was not as prevalent, and it's an effective tactic if the news is relevant to the person. Joe Pulizzi (@joepulizzi) with Content Marketing Institute (@cminstitute) sends an email newsletter every day, and it remains one of that company's most highly engaged with emails. People engage with it because the content is relevant and warranted.

In Figure 10-10, the amount of information has been condensed to a single topic, yet the amount of content remains high. This email from ReadyTalk is advertising a new webinar. It is sent from the marketing team to people in their database who would find this webinar helpful.

The nurturing email in Figure 10-9, sent from a salesperson, was used to help nurture sales leads after they were already engaged with a salesperson. This type of message gives the sales team the ability to have a much larger reach while keeping salespeople laser-focused on only the leads who want to talk. The email contains only one topic and is short on content. It's also highly personalized and appears to be written by one person, intended for the recipient.

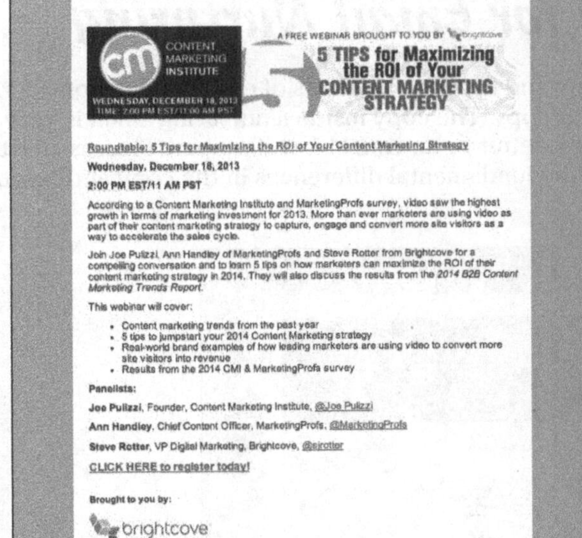

A FREE WEBINAR BROUGHT TO YOU BY brightcove

CONTENT MARKETING INSTITUTE

WEDNESDAY, DECEMBER 18, 2013
TIME: 2:00 PM EST/11:00 AM PST

5 TIPS for Maximizing the ROI of Your CONTENT MARKETING STRATEGY

Roundtable: 5 Tips for Maximizing the ROI of Your Content Marketing Strategy

Wednesday, December 18, 2013

2:00 PM EST/11 AM PST

According to a Content Marketing Institute and MarketingProfs survey, video saw the highest growth in terms of marketing investment for 2013. More than ever marketers are using video as part of their content marketing strategy to capture, engage and convert more site visitors as a way to accelerate the sales cycle.

Join Joe Pulizzi, Ann Handley of MarketingProfs and Steve Rotter from Brightcove for a compelling conversation and to learn 5 tips on how marketers can maximize the ROI of their content marketing strategy in 2014. They will also discuss the results from the *2014 B2B Content Marketing Trends Report*.

This webinar will cover:

- Content marketing trends from the past year
- 5 tips to jumpstart your 2014 Content Marketing strategy
- Real-world brand examples of how leading marketers are using video to convert more site visitors into revenue
- Results from the 2014 CMI & MarketingProfs survey

Panelists:

Joe Pulizzi, Founder, Content Marketing Institute, @Joe Pulizzi

Ann Handley, Chief Content Officer, MarketingProfs, @MarketingProfs

Steve Rotter, VP Digital Marketing, Brightcove, @sjrotter

CLICK HERE to register today!

Brought to you by:

brightcove

Figure 10-9: An email blast sent to inform people of an upcoming webinar.

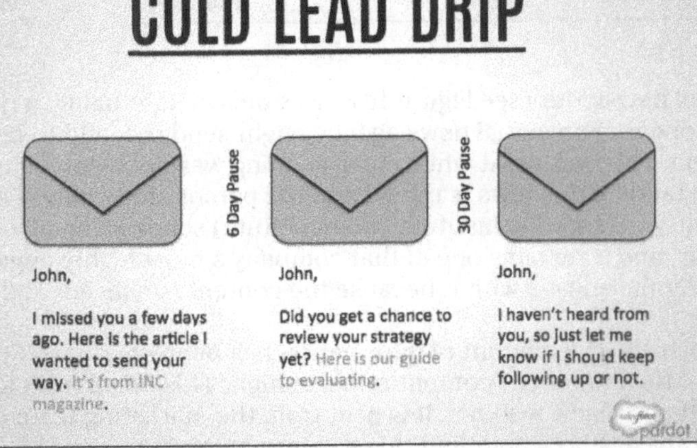

Figure 10-10: A good example of a one-to-one email used in a nurturing program.

Learning the importance of the subject line

The subject line is one of the main reasons your email gets opened. People do not randomly open emails; they open only the emails that feel relevant to them at the time. The main reason they won't open them if they are not relevant is simple: People get too many emails per day to read them all. Here are the basic stats on emails sent per day:

- 294 billion emails sent every day
- 12 billion emails sent every hour
- 200 million emails sent every minute

A person can disqualify an email in 1/20 of a second. So if your subject line is not relevant, don't expect it to get opened.

For your emails to compete with the volume of emails your prospects see in their inboxes every day, your subject lines have to be as relevant as possible. Behavioral tracking in marketing automation is one of the main factors that can help you create relevant subject lines.

Using a stage-based tone and dynamic content

You need to learn to write in the correct tone and include relevant points of interest to your leads, so use the stage-based concept of lead generation. Each stage has the goal of getting the person to the next stage, and finally to the MQL stage.

- **Stage 1:** When working with early-stage leads, try to keep the subject lines light and personal, with no company branding in them.
- **Stage 2:** In this stage, people are more educated about your product and have engaged with you before. Try to use subject lines that help reinforce their interest, but do not push your product.
- **Stage 3:** Now people are about to set up demos, so you can push the reasons that your company/solution is better in your subject line.

When nurturing a person through her interest in your product, you can add something of particular interest to her to make your messages even more relevant. You can use dynamic content to add words to your subject line or the body of your email. Dynamic content easily allows you to add specific interest based on a person's behavioral data. This feature works like a mail merge field, whereby the email looks at a specific field in the database and populates it with whatever lives in that field. Figure 10-11 shows an example of dynamic text within the email.

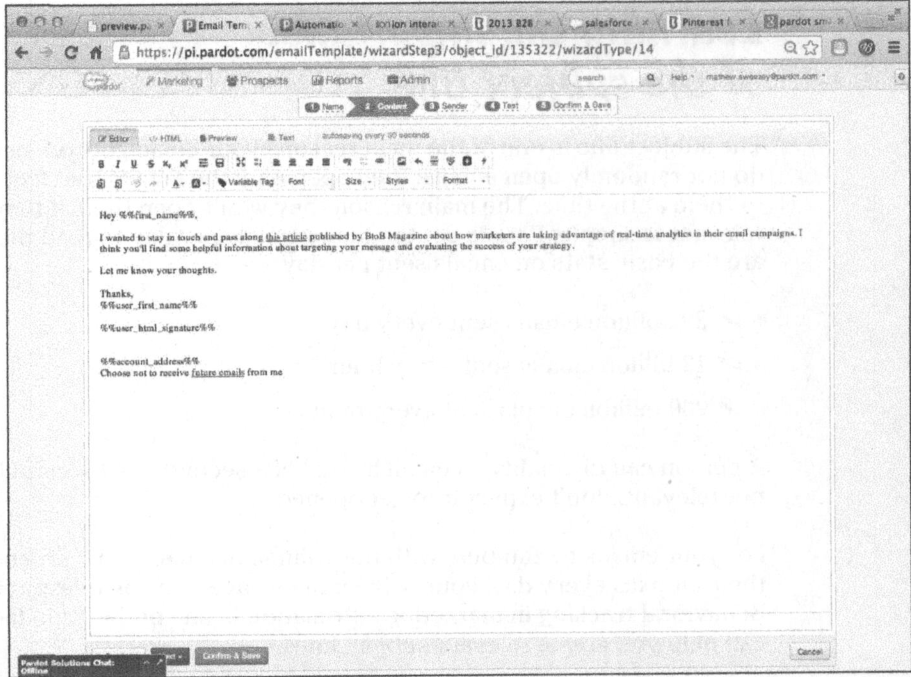

Figure 10-11: Use dynamic content in a subject line.

Most people think that dynamic content saves them the time of having to create many different emails. This belief is false. Both ways require you to create the same content, and both ways require the exact same testing. So you don't reap a large time savings on creation; instead, you gain an easier way to manage very complex sending requirements.

Writing with a personal tone

Your email copy should use a personal tone. Here are some easy tips to help you ensure that you're using such a tone:

- **Test it:** Send what you think is a good email to ten people in your company. Ask them to tell you whether they thought that this email was written just for them. If they feel it was, you're fine. If they don't, try again.
- **Copy others:** If you get an email from someone and you engaged with it, mimic the language. Look at why you engaged and then style your message with the same kind of language. If it worked on you, it will work on someone else.
- **Scan your inbox:** Scan your inbox for emails sent from you to your friends, and from them to you. These emails will have the highest engagement of all emails ever sent out of your inbox. Look at how you write and how they write. Notice the tone and the words used. Copy this same cadence, tone, and writing style when you send nurturing emails.

Stop writing with the "golden pen"

My father was a used car salesman for part of his life, so I can talk about this profession with a bit of humor. If you were to ask people whether they trust used car salesmen, most would likely answer no. In fact, Gallup conducts a poll to see which professions are trusted and not trusted. Salespeople always fall at the bottom of the list. Lower than lawyers and congressmen! Why is this?

It has to do with the way they talk. Have you ever heard the expression "He can sell ice to an Eskimo?" It refers to a person who can talk anyone into anything, and this is the reason people are put off by salespeople. No one wants to be taken advantage of by fancy manipulation. People believe that salespeople speak with a "golden tongue." The same holds true for mass emails. If you expect your single, perfectly crafted subject line to convert everyone who reads your emails, you are writing with the equivalent "golden pen."

Effective Calls to Action for Lead Nurturing

The call to action (CTA) is the goal of every email. The CTA is a very tricky thing, because you are asking someone to do something. This is one of the reasons content marketing has become so big. It disguises your CTA and makes it appear helpful to the person, when really it is serving your needs just as much. Good CTAs always do the following:

- **Include hyperlinks:** Never attach a file or embed a video. Instead, use a hyperlink to direct people to assets. This approach gives you the power to track engagement.
- **Point to relevant information:** Relevant information may just be a tweet you found. It might be a video, or anything. A great feature of the Internet is that everything is accessible via a link.
- **Use creative copy for your hyperlink:** Having a "click here" link increases your odds of being trapped by a spam filter. Instead, try using techniques like the ones shown in the nurturing email in Figure 10-12. The hyperlink is at the top of the message, is half of a sentence, and talks about something the prospect might like.
- **Appear close to the top of the message:** Traditionally, people put the CTA at the end of an email. They clutter up the first half of the email with a description of why you should click the link. Try reversing this order to increase conversions. Keep your copy short and your link high in the email.

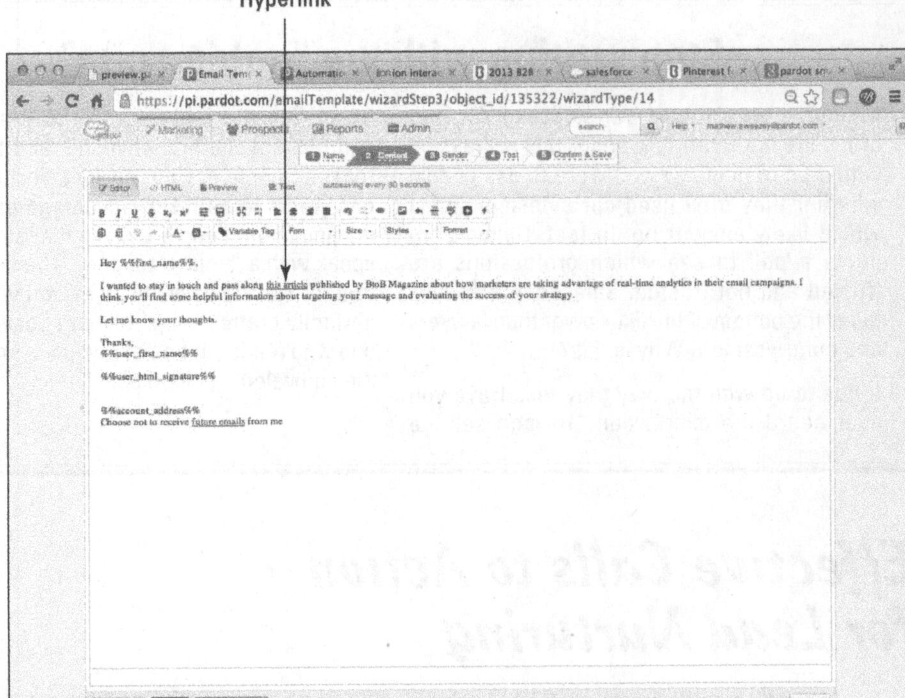

Figure 10-12: Use a hyperlink in your nurturing email CTAs.

Using creative CTAs to help increase engagement

Most companies use CTAs in the form of links to articles, content, or their website. These CTAs usually provide content, which is great, but you can also use CTAs for other purposes to get more engagement from them. Using CTAs also gives you more ways to mix up content in your nurturing program. Try placing CTAs in the following ways:

- **Ask for comments on the blog:** A great use of nurturing can be to help drive comments to your blog. Comments on your blog give your post more validity and make it more engaging. Getting comments can be tough, so try asking for them through a nurturing campaign.
- **Ask for feedback:** One way to ask for feedback is to send an email follow-up to your white paper. Ask for feedback on how helpful it was. You'll get an engagement, and you'll get feedback.

- **Ask for recommendations:** If you are nurturing current clients, dedicate an email to asking people to recommend your company. This request can help you drive recommendations and give you other engagements beyond just sending content. Also, if clients do make recommendations, make sure to thank them.
- **Survey people:** Surveys are a great way to get new content for articles. Try sending an email with a short survey asking people to help. You can offer them first dibs on the new research you produce, or invitations to a webinar available only for those who give feedback.

Increasing engagement by better targeting of CTAs

The number-one mistake with CTAs is asking people to do something when you know they don't want to do it. That's an easy concept to grasp, but when you're mass emailing to large numbers of people, realize that the majority of them don't want to hear from you. In a nurturing campaign, a lot of them are not expecting to hear from you, either. Learn to increase your engagement rates with CTAs by focusing only on prospects who you know would like what you are sending. The easiest way to do this is to match your CTA with your lead stages.

- **Stage 1:** For early-stage leads, try to keep the CTAs linked to helpful, short pieces of content. Remember that it's about them, not you, at this stage.
- **Stage 2:** At stage 2, people are more educated about your product and have engaged with you before. They also most likely need to convince others of the idea. Consider using social proof such as case studies and examples of how others benefited.
- **Stage 3:** People at this stage are about to set up demos, so go ahead and push why your company/solution is better in your subject line. Send the heavy buyers' guides to help them make a better decision. They want to know why you are best at this stage, so tell them.

Following the concept of matching your CTA and content to your stage will greatly help you increase your conversion rate on your nurturing emails.

Signature links may hurt sending rates

Putting hyperlinks in email signatures is very popular. It's a good practice for personal emails, but in mass emails or nurturing emails, these links can hurt your sending rates. Because I suggest sending short emails, be careful with the number of links you include in an email. Try to restrict yourself to one hyperlink for every few lines of text in your email. This ratio of text to hyperlinks helps ensure that your email does not appear "spammy" to spam filters.

Improving Email Deliverability with Email Authentication

Email authentication is likely to be new to you if you have never used an advanced email tool. Email authentication is very similar to your CNAME, which I go over in Chapter 4. It gives the Internet a way to correctly verify where the email is really coming from. Each spam filter uses a different email authentication method, and a list and the methods used appears in Figure 10-13. The purpose of email authentication is to assure mailbox providers that your emails are coming from your email domain and not a spammer who hijacked your IP address. You should plan on setting up as many types as your vendor will allow.

Email Authentication Checking by ISP

ISP	DKIM	DomainKeys	SenderID	SPF
AOL	☑		☑	
Gmail	☑	☑		☑
Hotmail/MSN			☑	
Yahoo!	☑	☑		

Source: Email Sender & Provider Coalition Authentication Report

Figure 10-13: Email clients and the email authentication they use.

Determining the Pace of Nurturing Emails

The pace of a nurturing campaign helps you to very effectively manage a relationship over a long period of time with very little effort. Here are the basic rules of pacing, as well as some specific tactics to use in any nurturing campaign to make them more effective.

- **Follow general pace rules.** The general rule of pace is 6-45 (that is, send emails at least six days apart but no longer than 45 days). I have seen many consultants suggest different time frames, but these are the time frames I teach. The reason is that a work week has five days, and having your emails sent at a minimum of six days apart is a fail-safe method of preventing two emails in one week. On the other hand, if you are not dropping an email to someone every 45 days, you're very likely to fall off that person's radar. (I got the 45-day number from my bestselling sales rep.)

- **"Set" things up.** I'm a firm believer in using sets within your nurturing programs. A *set* is a group of emails that are sent in quick succession, followed by a long pause. Figure 10-14 shows a set of emails in a long nurturing program. The idea behind a set is to go hard and then slack off. If going hard didn't work, and you keep it up, you'll burn out your lead. So learn to work hard in sets, followed by long pauses to be respectful of the prospect's level of interest.

Drip Logic

▶ Start
↓
1. Send email Nurturing - Introduction ✖
↓
2. Pause 6 days ✖
↓
3. Send email Nurturing - Personal Note 1 - Case Study Follow Up ✖
↓
4. Pause 6 days ✖
↓
5. Send email Nurturing - Personal Note 2 - Case Study Follow Up ✖
↓
End

Figure 10-14: A set of emails in a nurturing program.

- **Act natural.** The main goal of nurturing is to have the email appear to be coming from a person. People do not send emails at the same time on the same day every week. So mix it up. Keeping a random pace is good practice. Figure 10-15 shows a random time pace (6, 8, and 13 days) between each email sent in the nurturing program. This random pacing is very important when you run sales-support nurturing programs.

Drip Logic

▶ Start
↓
1. Send email Nurturing - Introduction ✖
↓
2. Pause 6 days ✖
↓
3. Send email Nurturing - Personal Note 1 - Case Study Follow Up ✖
↓
4. Pause 8 days ✖
↓
5. Send email Nurturing - Personal Note 2 - Case Study Follow Up ✖
↓
6. Pause 13 days ✖
↓
End

Figure 10-15: Emails sent at different times to appear random.

- **Realize that a long sales cycle means long pauses.** When you have a lengthy sales cycle, lasting many months or years, you have a long time to get the lead into a sales-ready state. Trying to force the lead to that state only damages your chance to build rapport. So pause for longer periods of time between each email if you have a longer sales cycle. The same concept goes for short sales cycles. If you have a short sales cycle, you have a shorter period of time to convert the lead, so you may have to take a more aggressive pace.

Ending Nurturing Programs

A nurturing program ends in one of two ways: The lead either converts along the way or makes it all the way to the end of the program. Those two scenarios are the only options the lead should have. Here's how to deal with both situations:

- **Leads who convert:** If a lead reaches your goal, she should be removed from the nurturing campaign. You can remove the lead through an automation rule, and with some tools, the automation rule is built in combination with the nurturing program. Regardless of how you set up the removal of the lead from the program, just remember to remove people from the nurturing program after they have converted.
- **Leads who don't convert:** Leads who don't convert along the way will make it to the end of your nurturing program. You should deal with these leads in a very specific way, using one of the following basic techniques:
    - *Use a list.* If the lead makes it to the end of the campaign, you can have a list that is auto populated with a segmentation/automation. This should remove the person from the nurturing campaign and put him on a special list. You can then use this list as a holding pen, or as the beginning of another nurturing campaign.
    - *Create a task.* If the lead is on a sales-support program, consider letting your sales rep know that the lead has finished being nurtured. The sales rep can then decide what to do next with that lead. The rep may want to reach out with a phone call or add the lead to another campaign. The point is to let the salesperson control the next step.
    - *End with a nice note.* You may want to have the last email in your nurturing program be a "break-up" email. This is a common practice for getting an engagement. Your email may read very much like the email in Figure 10-16. The tactic is similar to what magazines do when they put "This is your last issue" on the cover of the last magazine in your subscription.

%%first_name%%,

It's been a while, and I wanted to check in to see if you still want me to send you some information from time to time. Just let me know if you could so I'm not sending you things you're not wanting.

It's really easy to let me know, just click the option you'd prefer.

I'm good and don't need any more information.

I like your content, I'm just busy. Keep it coming.

Sincerely,
%%user_first_name%%

%%user_html_signature%%

Our mailing address is:
%%account_address%%

unsubscribe from this list | update subscription preferences

Figure 10-16: A break-up email used to end a nurturing program.

Case study: Building a killer email nurturing program

Here's how a real business, KANA Software, executed its drip programs (including some of the best practices it used).

The Problem the Company Solved with Nurturing

Before implementing drip campaigns, the company had sent well over 1 million emails with an average click-through rate (CTR) of 3.66 percent. KANA Software wanted to create a way to move its prospects through its marketing and sales funnel based on the different software lines the company sold. The overall goal was to engage with the company's database, have a conversation with those prospects, and then pass them along to sales.

How the Company Did It

To accomplish these goals, KANA Software turned to lead nurturing. The company decided to implement drip campaigns by going through a five-step process, outlined in the following paragraphs.

Step 1: Define goals.

Here are some of the goals KANA Software came up with prior to setting up its lead-nurturing campaigns:

- Target prospects via email nurturing campaigns with relevant content based on previous-offer downloads.

(continued)

(continued)

- Move "latent" leads through the funnel and reengage them.
- Show that CTR can be increased through targeted campaigns.

Step 2: Create a checklist.

Before building out a drip campaign, you should create a checklist of all the necessary materials and steps. KANA's checklist looked like this:

- Identify content and paths.
- Create lists.
- Create landing pages.
- Tag URLs (using custom redirects and UTM parameters).
- Draft email templates.

Step 3: Identify content and paths, but keep it simple.

At first, KANA Software created a complicated diagram to map the content that would be used in the company's drip campaigns, along with the paths that prospects could take. When describing their process, the team at KANA commented that they could have kept things a lot simpler. For example: Did the prospect click a link? Yes? Have a sales rep call them and mention their interest.

Step 4: Build drips.

When it comes to actually building the drip campaigns, KANA Software provided the following tips:

- Choose names for your drips that are scalable and easy to remember.
- Think about your audience's time zone.
- Use tags for information such as product interest, language, and geography.
- Pay careful attention to the tone, style, and wording of actual drip emails.
- Know who your audience is and who it isn't. (Use suppression lists to keep certain people from getting drip emails.)
- Stagger start times of multiple drips to prevent sending too many emails to a single prospect.
- Consider pauses and how these match the pace of your sales cycle.
- Tag recipients who pass certain stages so that you can identify what kind of content they engaged with.

Step 5: Review and tweak.

After you've launched your first drip campaign, you need to evaluate it to see whether any areas need improvement. These are some of the questions that the team at KANA Software asked themselves when reviewing their campaigns:

- Why are click-through rates higher in one email than the other?
- Are pauses too long or too short?
- Where do people stop engaging or start to fall off?
- Are we meeting our goals and can we do better?

The Results

After evaluating its campaigns, KANA Software was pleased to find that its targeted, lead-nurturing campaigns had succeeded in moving leads through the sales funnel, increasing click-through rates, and driving engaged traffic. The company reported the following statistics:

- The average click-through rate on its drip emails was three times higher than its normal blast email click-through rate.
- Submission rates were higher than on the company's cost-per-click landing pages (34.19 percent versus 2.63 percent) and drove more engaged traffic to its site.
- Site visits originating from drip emails lasted an average of 3:02 versus a 1:56 average visit time for all traffic.

Part IV

Mixing, Scoring, and Reporting

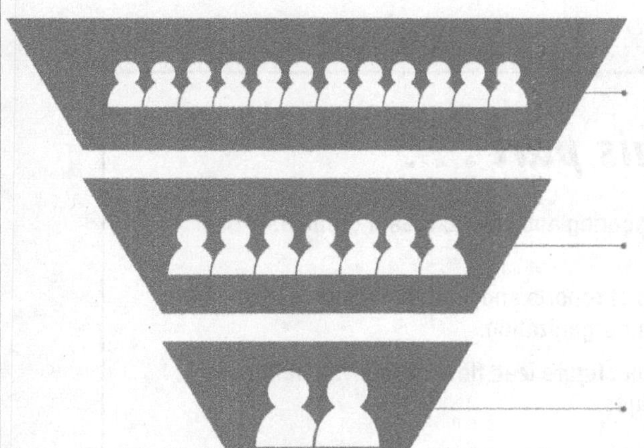

A snapshot of your Lead Funnel at any given time.
Stage 1: Leads are the farthest from MQL, and the least valuable asset at this moment in time based on likelihood to convert to MQL.
Stage 2: Leads are farther along than stage one, and more valuable because of this. However they still do not meet stage 3 criteria, and will take longer to convert than stage 3 leads.
Stage 3: Leads are going to convert to MQL within a short period of time, making them the most valuable and time sensitive of the lead funnel.

You can download an article about lead scoring at `www.dummies.com/extras/marketingautomation`.

In this part . . .

- Get to know lead scoring and how to create great lead scores.
- Explore new types of reports and learn how to prove your marketing value to your organization.
- Learn how to predict future lead flow to help you better estimate future revenues.

Chapter 11

Combining Automation with Other Marketing Programs

In This Chapter

- Combining social media efforts with marketing automation
- Using video in marketing automation
- Integrating offline events

If you're a modern marketer, you're likely involved in many types of online marketing such as search marketing, email marketing, and content marketing. Managing multiple types of marketing usually means struggling with multiple tools and data that needs to be imported and exported from one tool to another. Marketing automation provides significant value because it is a single tool that replaces many of your disparate unconnected tools and data-sharing practices.

In this chapter, I show you how to connect your marketing automation tool with all your marketing efforts. Tying these endeavors together allows you to track the ROI on webinars, YouTube videos, and other external marketing efforts. The chapter also covers integrating social media with your new marketing automation tool to help you prove the value of your social media efforts.

Placing Marketing Automation at the Center of Your Marketing

Without marketing automation, all your marketing data is locked inside each of your individual marketing tools unless you export it. When you add marketing automation, your data is free to be shared among marketing tools without the need to manually export anything.

Freeing your data also allows you to leverage it for advanced personalized campaigns. The key to marketing automation is not to automate only individual campaigns you are running. Rather, marketing automation is most powerful when you leverage data across multiple marketing tactics to create individually targeted marketing campaigns that are relevant to each individual you're marketing to. This is how you drive a larger increase in engagement.

The following list describes the most common channels that marketers use. If you're using these marketing channels, you are likely to have new data points available to you after you implement marketing automation:

- **Paid ads** give you data points on keywords and ads a person engaged with. With this information on the single prospect record, you can now track the lead all the way to a closed opportunity to prove the true ROI on any search term or paid ad.
- **Email marketing** gives you data from opens, bounces, clicks, and post-click activity. With marketing automation, you can track past the link click. So if someone clicks your link and then goes to your pricing page, you can easily identify this prospect as a sales-ready lead and even have your lead passed to sales in real time when this happens.
- **Social media** gives you the ability to include conversations and content in a person's scoring model. Use social media engagement to drive your next personalized email.
- **Websites** give you the specific pages and actions a person engages with while on your website. With the single prospect view, every web page is logged on to a record so that sales can call the leads who looked at the website.
- **SEO campaigns** give you data points on the specific search terms each person uses for a search. With the single-prospect view and automation, you can segment and email the leads who searched for your competitors' keywords.
- **SEM** gives you data on the search terms people use. Marketing automation allows you to track the paid search terms that people engage with to find you. This information on prospects can help you segment incoming leads based on their specific interest because you know the exact SEM words they engaged with. By tracking search terms and tying them to specific prospects, you can find out what features they are interested in and what problems they have. This tracking can even let you know whether prospects were searching for a competitor when they found you.
- **Video marketing** gives you data on how interested a person is in a topic based on which videos she watches and for how long.
- **Event marketing** allows you to keep up with offline engagement and use data captured at your events in your follow-up campaigns. With marketing automation, you can also understand the influence of events on opportunities, as well as provide ROI for events.
- **Webinars** give you information on what topics a person finds relevant.

Case study: Placing marketing automation at the center of your inbound marketing strategy

Prior to implementing marketing automation, Mediacurrent had an inbound marketing strategy but no formal process in place for following up with leads in a timely manner. The company was also dealing with a fragmented reporting structure and an unfocused content strategy that didn't address buyer needs as well as it could. With marketing automation, Mediacurrent was able to begin creating a scalable inbound marketing strategy that cut down on manual processes and increased marketing and sales efficiency.

The Solution

The Mediacurrent marketing team uses inbound marketing to build trust, foster relationships, and drive credibility within the open-source software community. But in order to achieve its long-term goals, Mediacurrent needed to produce and present the right educational resources to the appropriate audiences at exactly the right time. After defining its buyer personas and auditing its content, Mediacurrent started using lead scoring and grading to help the company focus on its most promising leads. Attributes such as title, industry, and revenue contributed to a lead's grade, while a scoring system was put in place to track and score leads with the greatest interest. Having a defined process in place to qualify leads helped to align Mediacurrent's sales and marketing teams, leading to more unique opportunities for collaboration.

Leads that received a grade of A and/or a score of 100 were automatically turned over to sales for follow-up, whereas leads who didn't quite meet the 100-point threshold were placed on lead-nurturing tracks. Prospect behavior was then tracked using the company's marketing automation lead-tracking functionalities, which catalogued the pages that prospects were visiting and gave a clearer indication of their interests, the stage in the sales cycle, and the effectiveness of Mediacurrent's content. This helped Mediacurrent's sales team target their conversations accordingly.

Based on the responses to its content, Mediacurrent began revamping all the calls to action on its website by offering similar resources that readers might be interested in, leading to a 129 percent growth in content conversions year over year. Mediacurrent also began combining its CRM reports, Google Analytics, data from custom redirects, and its marketing automation's life cycle reporting to pull numbers on lead generation, cost per lead, and sales follow-up activity — giving the company hard data that could speak to the success of its inbound marketing strategy.

Results

Within 12 months of implementing these processes and technology, Mediacurrent saw the following results:

- 53 percent increase in organic search traffic, which meant more white paper and ebook downloads
- 40 percent increase in regular email subscribers
- 23 percent increase in leads assigned to the sales team
- 129 percent year-over-year growth in content conversions
- 55 percent of viable leads closed on

Each of these channels connects to your platform but may require additional integration. Finding a solution that natively accommodates most of your marketing channels and tools is best. The more direct integrations a tool has, the higher the cost is likely to be. Make sure to weigh the costs and benefits of having to import one or two data sets on a regular basis versus having it fully connected.

Leveraging Social Media with Marketing Automation

Social media has recently taken on a new form. For the purpose of this chapter, and all future marketing, you should consider anything that happens online to be social. For example:

- Your blog allows for social sharing
- Your Twitter feed is social
- People are copying your white papers to LinkedIn
- People are talking about your company on Facebook

The next sections show you how these social interactions tie in with marketing automation.

Syncing social media with marketing automation

You have two ways to sync your social media with your marketing automation tool:

- **Syncing social media when your marketing automation tool can execute social campaigns.** Some marketing automation tools have social media post abilities in their tool sets. Others don't. If your tool does allow you to execute social campaigns, you don't need to take any actions to sync your campaigns; the syncing should already be done for you.
- **Syncing social media campaigns to marketing automation when using separate tools.** If you're using different tools, you can connect the two by syncing the URLs, as shown in Figure 11-1. In this figure, I created a custom URL in my marketing automation tool and pasted it into HootSuite. This allows my marketing automation tool to track the link clicks but allows HootSuite to send it out across its network.

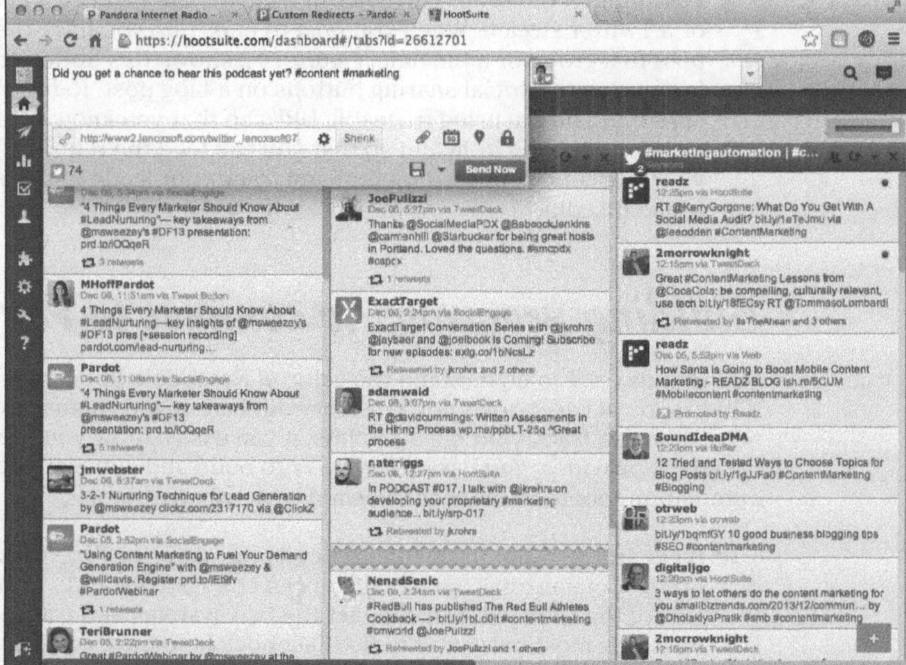

Figure 11-1: Integrate your disconnected marketing automation tool with social sites.

Leveraging LinkedIn with marketing automation

LinkedIn is a very powerful social media channel for most businesses. For consumer packaged-goods brands and other non-B2B companies, it has little value. If you run marketing for a B2B brand, here are some ways to use LinkedIn and marketing automation together:

- **Posting to groups:** This is the most effective way to use LinkedIn and your marketing automation tool. A LinkedIn group is a content channel. It does not create content for you, but helps you distribute it. So if you are following the trends in a group, all you need to connect the group with your marketing automation tool is to make sure that you have a way to track the URL posted to LinkedIn. To make this connection, you create a dedicated landing page for the content, using custom redirects, or create special versions of the content only for LinkedIn. Regardless of which approach you choose, the goal is to make sure that you know where your leads are coming from and can get this information into your marketing automation tool. The URLs allow you to do this.

- **Posting to a timeline:** Timelines in LinkedIn are just like a Facebook feed or a Twitter stream. When you post to LinkedIn, you have the option to post to a group or a timeline. Figure 11-2 shows this option that appears from using the social sharing buttons on a blog post. Remember to make sure that you are using traceable URLs so that you know where your leads are coming from and so that you can feed the required data into your marketing automation tool and track your leads that are generated from LinkedIn.

Building programs to connect to Facebook

B2C brands tend to understand the value of Facebook, but convincing many B2B brands of Facebook's power is very difficult. If you can use marketing automation to track your engagements, it can easily show you the value Facebook provides. You have a few ways to build and connect your marketing automation tool to Facebook. Some are easier than others:

- **Basic integration:** Basic integration is the same for Facebook as any other social media channel. If you can control your URL, or the destination of the URL, you can connect the two systems and track your lead flow. The most basic way to use Facebook is to have a page and allow people to Like your page. Receiving Likes can help provide social proof of the viability of your company.

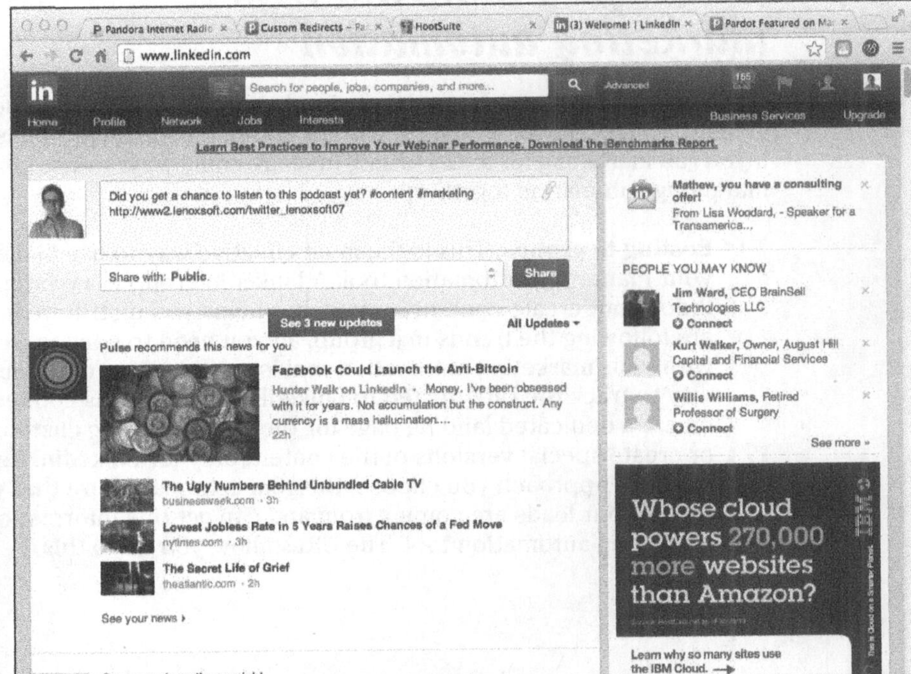

Figure 11-2: Posting to a timeline or group is an option in LinkedIn.

- **Intermediate integration:** If you are a more advanced Facebook marketer, you might be using Facebook ads. If you are using Facebook ads, they integrate with marketing automation in the same way as any other paid search medium. You need to make sure that you're using custom URLs or driving leads to a specific landing page. Either of these methods allows you to track effectiveness. I call this intermediate integration because it requires you to know how to do paid placement ads in Facebook. This knowledge is not something most people have.
- **Advanced integration:** If you're an active marketer in Facebook, you can get into very advanced integrations. Facebook allows for the insertion of iFrames into your pages. That way, forms created in your marketing automation tool can be posted to your Facebook page, giving you a lead capture form inside Facebook. Because a lead capture form is already native to your marketing automation tool, no integration is required for setup. I call this advanced integration because posting iFrames into Facebook requires IT help if you're not familiar with the use of iFrames.

Integrating Video into Social Media

Video is a massive social media tool. It can be used on any medium. If you are not doing video now, you should be. Videos are the hottest engagement method currently online. You can read tons of stats on their power. Do you think your prospects watch more TV or read more books? Answer: They watch more TV. That's why video is such an awesome tool with social media. You have three ways to integrate video into your marketing automation mix:

- **Basic:** The most basic integration you can have between your videos and your marketing automation tool is to simply post video to your website. Because your marketing automation tool knows what pages a person looks at, you can easily see whether someone visits the page your video is on. This visibility allows for all automations such as scoring, routing, and nurturing.

  Posting video to your website is not the best way to use it, but it is better than nothing. It also is the easiest to set up, and you can do it with any video platform, from YouTube to Vimeo. Your call to action can be on the page or you can embed it at the end of the video. You can even have a form below the video without editing your video file at all. All these options are easy, and you can handle them without any technical knowledge.
- **Intermediate:** If you want a tighter integration between your videos and your marketing automation tool, you can embed calls to action within your video. This functionality depends on your video-hosting tool. More advanced tools such as Wisita are very specific for B2B marketing and have simple tools to allow you to insert forms into your videos. These video-hosting tools do not require you to have any special software or video equipment.

- **Advanced:** Advanced integration requires that both your video platform and your marketing automation tool allow for this type of connection. You can check with your vendor to see which video platforms the vendor integrates with. By connecting your video platform to your marketing automation tool, you can see how much of a video each person watched and then run automations and scoring based on a person's engagement with a single video. This technique is super powerful and not that hard to set up.

Driving Leads to an Event with Automation

Marketing automation can lend a hand in advertising and managing your event. You can market offline events without marketing automation; however, you'll have a harder time keeping up with registrants, and you'll likely lose valuable insights into who is coming from where. You'll also struggle with keeping your communication consistent across all marketing channels. Using marketing automation helps you save large amounts of time, gain valuable insights on people so that you know what is relevant to people, know where they came from, and be able to do a much better job at lead follow-up and reporting on the effectiveness of your event.

The following sections show you how to use marketing automation to promote an event across multiple channels, send out email invitations, manage the event, and send post-event communications.

Setting up event registration

To begin marketing an event, follow these simple steps:

1. **Create the event registration page.**

   I suggest using Eventbrite to manage your events. Eventbrite has connections to many marketing automation tools, making events very easy to manage. It's also free to use if your event is free to attend. Figure 11-3 shows Eventbrite's tool.

2. **Build the landing page.**

   After creating your event registration page, you need to put your registration form onto a landing page. Figure 11-4 shows an Eventbrite registration form on a website landing page. If you are doing a webinar, you need to use the webinar registration page given to you by your webinar platform. If you're not doing a webinar or using Eventbrite, I suggest creating a form in your marketing automation tool to capture registrations.

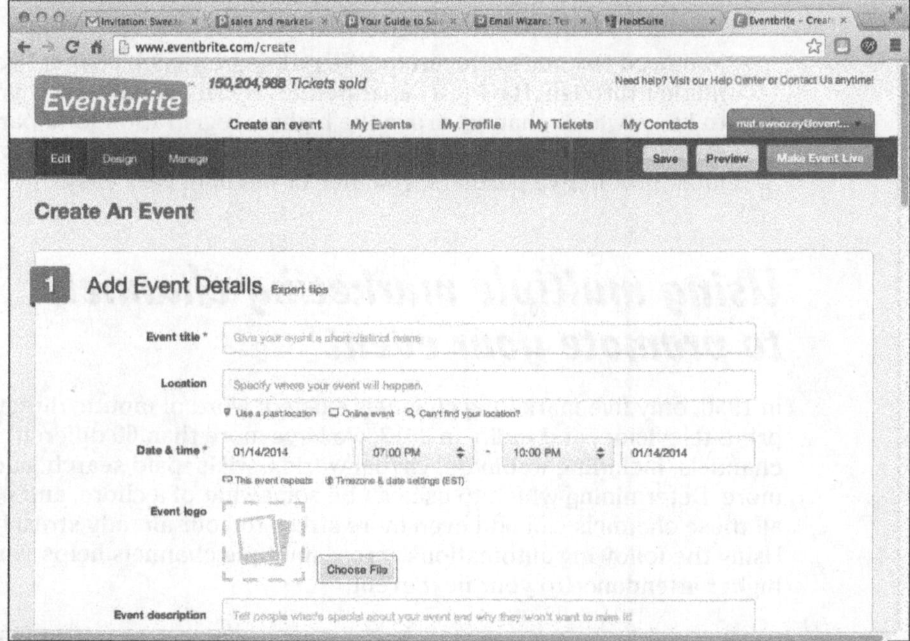

Figure 11-3: Use Eventbrite's event management solution.

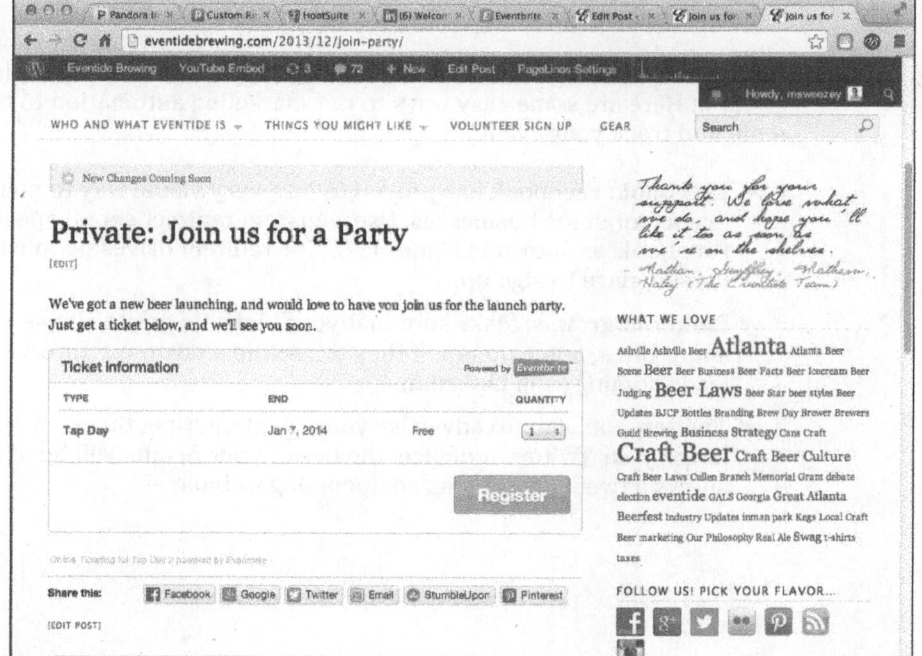

Figure 11-4: Embed your registration form on a landing page.

3. Create a custom redirect.

You need to create a separate URL redirect for each channel you plan to market through. Having a separate URL is critical only when you want to know which channel drove the highest registration for a particular event. Seeing which link was clicked the most makes reporting on your most productive partners, channel, or medium very easy.

Using multiple marketing channels to promote your event

In 1950, only five marketing channels existed: word of mouth, direct mail, print, television, and radio. In 2013, we have more than 60 different marketing channels, including webinars, virtual worlds, wikis, paid search, and so much more. Determining which to use can be somewhat of a chore, and managing all these channels can add even more stress to your already stressful day. Using the following automations across multiple channels helps you drive higher attendance to your next event.

Create a separate traceable URL for each channel. A traceable URL makes reporting on the ROI of each channel easy. Creating the traceable URL, and being able to associate it with revenue, are activities that you cannot do without marketing automation!

When you're putting on an event, you need to make sure that people know about it. Here are some easy ways to use marketing automation to help promote and track your event:

- **Facebook:** Facebook has proven to be a very viable way to market events for some businesses. Use a custom redirect set up specifically for Facebook, as shown in Figure 11-5. The redirect drives people to your landing page to sign up.
- **LinkedIn groups:** Make sure that your LinkedIn group allows you to share URLs. Some do not. If they do, set up a custom redirect to track leads coming from LinkedIn.
- **Twitter:** You want to advertise your event multiple times on Twitter. The larger your Twitter audience, the better your results will be. Figure 11-6 shows a tweet advertising an upcoming webinar.

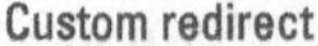

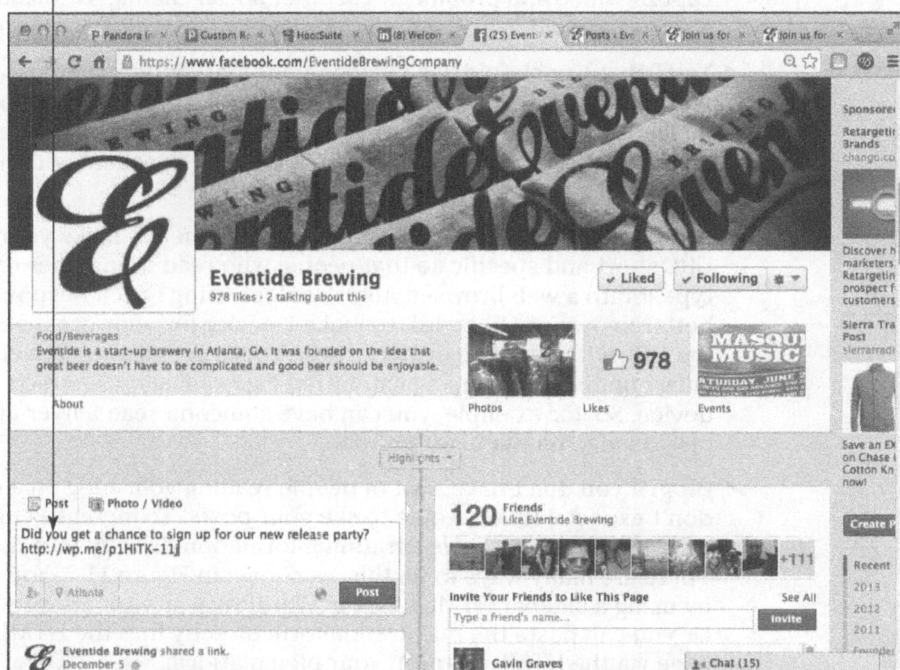

Figure 11-5: Use a custom redirect to drive Facebook visitors to your event.

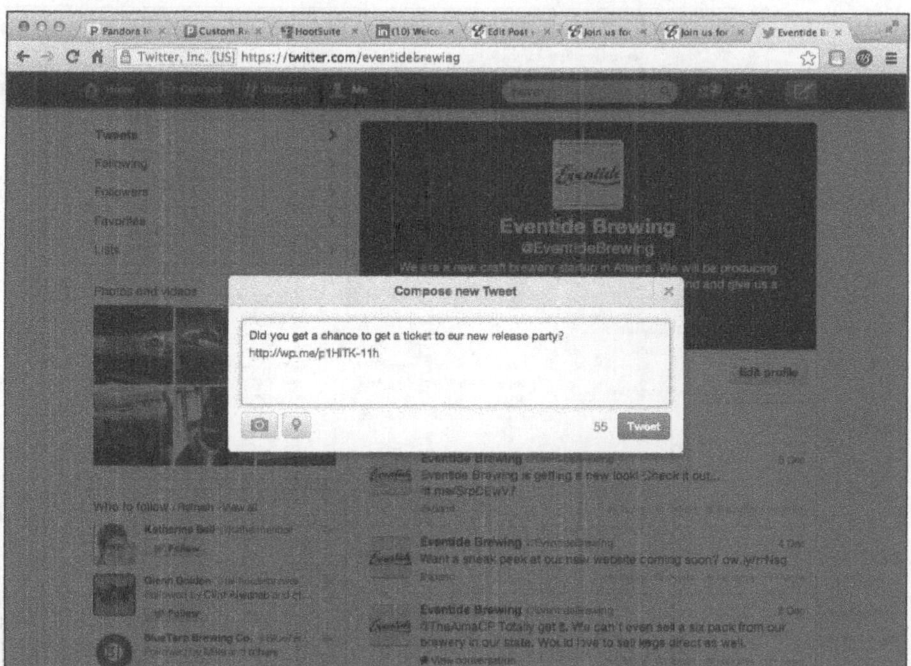

Figure 11-6: Tweet your events to a large audience.

- **Vine:** Vine is a social media channel launched in 2013. You can use Vine to capture video and promote it via other social channels. Consider shooting a six-second video explaining what people can expect at your event.
- **YouTube:** You should use video in your marketing regardless of whether you choose YouTube or another video site to host your video. Consider mixing shots from your other events. Try to show as many people as possible in every shot, and highlight keynote speakers and their accomplishments. Basically, you're creating a trailer!
- **Direct mail:** If you're advertising with print media, make your custom URL short and specific so that people who read it on paper can easily type it into a web browser. Also consider using Quick Response codes, better known as QR codes, to make it easier for your prospect to access the URL with a mobile device. These codes are easily scanned with a smart phone to pull up a customized experience on a person's mobile device. So, for example, you can have someone scan a flyer and instantly play a video on that user's phone.
- **Blog:** If you don't have a lot of people reading your blog on a daily basis, don't expect a lot of people to see your posts. To increase engagement with your blog, paste registration information directly into the post. There are many ways to do this, as shown in Figure 11-7. You can do this by using a sidebar HTML block in WordPress or your chosen blog tool. Or you can paste the registration form directly into the HTML of the page via the HTML editor in your blog platform.

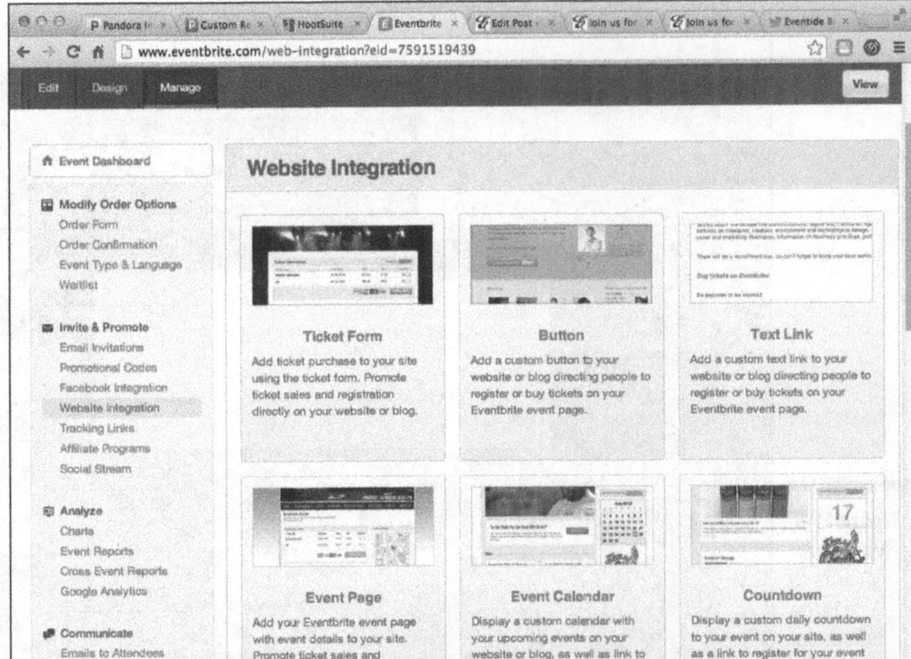

Figure 11-7: Blog posts promoting an upcoming event should include easy registration.

You can remove the need to click off the page by embedding your registration form on the page you are advertising. You'll capture more leads than you would by asking prospects to leave the page and register on another page.

Staying relevant after an event

Your event is only one part of your marketing automation campaign. If your event generates leads, you need to follow up with them. A typical event also has many more registrants than actually attendees. Don't follow up just to say thank you to those who attended. Use marketing automation to deliver content to those who couldn't attend, as well. Your follow-up should be broken up into three parts:

- **Content:** Take as many photos, videos, and audio recordings as possible at your event. Capture every speaker and get a copy of the speaker's slides. All this content becomes great follow-up material. Break your content into long- and short-form content. *Long-form content* is any content that exceeds a few pages. Usually this content consists of ebooks, white papers, and full analyst reports. *Short-form content* is very short.

  If you take a white paper (long form) and break it down into specific sections, you have a short-form piece of content. Using both forms of content results in a lot of content for both inbound marketing and outbound emails. Your long-form content helps you identify more sales-ready interest, and your short form content works as teasers for the long-form content.

- **Follow-up nurturing program:** Try to kick off your nurturing campaign the day after your event, and run it for seven to ten days after the event. This length of time should allow you to have two to three follow-up emails delivering content around your topic.

- **Automation rules:** You need automation rules to help you manage all your follow-up. Your automation rules add people to nurturing campaigns, change their scores based on attending the event, and pass sales-ready leads over to sales. Ensure that you have the following automation rules set up to help you manage your leads correctly:

  - Score leads for signing up. Your score depends on the sales readiness of your webinar. If the webinar presents a product demo, score higher. If it is an educational webinar, score lower.
  - Notify salespeople if any of their leads attend a webinar.
  - Put everyone who signed up on a drip nurturing program.
  - Identify sales-ready leads and pass them to sales. (You should have already created this rule, but if not, make sure to do so now.)
  - Attach the leads who signed up for your webinar campaign so that you can track its effectiveness.

Chapter 12
Scoring Leads

In This Chapter

- Recognizing basic scoring concepts
- Building your first scoring model
- Choosing actions and behaviors to score
- Monitoring your scoring model

Scoring is a method of assigning numbers to one or more actions or behaviors taken by a prospect or customer. With scoring, you can quantify varying levels of engagement with your marketing programs. A *score* — the actual number you choose to assign — is both a data point and a field in your database. Any field in your database can have an associated score by assigning a number based on the data in the field. You can also use scores to trigger future automations in response to an action or behavior that pushes the score over a certain threshold.

You can use scoring for lead qualification, segmentation, cold leads identification, and much more. Scoring leads based on their interactions allows you to measure their interest and sales readiness.

In this chapter, I explain the basics of lead scoring. I show you how to create a proper lead-scoring model and how to use scoring information for personalization, targeting, and other activities to help you drive more engagements in the future.

Recognizing Basic Scoring Concepts

Scores are used for measurement. They can tell you whatever you ask them to tell you. For example, a score can tell you when leads are cold, when they are hot, whether they are likely to churn, how many times they have logged in to your application, or whether they are interested in a specific piece of your solution.

In order for scores to tell you what you want to know, you need to first understand what a score represents and how scores can be associated with actions, behaviors, and data to identify leads with the characteristics you want to take action on.

The next sections explain the most common scoring uses and how to combine scoring with grading. Understanding the basic concepts of lead scoring will also help you to craft a great scoring model. I discuss crafting a scoring model later in this chapter.

Understanding what a score can tell you

You use scores to measure all kinds of engagement. The goal of lead scoring isn't to measure the engagement, however. The goal is to determine what the engagement means and how valuable the engagement is based on your company's sales process. Before you start scoring and building scoring models, make sure that you understand these three common lead-scoring goals:

- **Sales readiness:** If you want to measure a person's sales readiness, score her based on interactions with sales-ready content. That way, each sales-ready asset she engages with adds to or subtracts from her overall sales-ready score. Set your overall score equal to a level of interaction that a prospect typically exhibits when she's ready to talk to a salesperson.
- **Product interest:** If you want to measure a person's interest in specific products or services, consider combining multiple scores, one for each product or service line of interest. That way, you can see the level of interest across multiple products.
- **Cold lead indication:** Scores show activity. So if no increase in score occurs over a period of time, you can pinpoint the score that identifies an inactive prospect as a cold lead.

Scoring behaviors versus actions

Actions are engagements with your marketing assets. For example, clicking a link is an action. *Behaviors* are exhibited by a person but not expressed in terms of actual engagement with your marketing assets. For example, inactivity is a behavior but not an action, because an inactive person by definition does not engage in any of your marketing assets. Knowing the following behaviors can help you create and refine your scoring model:

- **Lack of activity** is a key reason for a salesperson to reach out. Inactivity might also be a good reason to lower a prospect's sales-ready score. Both of these automations can help you identify trends in behavior and appropriately take action.

- **Length of video play** should be thought of in terms of percentage of play rather than time. For example, if a person watches one minute of a one-minute video, he shouldn't be scored the same as a person who watches 10 percent of a ten-minute video.
- **Number of pages viewed** assumes that the more pages a person downloads in a visit, the more engaged he is. When you score total number of pages, make sure that you are scoring people based only on pages that help you identify them as sales ready. Don't include your home page, careers page, or any other pages not connected to your selling cycle.

Discovering the best opportunities with account-based scoring

A committee, rather than a single person, makes many of the organizational purchase decisions. When leads are identified with a marketing automation solution, they can also be associated with an account. Identifying more members of the decision-making process and calculating their collective score is a powerful technique for identifying the most sales-ready accounts.

Account-based scoring is a way to identify groups of leads related to the same purchase decision under the same account, as shown in Figure 12-1. Scoring leads based on an account of multiple buyers gives a much clearer picture of the sales readiness of a business and can easily be used as a tool to help you identify the very best sales opportunities rather than just the best individual leads.

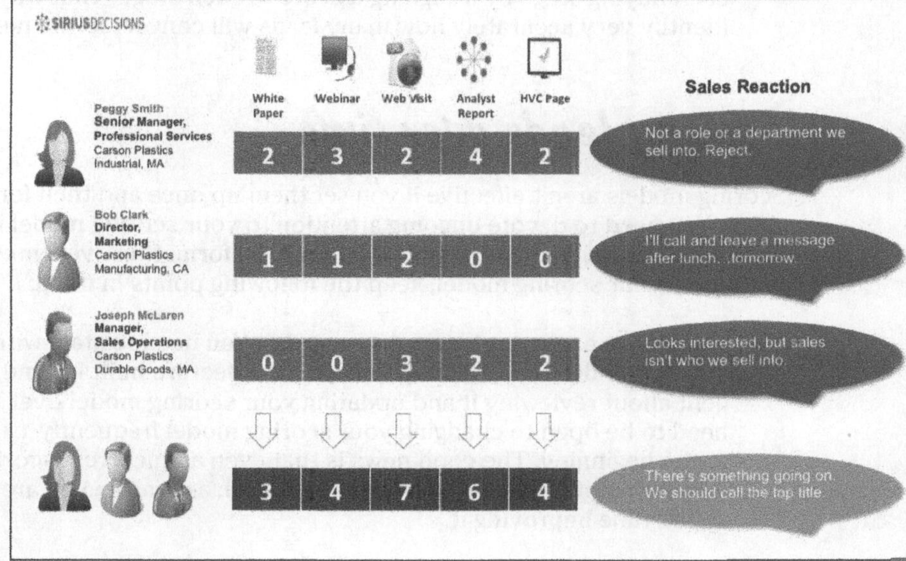

Figure 12-1: Account-based scoring includes the company and each person involved in the purchasing decision.

Understanding account-based scoring is an especially large benefit of marketing automation for B2B companies with complex sales cycles.

Taking action on lead scoring

You won't get the full value out of scoring unless you use your scoring model to recommend actions based on the scores. Here are the most common actions you can take based on your lead-scoring model:

- **Lead Qualification:** Using lead scores as data points for lead qualification is the most common use of scoring. To qualify leads based on a score, you need to have an automation rule to monitor lead scores, looking for those leads that match specific criteria. The leads that match the criteria are then assigned to the correct salesperson.
- **Segmentation:** A powerful use of segmentation is to sort your database by lowest lead scores. After you have this segment, you can give the segment a special campaign with the goal of driving more actions. Or, sort your database to find the leads with the highest scores and give them all a personal interaction on Twitter. Looking at score for segmentation opens your eyes to new possibilities in the future.
- **Lead nurturing:** Leads showing inactivity have scores that aren't increasing over a period of time. Use lead scores to identify cold leads based on inactivity so that you can place them on a lead-nurturing track.
- **Reporting:** Scores can help you identify where a lead is in the buying process. Look at your database and track the percentage of your leads in each buying stage by assigning a score to each stage. That way, you can identify very accurately how many leads will convert to the next stage.

Scoring leads over time

Scoring models aren't effective if you set them up once and then forget about them. You need to devote ongoing attention to your scoring model if you want your scoring model to give you relevant information over time. When setting up your scoring model, keep the following points in mind:

- **Scores are a constant work in progress.** You need to start with a basic scoring model (some tools come with this feature built in) and be diligent about reviewing it and updating your scoring model over time. You need to be open to changing your scoring model frequently, especially at the beginning. The good news is that even an incorrect scoring model is more helpful than no scoring model at all, as long as you are willing to spend time improving it.

- **Scores can go up and down.** An increase in score helps you to measure sales-ready actions, and a decrease in score helps you track a lack of engagement over a period of time. Remember to keep these uses in mind when setting up your scoring model.
- **Scores are relative to time.** Scores matter only at the time they are created. For example, a person who racked up a high score last year is not as likely to be sales ready this year. Scores are timely and should reflect the time of inactivity in more advanced scoring models.

Combining lead scores and lead grades

Lead scoring is often confused with lead grading, but these two models have different uses, as follows:

- A *lead-scoring model* is the method for measuring interactions or behaviors. You use lead scoring to measure a person's sales readiness. Determining sales readiness is typically based on interactions with marketing material and campaigns. Common actions to score are
  - Page views
  - Email clicks
  - Downloads
  - Search terms
  - Campaign touch points
  - Form completions
- A *lead-grading model* is the method for measuring demographic qualities of people. You use lead grading to measure a person's demographic fit. Grades are based on fields in your database and usually use an A-to-F scale, just like the grades you received in school. Common criteria to grade are
  - Job title
  - Company size
  - Company location
  - Company revenue
  - Software used by company
  - Industry

Figure 12-2 shows a person's lead score based on her interactions with marketing assets, whereas her lead grade is measured from her job title and company size.

Figure 12-2: Lead score and lead grade derive from different aspects of a lead.

You need to use lead grades as separate database fields in conjunction with your lead-scoring model or you run the risk of sending highly active sales-ready leads to salespeople when they are actually a bad demographic fit. For example, if you base lead scoring only on engagement with your marketing, your scoring model could identify a college kid doing a research paper as a hot prospect because of his level of activity. If, however, you're targeting VP-level retail brand managers, your high-scoring college student should be filtered out by a low grade based on the absence of a job title.

If you separate lead scores from lead grades in your database instead of combining them into one score, you can more clearly see the level of opportunity fit on a demographic and activity basis. Separating the two numbers from each other is the easiest way to rule out prospects who are active yet unable to make a purchase decision.

Finding diamonds in the rough

QlikTech, a business intelligence software company, had a problem. The company was using telesales in its sales process to help qualify leads, but telesales teams followed up with every lead that came in. Because QlikTech was a global company, it had more leads to call than time in the day. The telesales team spent most of their time trying to find the sales-ready leads, but couldn't find them all.

QlikTech decided to implement a marketing automation solution and a lead-scoring model and quickly found that leads who obtained a score over 50 were six times more likely to become opportunities than were leads with no score. This data helped the telesales team to easily identify the leads they should be calling, and it left the others to be nurtured by the marketing team into sales-ready leads.

The combination of lead scoring and lead nurturing changed the way QlikTech's marketing and sales teams operated and helped to close more deals in a shorter time frame than ever before.

Knowing When to Score Prospect Actions

Not all actions should be measured and scored. Keeping your processes and automations as simple as possible makes your application much easier to manage. Lead scoring is supposed to clue you in, not give you the perfect picture. The following sections show you which actions to score and which details to score in the actions you choose.

Identifying key actions for scoring

Identifying your key interactions is a must. Fortunately, it involves an easy two-step process:

1. **Define your lead stages.**

   You should have three basic stages in your marketing cycle in addition to the stages of the buying cycle, as shown in Figure 12-3. These stages are the basis for your scoring model.

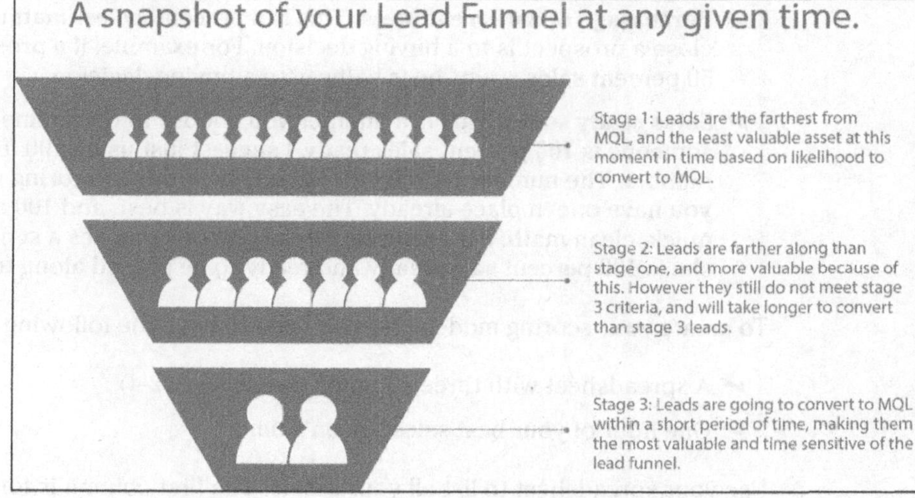

A snapshot of your Lead Funnel at any given time.
Stage 1: Leads are the farthest from MQL, and the least valuable asset at this moment in time based on likelihood to convert to MQL.
Stage 2: Leads are farther along than stage one, and more valuable because of this. However they still do not meet stage 3 criteria, and will take longer to convert than stage 3 leads.
Stage 3: Leads are going to convert to MQL within a short period of time, making them the most valuable and time sensitive of the lead funnel.

Figure 12-3: Your marketing cycle should have three stages.

2. **Associate actions and content with your stages.**

   After you have laid out your three stages, place your key actions in the appropriate stages in the form of a timeline. Examples of key actions are downloading a specific white paper and filling out a certain form. You need to ask your current customers which assets they interacted with, and when. Alternatively, you can look at your historical data and try to figure out this information.

Using your phone to call current customers and interview them about their engagement with your content makes associating actions and content with your stages much easier. Customers help you refine your content to match your stages and let you know where each piece of content belongs on the timeline.

When you're looking at where to place an action or asset on your marketing stage timeline, try to determine how each stage relates to a prospect's progress through a decision-making cycle. For example, prospects in the first stage may have very basic needs and understanding. Prospects in the second stage may understand their basic needs but not have consensus from their company to investigate further. Prospects in stage three may be evaluating which companies to contact to set up demos.

Building Your First Scoring Models

Scoring models should start as very basic and grow more elaborate over time. It is critical not to start with a larger scoring model. To begin, you need to understand the following terms:

- **Percentage of sales readiness:** This is a percentage estimating how close a prospect is to a buying decision. For example, if a prospect is 50 percent sales ready, he is halfway to a buying decision.
- **Sales-ready score:** This is a number you choose to determine when someone is 100 percent sales ready. I suggest just using 100 for this number. The number will change based on your lead-scoring model if you have one in place already. The easy way is best, and 100 allows for quick, clean math. For example, when someone reaches a score of 100, she is 100 percent sales ready and ready to be passed along to sales.

To create your scoring model, you also need to have the following in hand:

- A spreadsheet with three columns (see Figure 12-4)
- One hour of your best salesperson's time

Use your spreadsheet to list all your assets. The first column is for the name of the asset, the second column, the stage of the asset, and the third column, the score of the asset.

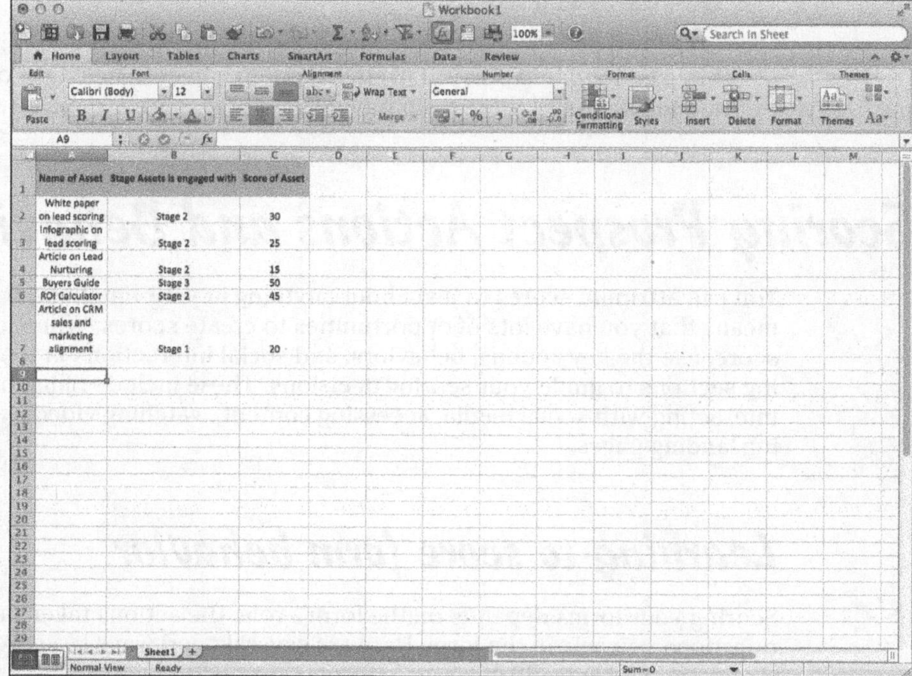

Name of Asset	Stage Assets is engaged with	Score of Asset
White paper on lead scoring	Stage 2	30
Infographic on lead scoring	Stage 2	25
Article on Lead Nurturing	Stage 2	15
Buyers Guide	Stage 3	50
ROI Calculator	Stage 2	45
Article on CRM sales and marketing alignment	Stage 1	20

Figure 12-4: Use a three-column spreadsheet for your lead-scoring model.

To create a score for each action, get help from your best salesperson, because that person is the best judge of which actions deserve which scores. Follow these two steps:

1. **Ask your salesperson, "If a person took only this action, how sales ready would this person be?"**

   Ask for this number as a percentage. Then multiply the percentage by your sales-ready score to determine the score for your action, as shown in Figure 12-5. For example, if your sales rep thinks that reading a white paper amounts to a prospect who is 30 percent sales-ready, and your sales-ready score is 100, then your score for the white paper is 30, because 30% x 100 = 30.

(How sales-ready the prospect is (using a percentage) if he/she does this one action by itself.) × (Sales-ready score — I always suggest using 100 points.) = Score

Figure 12-5: The formula for creating a score for an action or behavior.

2. **Give the asset a score.**

   Give the asset the score from Step 1 and record it in your spreadsheet. Keep in mind that you will need this spreadsheet to manage your scoring model in the future, so keep it handy.

Scoring Prospect Actions and Behaviors

You can attribute scores to just about anything in your database, which means that you have lots of opportunities to create scores. When learning to score, use the key actions, behaviors, and social interactions in the following sections to guide your scoring decisions. These include filling out forms, interacting with social media, accessing content, watching videos, and visiting landing pages.

Learning to score form behavior

Scoring your forms depends on the form's role, the actions taken, and the questions you ask on the form. Here are several good ways to score forms that your prospects fill out:

- **Forms for downloading content:** When you score a form used by prospects to download content, the form should have a score associated with the completion of the form. Use the sales-ready score of the content to determine the appropriate score for the action of filling out the form.
- **Contact Us forms:** If your form asks a prospect for contact information, it should be scored as instantly sales ready when a prospect fills it out.
- **Scoring answers to questions:** You should use the questions you ask on a form to raise or lower a person's grade, not score. Questions should be considered qualifying questions that help you weed out the good leads from the bad leads. However, you should consider the completion of the answer form as a scored action. I discuss the difference between scoring models and grading models in the "Combining lead scores and lead grades" section, earlier in this chapter.
- **Scoring complementary actions:** When a form protects a piece of content that is emailed to a person after the form is filled out, you should score the content, the email open, and the click to retrieve the content. Ask your sales team for help to correctly score each of these actions separately.

When crafting your scoring model, remember that many of these actions happen in succession, so make sure to understand the full scenario a prospect might go through so that you don't overscore prospects. For example, if a person downloads a document by filling out a form, you are likely to have a score for the form completion, the email being sent, the email being opened, the email link being clicked, and the white paper being downloaded. Overscoring causes you to pass on prospects who are not actually sales ready; you only think they are because you artificially bumped up their score without realizing it. Make sure you understand the steps a person will be taking so that you are not overscoring someone for a basic action.

Scoring prospect interactions with landing pages

Landing pages are scored like forms because landing pages usually have forms that trigger an email to the person who fills out the form. The main difference between scoring landing pages and scoring forms is the fact that landing pages are accessed via a URL 100 percent of the time. This means that you can have two scored actions — one for accessing the landing page and one for filling out the form. You can also get more detailed by scoring the click on the landing page link, the viewing of the landing page, time spent on the landing page, and any subsequent actions. Here's how you should score the most common landing page actions:

- **Score the landing page link** based on the stage of the content behind the form or on the page itself.
- **Score the page view** as a very basic score, and the completion of the form as the highest score.
- **Score any content served up** from a landing page higher than content accessed from an email blast.

Remember that your prospect went through a lot of steps to access your content, so make sure that you're accounting for the number of steps to determine the prospect's desire to read your content.

Scoring using custom redirects

A *custom redirect* is a term given to a URL that directs you to another page. When your company, for example, has partnerships with different businesses that drive leads or traffic to your site, custom redirects are a very powerful tool to help you determine your best partners. They allow you to give a different URL to each partner and track all the leads from that single partner. For example, you might give each partner a specific URL but have each URL drive leads to the same web page. Then, if you ever need to change the URL or create another one for each partner, you never have to change your website to track where your leads came from. You may also have a link on another site that you control. For example, if you have a button on your YouTube page directing people back to your website, you can use a custom redirect to score someone who clicks the link, and you can create a special automation for when this happens.

Scoring on web interactions

Any URL can be tracked. Most web content has to be accessed via a URL regardless of who hosts the content.

To score web interactions and identify sales-ready leads, you should break your web actions down into sales-ready actions and general actions as follows:

- Score any actions not related to a buyer's journey as a *general action* that does not increase the sales readiness score. For example, many people attach a score to every URL. But not all URLs visited are indicators of sales readiness in a prospect.
- Score any actions related to a buyer's journey as a *sales-ready action* that increases the sales-readiness score. For example, the URL of a pricing page on your site and the URL of your product features and benefits page are good examples of pages that are probably indicators of sales readiness in a prospect.

Scoring on downloads

When you score downloadable content, remember that your goal is to score the person interacting with the content, not the value of the content itself. Scoring the person involves looking at the proximate cause of the download and including that action in the download score. For example, a score for content downloaded from an email should be lower than a score for content downloaded from a landing page after a Google search. That's because a person who proactively searches for your content is probably more interested than a person who passively receives an email. Your marketing automation system can tell you whether someone was searching through one of your search engine marketing campaigns or one of your email campaigns, and apply your chosen scores accordingly.

Scoring on email engagement

You can break down email engagement into two specific actions:

- **Email opens:** An email open should never be scored. It is a false indicator of interactions. An email open is marked whenever the email is displayed, not read. This means that it can just pop up in the preview pane and be considered opened by an email tool. Having an email marked as read when it wasn't occurs because of how email opens are tracked by marketing automation applications, and every application uses the same technology for this tracking. So scoring email opens doesn't help you determine a sales-ready prospect.

- **Email clicks:** If you are using email campaigns to build rapport over a long period of time, a person is likely to click many emails. Each score you assign should represent a specific step in the prospect's journey. For example, clicks on emails sent to keep in touch with inactive prospects should be scored very lightly compared to emails sent to prospects who recently signed up to be contacted.

In addition to clicks and opens, you should consider how each email was sent. For example, score an email triggered by a form submission higher than an email blast to everyone on your list. I discuss working with emails in detail in Chapter 10.

Correctly scoring search terms

Start out with a general score for all search terms and move to a more meaningful scoring model over time. Your general scores tell you which search terms are predictors of sales readiness and which ones are not. For example, you might start out thinking that people searching the term "pricing" are at the end of the buying cycle, only to find through your general scores that they are at the beginning of that cycle. In that case, lowering the score for the pricing term makes sense.

When asking your clients about their buyer's journey, make sure that you understand how their search terms change over the course of their journey. A recent survey conducted by ExactTarget, an email service provider, shows that people change their search terms two to three times during their buyer's journey. This means that you will likely need to score many different search terms.

Scoring social media interactions correctly

Proving ROI on social media campaigns can be difficult. That is, it's difficult until you have marketing automation and it becomes very easy to see who interacts and where in the sales cycle the interaction occurs.

Each social media post, such as a tweet, Facebook post, or LinkedIn post, contains a URL. Figure 12-6 shows a custom URL being used to attach this lead to a campaign. Adding the lead to the campaign will make it very easy to show ROI on the social channel I post this link to.

The URL you should use for scoring is the URL your marketing automation tool gives you, as shown in Figure 12-7. Most tools also let you attach a piece of content to a campaign and a score for future automation. When you copy your social URL and paste it into your messaging application, it will be sent and tracked by your system.

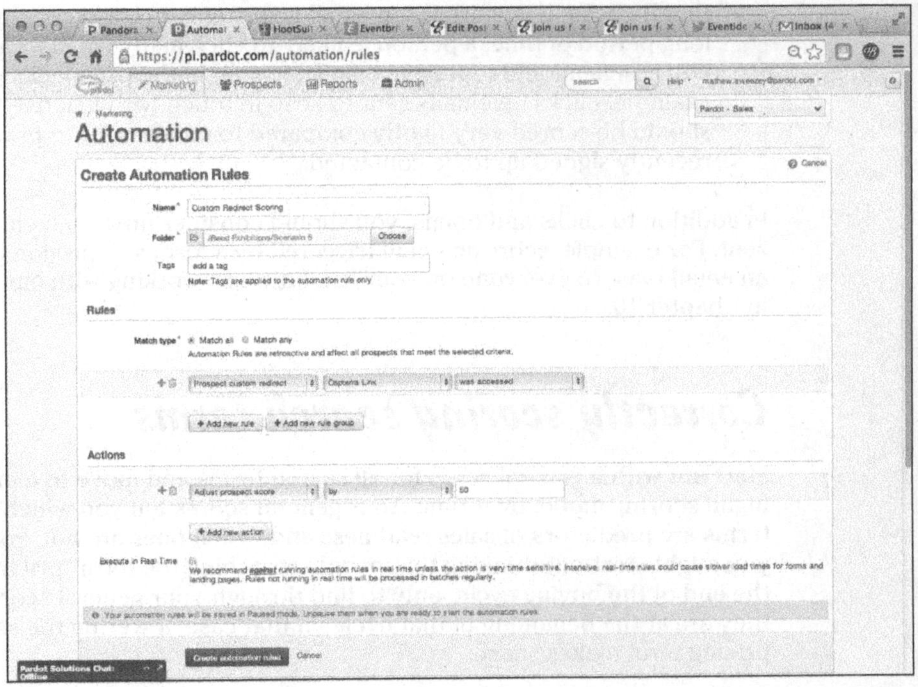

Figure 12-6: Score social posts using the URLs from the posts.

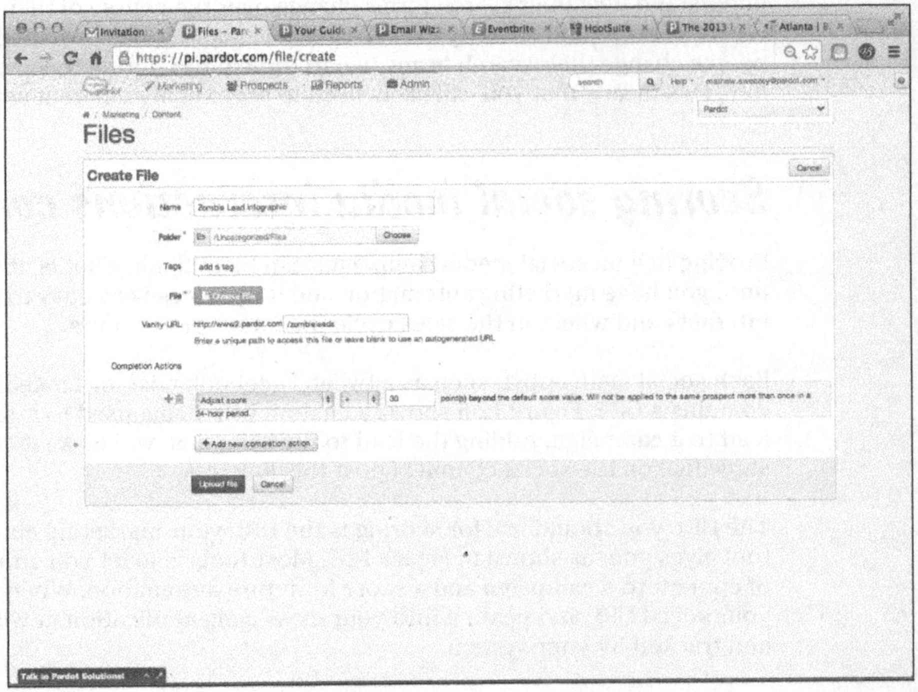

Figure 12-7: Use the URL provided by your marketing automation tool to score social URLs.

Keep in mind that social media Likes, follows, retweets, blog posts, and other non-URL interactions should not be scored as sales-ready actions. They should instead be scored for other types of measurement, such as identifying your happiest customers. For example, score blog posts when your content points to a stage in the buyer's journey, but not when posts contain content about your company culture.

Advanced Scoring Models

Many people use marketing automation to help determine sales-ready leads, but many advanced lead-scoring models exist as well. I suggest waiting until you are capable with your tool before getting into advanced models. In fact, I suggest waiting until you have been running your tool for a minimum of one year.

Learning to use advanced scoring helps you show a lot more value from your marketing automation tool, and it helps your company drive additional revenue from the same tool. The next sections show you how to leverage more of your marketing automation tools by using scoring models to identify your best customers, your most active people, and your unhappy customers.

Using lead scoring for a net promoter score

A net promoter score is a modern way to identify your best customers and help focus your marketing on the best and worst customer attitudes. By identifying your happiest and unhappiest customers, you can easily focus your time on mitigating churn and encouraging the happiest people to promote your brand.

You can buy special software to help you manage your net promoter scores, or you can use your marketing automation tool for this purpose. To ascertain your net promoter score, use a score field to determine how active someone is with your marketing over a period of time. For example, people who read your blog on a daily basis and read every white paper should score highly.

You can also build a form in your marketing automation tool to ask the standard net promoter score question, which is, "On a scale of 1 to 10, how happy are you with our company?" This information can go into a custom field in your lead record to score the happiest and unhappiest clients.

Scoring multiple buyers for sales readiness

If you are selling into a B2B account, multiple buyers may be involved. In these cases, you need to use *account-based scoring* to score every buyer associated with an account to determine the sales readiness of the whole account.

You have a few different ways to score multiple buyers as one account. If your tool allows for account-based scoring, ask your vendor how to set up multiple-buyer scoring. If your tool does not have account-based scoring out of the box, you can still set it up in your CRM using the following steps:

1. **Create a custom field in the account record and name the field Account Score.**
2. **Populate the custom field with scores.**

   Use the coding language of your CRM to set up an automation. That way, you can have all individual scores under the account summed together. You may need your CRM admin if you are not familiar with coding in your CRM.
3. **Connect to your marketing automation tool.**

   The field you created in Step 1 needs to be connected to your CRM. I discuss connecting custom fields in Chapter 4.

Using tally fields for scoring

If you have multiple stages in your buyer journey, you can determine the score for each asset in each of your stages using tally fields. Tally fields are a type of number field that increases only by a single number each time, as in keeping a tally. You have to guess at first, but you can eventually count how many interactions a person has in each stage. That way, you can easily determine the correct lead score for each interaction within a stage, as shown in Figure 12-8.

When you have a sizeable set of data, you can look for trends. For example, if you use 100 as your sales-ready score and the average person engages with five pieces of content in stage one, three pieces of content in stage two, and four pieces of content in stage three, you can break your scoring model into 12 equal parts. That way, you can easily score each action with a score of eight points. You can then move the score up or down depending on the suggestion from your sales team as to the importance of the action.

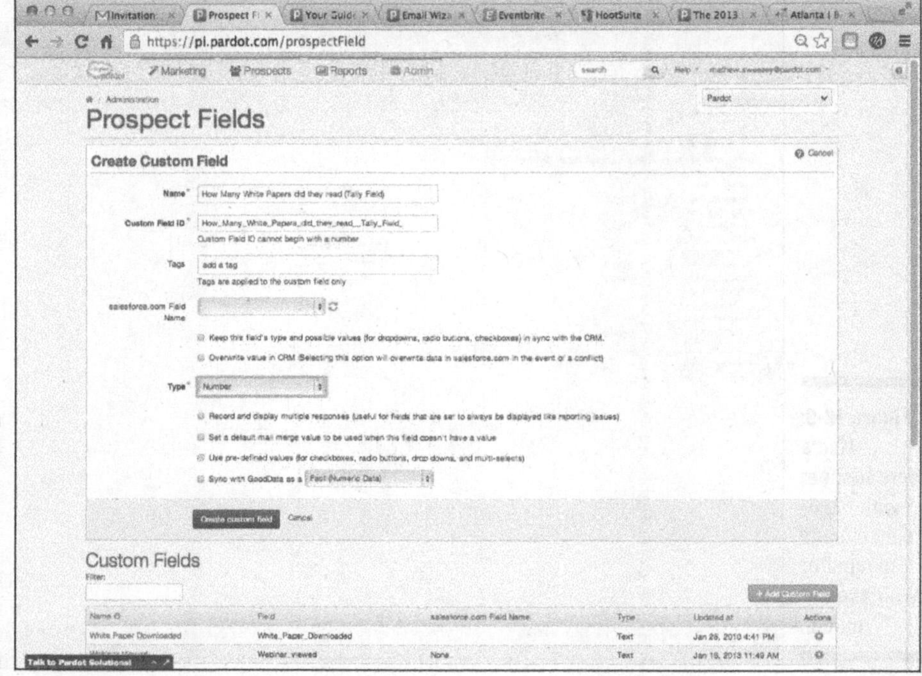

Figure 12-8: Add a tally field to track multiple buying-cycle stages.

Monitoring Your Scoring Model

Scoring models are living and constantly changing. If you set up scoring once and never touch it again, the results will be only as good as your first guess. So, you should plan a schedule of evaluation and reconfiguration. I suggest looking back 60 days from your first attempt. After that, look back every 90 days.

The next sections show you how to monitor your scoring models over time so that you can continually improve them and maintain accurate scoring.

Learning to use the multiple-column approach

When your scoring model changes, use a spreadsheet with multiple columns to keep track. The spreadsheet is your living document to help you track your changes and make sure that you have all your items together. Figure 12-9 shows a scoring model that changed with notes from salespeople.

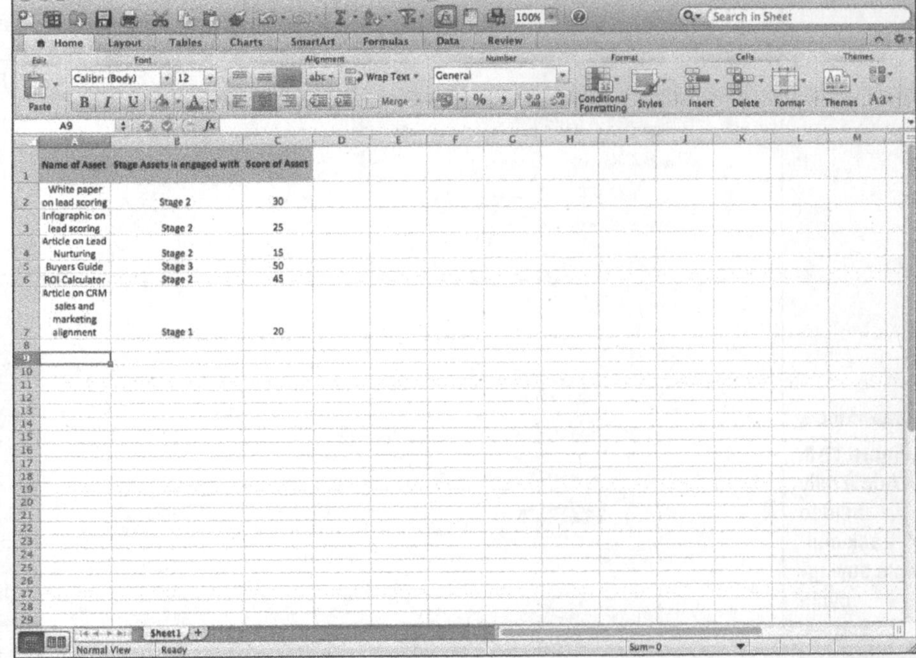

Figure 12-9: Use a spreadsheet with multiple columns to monitor your scoring model.

When reviewing your scoring model, add a new column for any revisions. This column helps you keep up with changes in your scores and is particularly useful when you're involved in future revisions and need to remember where you started, and why your scores are where they are.

Making use of score degradation

Score degradation is the process of lowering someone's score, which helps you to make sure that your current score is an accurate reflection of a prospect's sales readiness.

Score degradation is based on unseen behavior rather than direct action. For example, lack of activity is a reason to degrade a score. Score degradation also happens when a prospect visits specific pages. The most common page for score degradation is the careers page on your website, because someone visiting your careers page is more likely to be looking for a job than to make a purchase.

When degrading a score, you should do it over a period of time. Some tools allow you to degrade a score over time by a percentage of the total score, or by a specific number. I suggest refraining from ever degrading a score to zero. A zero score removes all past interest, which makes it hard to segment based on past activity. Instead of degrading to zero, create a minimum equal to 50 percent of the total sales-ready score as a starting point. That way, you can still show activity while keeping leads out of the hands of your salespeople.

Using a checklist for refining your scoring model

When you refine your scoring model, use the following checklist to ensure that you're evaluating the correct people, the correct amount of time, and the right assets:

- **Look at the ratio of sales-ready leads being converted to opportunities.** A low ratio of sales-assigned leads to closed deals can be an indicator of a bad scoring model.
- **Ask your salespeople how they feel the leads are doing.** If the sales reps don't like their leads, it can be an indicator of a bad scoring model.
- **Ask salespeople how they feel about the actions the leads are exhibiting.** Do they see a trend with specific actions? Salespeople can usually identify trends in leads, and they can become aware of new actions that need to be included or excluded from a scoring model faster than marketing in most cases.

Your salespeople are a key to helping you to refine your scoring model. Marketers often pass leads to sales based on activity alone, but salespeople know which leads are the most sales ready. Salespeople can help you confirm or deny your activity-based assumptions.

Chapter 13

Generating Reports

In This Chapter

- Understanding the correct metrics to use
- Defining MQL reports
- Leveraging SQL reports
- Gauging the true value of marketing

Understanding how to prove the value of your marketing efforts is the best way to grow your department. Marketing used to be a very subjective art. Still today, most marketers are looked at as money pits, where money goes in and no tangible results come out. But marketing automation changes the notion that marketing has no value, because lead tracking and CRM integration allow you to see every touch point and the resulting impact to your organization and bottom line.

Marketing automation includes many of the same metrics you have without marketing automation. Open rates, click rates, and bounce rates are all the same. The major difference between your current reporting and reporting with marketing automation is the fact that the reports generated with marketing automation can help you understand your lead flow and the value of a campaign. You can measure the size of your lead funnel, the speed at which a lead moves through the funnel, and the efficiency of your funnel to convert a lead into an opportunity.

Marketing automation gives you more data than you are probably used to having. With a single tool doing the job of many former tools, you have the ability to see a lot of information you never had access to before. Don't try to dig too deep at the beginning. You can easily get analysis paralysis with marketing automation reporting because you can get lost in the amount of data you need to sift through. Keep your reports short, simple, and easy at this stage.

In this chapter, I show you how to craft your marketing automation campaigns so that you can generate these reports. I also help you better show the value of your efforts by setting up Marketing Qualified Lead reports, and you see how to read these reports to refine your programs.

Understanding Appropriate Reporting Methods

Marketing automation allows for new ways of marketing and reporting. Following are three appropriate reporting methods that you can use to measure your results, evaluate how people move through your marketing stages, and track how effective your marketing is:

- **ROI reporting:** *Return on Investment (ROI) reporting* tells you how much money your marketing campaign returned for each dollar spent. To use ROI reporting appropriately, use it only when money is spent at the start of a campaign and money is returned at the end. ROI reporting is usually a long-term report for lead sources.

  For example, if you paid $100 to acquire a lead with a paid search campaign, your ROI reporting could last for months if it takes months for a lead to make a purchase. I discuss ROI reporting in more detail a little later in this chapter.

- **Velocity reporting:** *Velocity reporting* tells you the speed at which a lead moves through your funnel. This is a very important metric, with no way of being tracked without marketing automation. Using velocity reporting appropriately allows you to increase the speed at which a lead converts. That way, you can increase the number of leads in a given time period and close more leads sooner.

  Closing more leads faster means having money in your bank sooner, which has more value than money in the bank later. This is especially true for software-as-a-service (SaaS)-based or recurring revenue businesses. Money in hand today is worth more than money in hand tomorrow. I explain velocity reporting later in this chapter, in "Gauging Future Lead Flow by Tracking Lead Stage."

- **Efficiency reporting:** *Efficiency reporting* compares the number of leads generated to the number of leads lost as a percentage over time. For example, if you generate 100 leads today, and 50 leads convert to sales-ready leads while the rest are lost, your efficiency of leads is 50 percent.

  Using efficiency reporting appropriately helps you understand whether you're attracting the correct people as leads. Because good leads have a much higher efficiency than bad leads, your efficiency reporting helps by showing you whether you are wasting money attracting leads who never convert.

Implementing Marketing Qualified Lead Reports

Marketing-qualified leads (MQLs) are leads that meet the basic requirements to leave marketing's hands and be passed to sales. Most leads that come in to your funnel will, you hope, be converted to an MQL that is passed to the sales team. After the sales team members agree that the lead is qualified, they accept it and change it to a Sales Qualified Lead. (I discuss Sales Qualified Leads in the upcoming "Implementing Sales Qualified Lead Reports" section of this chapter.)

MQL reports can tell you a lot about your lead flow. The next sections show you how to understand and set up MQL reports, and how to use velocity and efficiency to evaluate your MQL leads.

MQL is a standard term used in marketing automation. If you use another term to denote a lead passing to sales, make sure that you also understand the MQL terminology and what it means to your lead funnel so that you can measure and report on your growth.

Understanding an MQL report

MQL reports are tools to help you manage and measure your lead hand-off process. When passing MQL leads to sales, you need to keep track of the number of leads you pass and the number of MQL leads accepted by sales. Giving sales the ability to accept or reject the MQL leads gives you a check and balance on your lead qualification process.

Most organizations have a set goal of leads they need to produce each month, and MQL is the report used to measure this goal. MQL reports tell you whether your department needs to produce more or fewer leads in the future. The efficiency of your MQL stage helps you determine whether your qualification for MQL is correct. Figure 13-1 shows the formula for determining your efficiencies within your MQL stage.

Figure 13-1: Use an MQL formula to determine the efficiency of your MQL stage.

$$\frac{\text{\# of SQL leads}}{\text{\# of MQL leads}} = \text{Efficiency of MQL leads}$$

To measure MQL efficiency, take the number of leads that reach the MQL stage and divide it by the number of leads that make it to the SQL stage. The closer you are to 100 percent, the better your efficiency.

If you're not currently being measured on MQL efficiency, consider advocating for this metric. Many companies find value in the percentage of leads moving from MQL to SQL as a measure of how good your marketing efforts are.

Setting up your first MQL report

Your MQL report is easy to set up in your marketing automation tool. The ways to do this differ according to your tool. Some tools have prebuilt MQL reports that automatically track all the leads you mark as sales ready. Other tools require you to manually set up MQL reporting.

To set up your MQL report, you need to obtain the following three data points:

- **How many people are MQL at a given time.** You need the ability to see the number of leads marked MQL over a period of time. A basic list with a sort-by-date field is fine. If your tool has a built-in MQL report out of the box, you don't need to do anything. If it doesn't, you need to create a custom list or create segmentation to keep up with this data for you.
- **How long it takes people to leave the MQL stage.** Time is used as a part of the formula. Just pick the time frame you want to measure results in. I suggest quarterly, biannually, and annually.
- **The cost of generating each lead in the MQL stage.** The simple way to calculate your ROI is to take your marketing budget over a period of time and divide it by your MQL number to arrive at what you're paying for each MQL lead. You should use this number to see whether you are spending more or less money over time to generate the same result. This number is a much more accurate representation of your direct results from specific actions, taking into account the time it takes for those results to yield results.

  You need to use a rolling average of costs over a period of time. So, for example, if you want to track how much it cost you to produce the MQL leads in Q1, and your average velocity of net new leads to MQL is 30 days, you need to account for your 30-day lag in results. To do so, account for your costs beginning 30 days prior to Q1, and stop 30 days prior to the end of Q1. The result tells you how much money you spent to generate the majority of the MQL leads.

Remember that the ROI report of a stage is not 100 percent accurate. You are assuming a lot of averages, and in marketing, people don't operate as averages. They operate as individuals. So use ROI reports as a guide. You'll notice that sometimes ROI can't explain why you had more leads, or fewer leads, during a time period. So look for large trends and understand this report as a guide, not a fact.

Creating SLAs with sales

A service-level agreement (SLA) is an agreement with your sales team to ensure that they are working leads in an appropriate time frame. Harvard University studied the follow-up times from leads after they were sales ready, along with the effect of follow-up times on close rates. The report shows that companies that try to contact potential customers within an hour of receiving queries are nearly seven times as likely to have meaningful conversations with key decision makers as firms that try to contact prospects even an hour later. Yet, only 37 percent of companies respond to queries within an hour.

Your SLA helps ensure that the work you are doing is not going to waste. Your SLA is your check and balance with the sales team to hold them accountable for following through on your efforts.

When you create your SLA, remember that the leads you pass over are qualified based on what you and your sales team agree on. So the leads should be good and should be accepted. Leads that are not called within the SLA time frame should be counted as wasting company assets and accompanied by repercussions of some kind. The duration of a lead in the MQL stage should be fixed by your SLA. That way, your velocity report will tell you whether the sales team is adhering to their SLA. If your SLA states that sales reps have two days to accept or reject any MQL lead, and your velocity is three days, you know that the sales team is dropping the ball and not holding up their end of the bargain.

Implementing Sales Qualified Lead Reports

Sales Qualified Leads (SQLs) are MQLs that the sales team accepts. After an MQL becomes an SQL, it is out of the hands of the marketing team and all reporting is based on the sales opportunity stage until closed. The next sections show you how to understand and set up SQL reports and how to use velocity and efficiency to evaluate your SQL leads.

Work with your sales team to craft an SQL workflow. Let them know how they will receive MQL leads, where to mark them as accepted or rejected, and what to do with the SQL lead after they get it. Usually, these parameters are up to you to dictate and set up. To mark the MQL leads as SQL, most companies use a field in the CRM tool that is synced back to the marketing automation tool. Lead Status is a good field to use for this purpose.

Understanding an SQL report

The SQL report tells you how efficient you are at creating leads for the sales team. Your MQL report lets you know how many you are creating, but SQL reporting lets you know whether the sales team agrees with your choice of leads. Because two teams are involved, the check and balance system has proven very effective at helping both departments work together.

When measuring SQL, use an acceptance rate to measure your efficiency. Your *acceptance rate* is the number of leads that reach the MQL stage divided by the number of leads that make it to the SQL stage, as shown in Figure 13-2. The closer you are to 100 percent, the better.

$$\frac{\text{Closed won deals}}{\text{\# of SQL leads}} = \text{Efficiency of SQL leads}$$

Figure 13-2: Use an acceptance rate to determine the efficiency of your MQL stage.

Setting up your first SQL report

Your SQL report uses some of the same data as your MQL report, but it can be a bit tricky to set up because it is dependent on data from sales. Here are the steps involved in setting up this report:

1. **Figure out how many people make it to SQL over a period of time, and calculate the cost of generating each lead in the SQL stage.**
2. **Choose a field to use for tracking SQL in your CRM.**

   I suggest using Lead Stage as the field for passing MQLs and asking sales to change the Lead Stage field from MQL to SQL. Use an automation rule. That way, when a lead is marked as sales ready, the Lead Stage field is also marked as MQL. This setup passes the leads to the CRM for the sales team to easily filter on, and then changes the field to SQL after salespeople accept the leads. Figure 13-3 shows a lead being marked MQL and SQL.

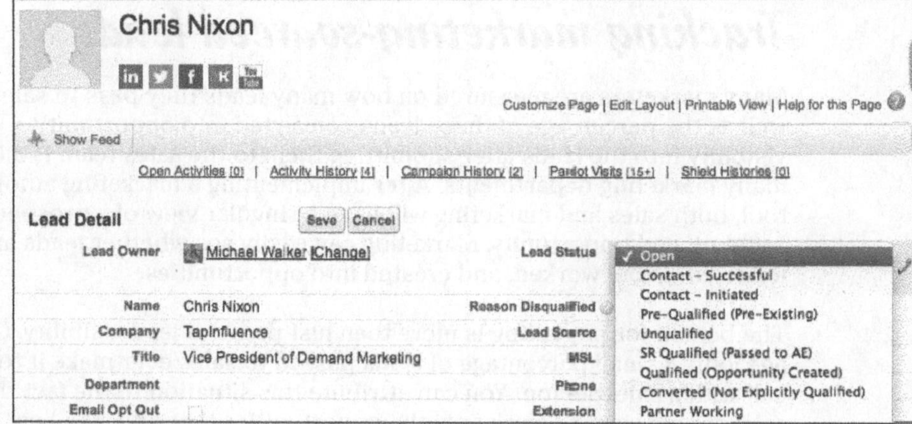

Figure 13-3: Pass leads to the CRM as MQL so that the sales team can change them to SQL.

3. **Measure lead flow into the SQL stage.**

   If your tool has this report out of the box, you do not need to do anything. If it doesn't, you need to create a custom list or segmentation to keep up with this for you.

   You also need the ability to see the number of leads marked SQL over a period of time. A basic list with a Sort by Date field is fine. Creating this list is an easy automation or segmentation that looks at a custom field in your CRM Lead Stage field and puts these people on a list.

4. **Measure your costs.**

   You have two ways to measure costs: simple and advanced. The simple way to calculate your ROI is to take your marketing budget over a period of time and divide it by your SQL number. For a more accurate representation of your direct results from specific actions, taking into account the time it takes for those results to yield results, you need to use a rolling average of costs over a period of time.

   For example, if you want to track how much it cost you to produce all SQL leads in Q1, and your average velocity of net new leads to SQL is 33 days (MQL average time plus your SLA from sales), you need to account for your 30-day lag in results. So account for your costs beginning 30 days prior to Q1, and stop 30 days prior to the end of Q1. This is the money that generated the majority of the SQL leads.

5. **Measure time.**

   Time is used as a part of the formula. Just pick the time frame over which you want to measure results. I suggest quarterly, biannually, and annually.

The SQL lead reports show you how many leads you are passing to the sales team and how many they are accepting. Many SQL reports are just a continuation of the MQL reports. So, if you have MQL reports, copy them and tweak them to get your SQL reports.

Tracking marketing-sourced leads

Many marketers are measured on how many leads they pass to sales, as well as the percentage of those leads converted into opportunities. Getting visibility into the leads after submitting them to the sales team is a bane for many marketing departments. After implementing a marketing automation tool, both sales and marketing will have a singular view of a prospect, lead, account, and opportunity. Marketing can easily see whether leads are being followed up on, worked, and created into opportunities.

The benefit for marketing is more than just presales lead visibility. On average, only a small percentage of leads passed to sales ever make it to a phone call with a salesperson. You can attribute this situation to the fact that salespeople want to work only the opportunities that offer the best chance to close this quarter, and don't want follow-up on fresh leads. Or sales reps might distrust the quality of the leads being passed on to them. Either way, a large number of leads passed to salespeople either can't or won't be worked for various reasons. By giving marketing the visibility to leads that are in the salespeople's hands, the marketing team can see the leads falling through the cracks and bring them back into the marketing funnel.

This capability can easily help the marketing team reach their revenue goals by getting more value out of leads already created. With the long length of many B2B sales cycles, the ability for the marketing team to pull leads back and track what happens to marketing-sourced leads has allowed many companies to drive more revenue out of their existing performance.

Looking at the Influence of a Campaign on a Lead

Determining what makes a lead take a specific action is, honestly, a fool's errand because it assumes that a lead exists in a vacuum and the only factor in the lead's actions is the campaign. However, I meet a ton of people who have to show campaign influence to a boss to prove their efforts. The following sections show you the best way to show the influence of your marketing efforts on your company's bottom line.

I don't recommend this theory of reporting, but I still show you how to create this report in case your company requires you to include it in your reporting.

Creating influencing campaign reports

You have many ways and many different types of reports to use to gather campaign influence data. The main factor for determining how you generate this report is your tool set. Some marketing automation tools can report on this easily; some can't. To know whether your tool has what it takes, ask the following questions of your vendor:

- **Is campaign influence built-in?** If your vendor says yes, ask one of the follow-up questions in the following bullets to further confirm the capabilities. If your vendor says no, see whether your CRM can determine the campaign influence, or ask your vendor what it would take to make this capability work in your marketing automation system.
- **How do I configure it?** If configuring the campaign influence capability is too complicated, evaluate your CRM as the option. A good tool should allow you to tag a prospect with every campaign and easily see the last campaign the prospect was engaged with before she converted. Even good tools that can track the last campaign can't always report on this, so be aware.
- **Can I use my CRM?** To use your CRM tool for this feature, make sure that your CRM can integrate with your marketing automation tool to pass on campaign information. Depending on your CRM, this process can be easy or complicated. Either way, you need your CRM admin to help set up this capability, as shown in Figure 13-4.

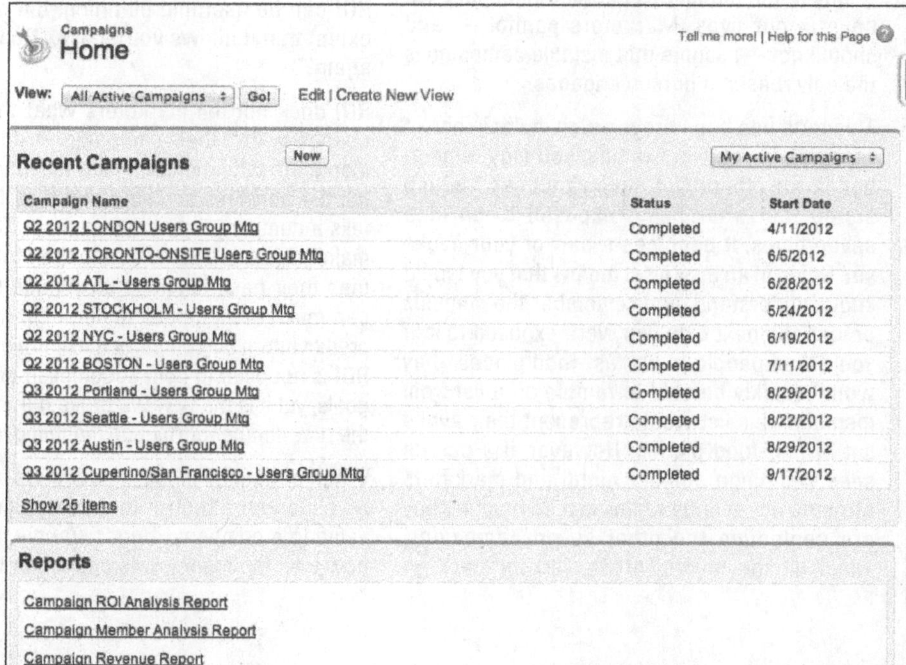

Figure 13-4: Your CRM may substitute as an influencing campaign reporting tool.

Be aware of the core flaws in attribution modeling

Despite its wide adoption and good intentions, attribution modeling has not done marketers any favors. This sidebar explores why attribution modeling devalues your role, points out the major flaws in its assumptions, and suggests other ways to consider looking at your data.

Attribution Modeling Assumes Too Much

Attribution modeling uses a linear progression of events to attribute value to each campaign in succession. If you saw this campaign and then bought the product, the purchase must have been a result of your previous marketing engagement, right?

This is the basic premise of attribution modeling. It assumes that all other events are held constant and that the only impact on your decision was the marketing campaigns you touched. This is the model's first major flaw.

The attribution model doesn't account for social perceptions, society's norms, personal beliefs, or any of the thousands of other influences we have in our lives. Marketers cannot — and should not —assume that a single campaign is the only reason a person engages.

This truth has been proven with multiple bits of research. A famous example you may remember is the "theory of seven touches," which stated that after being exposed to an idea seven times, it becomes a part of your evoke set. Being in an evoke set means that you would know, understand, and remember the stimulus or idea the next time you were exposed to it. If you asked people to list fast-food places, they would quickly be able to ramble off a list from memory. This list would represent their evoke set of fast-food places. However, if a person sees campaign number eight, and marketers attribute all revenue to this last campaign, they are neglecting the other seven campaigns, which did the majority of the work for them.

Attribution modeling does take multiple campaigns into account by suggesting that ROI should be shared across all of them. But this amounts to another giant fallacy because it assumes that each campaign had an effect on the prospect, or that she even noticed it at all. Marketers have no easy way to tell the effect of an ad on a person without asking that person, and even then, you never know, so you're making a lot of big assumptions on things that can never be proven.

Attribution Modeling Overemphasizes ROI

ROI allows you to prove the direct return on dollars spent. In the marketing world, this means showing the value of any campaign by tracking its direct impact on revenue. Now you come to the second big problem with attribution modeling: The model's focus on ROI forces a marketer to look only at spending, which is an unactionable, lagging indicator that is not tied to any core business goals or representative of any real marketing value.

ROI can be useful in planning, but only to the extent that it allows you to ask, "Do we do this again?"

ROI does not tell marketers what they should change within their campaign. It does not tell marketers why the campaign failed, nor does it tell the business anything about its future. ROI tells a company only about its past. Companies' main goals are usually tied to their future rather than their past, because they value things that can make them money faster, help them better predict future outcomes, or maximize efficiencies. ROI is not used to help accomplish any of these goals, yet it is the way we prove our value and is the only number attribution modeling focuses on.

When attribution modeling attempts to break up revenue and attach it to a campaign to prove value to a company, it does so only by showing how well the money was spent, not how well it helped accomplish business goals. This type of reporting keeps marketers from proving their real business value because it doesn't account for all the value marketing is actually producing — only how well marketers spent their budget in the past.

There Is a Better Way

A much better way exists to show the value of your efforts; you just have to look to find it.

Consider matching your efforts to core business goals. This alignment will help you to be truly indispensible, rather than be viewed as a cost center. Here are some items to measure and consider when it comes to proving the value of your marketing campaigns:

- **Know the time value of money (TVM).** This basic economic principle should be one of your major marketing value propositions. The TVM principle states that a dollar that comes in today is more valuable than a dollar that comes in tomorrow. This is because it can be put to work much more quickly, yielding a higher return. As a marketer, if you can help speed up the revenue cycle and bring money into the organization faster, you are driving real value.

  To speed the revenue cycle, you need to track the average speed of a lead moving though your life cycle. Knowing that your campaign has shortened the sales cycle by days equates to serious dollars over the course of a year. Think about it this way: If you have a 30-day sales cycle and you shorten it by two days, you gain an extra month of revenue each year. That's a massive increase in revenue!

- **Predict the future.** Knowing what the future holds is another major business goal. CEOs pay a lot of money to get reports on future outlooks, and many people are dedicated to predicting future trends. You should be one of them. Instead of just reporting on current lead flow, report on future lead flow. You can easily report on future lead flow with modern marketing technologies. Having the power to predict and deliver will help you become a valued asset to your business, taking the focus away from your efforts and keeping the focus on your results.

At its core, attribution modeling tries to answer some very complex questions quickly and easily. If you subscribe to the attribution model, make sure that you are aware of its shortcomings and consider investigating other ways to prove your value. Otherwise, you'll always just be looked at as a cost center and not a business driver.

Limiting factors of influencing campaign reports

Many issues crop up with using influencing campaign reporting. If you are the department asking for this report, I suggest asking yourself what you really want to find. If you are trying to find a silver bullet, you are on a fool's errand. Statistical averages are great to see on a large scale, but determining whether a campaign had a direct influence is very hard to prove. If 100 percent of your leads all convert on the same campaign, I suggest running the campaign to everyone. However, that still does not suggest that it had any bearing on a single deal closing. Using influence to identify effective campaigns is not always the best way, and there are other ways to identify great campaigns, which I walk you through. The reasons I'm against using influence reporting to evaluate the effectiveness of your campaigns are as follows:

- **People live in bubbles.** This type of report lacks in accounting for outside influences. Such influences can never be accounted for. So you run the risk of attributing significance to a campaign that might not have been significant at all.
- **Singular channels get the credit.** You can tie this report to only a single campaign, but you're marketing across multiple channels at one time. What if a lead is affected by social media, email, and your website all in the same day? In such a case, the last interaction shouldn't receive all the credit.
- **Attribution modeling doesn't work.** A conversion is not a singular action; instead, it's a combination of many smaller interactions moving someone toward a final action. Attributing all the work to a single campaign neglects the effort of your supporting campaigns and may lead you to rely too heavily on your "silver bullet" campaign. See the "Be aware of the core flaws in attribution modeling" sidebar for more about the problem with reading too much into one campaign's apparent effects.

Gauging Future Lead Flow by Tracking Lead Stage

One of the best uses of marketing automation is gauging future lead flow. Marketing automation can gauge future lead flow because it gives you visibility into your leads, telling you where they are and the average time you can expect them to move to the next stage. Tracking by lead stage allows you to plan for resource allocation and future business direction.

The following sections show you how to track your future lead flow by crafting a lead stage model and creating a baseline. You can create your lead stages at various levels, so I discuss the specifics. I also show you how to create a baseline to gauge your progress or failures.

Creating lead stages

Start by creating three lead stages. According to a research paper I published, titled "State of Demand 2013" and put out by ExactTarget in 2013 (`http://pages.exacttarget.com/EN-StateDemandGen`), the average lead goes back to Google to research a purchase three times before talking to a salesperson. The research also states that the higher the price of your product/service, the more stages you are likely to have. So start with three stages, as explained in the following list, and move up or down from there as time goes on if you feel it is necessary.

- **Lead stage 1 — No identified need:** Use your first stage to identify leads who are just beginning their journey for a solution. This means that most of the time, leads don't have a refined pain point yet. For example, when searching for marketing automation, it's common to search first for email marketing or something other than marketing automation.
- **Lead stage 2 — Identified need, no B.A.N.T.:** The second stage of a lead in your marketing cycle is a lead who knows what he needs but can't purchase yet. Remember, most B2B purchases happen with a committee, so a single person might push for the idea, but he has to have agreement from the entire team before he can set up demos or have the Budget, Authority, Need, or Timeline (B.A.N.T.) to purchase.
- **Lead stage 3 — The short list:** Leads in stage three have B.A.N.T. and are ready to set up their demos. A great statistic to keep in mind at this stage comes from the Consumer Executive Board. Its research states that after a lead gets to a conversation with a salesperson, he is already two-thirds of the way to a purchase. This means that he has a short list of solutions in mind well before reaching out to set up a demo. So the last stage of marketing is used to prove why the prospect should set up a demo with you.

Creating your lead stages is very easy. Either your tool is set up to run this report, or it is not. If it is not, you just need to create three custom segments to drive your reporting on lead stages. Ask your vendor before you start building anything to see how the vendor suggests accomplishing this report.

Understanding how to measure velocity through stages

Measuring the velocity of a lead through the stages is very important because each lead moves at a different pace. Understanding the group average makes it easy to predict with a great degree of certainty what will happen in the future. This is how you will calculate your future lead flow. To create this report accurately, you need to set up the following criteria:

- **Create lead stages.** Your lead stages need to be set up prior to developing a velocity report. You can either create a special report in your tool, if you can, or simply use lists to keep up with this information. I discuss lead stages in the previous section in this chapter.
- **Measure leads into each stage.** The number of leads that move into each stage is the first step to generating the velocity report. You need to be able to look back on this number as well so that you can compare lead volumes from one time period to the other.

- **Measure when the prospect moves to the next stage.** The difference between being in and out of a stage gives you your average time.
- **Use the lead score to measure stage.** Lead score is a great way to measure a person's lead stage. Score is great because it is a gross representation of a prospect's activity. The more activity the prospect engages in, the farther along in the cycle you can assume the prospect is. You can also get more advanced and use a lead score and a stage as separate data points in your tool. Lead stage in this case is changed only if the person starts to engage with content tailored for the next stage.
- **Measure average time in a stage**. This number gives you the core metric you are after. Knowing the average time spent in each stage tells you whether you are speeding up your leads through the marketing funnel.

You can take this report to the next level by also looking at the number-one conversions that drive someone into each stage and out of each stage. This tells you on average what the number-one actions or campaigns are that get someone into and out of a stage.

Building a velocity report

If your tool is set up for advanced reporting, you should have a velocity report available to you. If not, you need to build it. Building this report can be easy or hard depending on the tools you have at your disposal. Here are a few easy ways to generate the report you need:

- **Using a list.** If you can create custom lists in your application, you can create this report on a very basic level. It will require a lot of manual work, but it is possible. Begin by creating three different lists, one for each lead stage. The lists need to be fully dynamic so that people can be added and removed based on a data point such as a score.

  If you're just starting with stages, you might want to consider breaking your total sales-ready score into three equal parts. Lead stage 1 would be all leads with a score of 32 and under. Lead stage 2 would be scores of 33–66, and stage 3 would be 67–100.

  When using basic lists to keep up with your lead stages, remember to use a spreadsheet tool. Most lists don't keep up with how many people are on them every day. They can show you this number each day, but not record it for analysis. You need to log in to your application and log this data into a spreadsheet for analysis.
- **Using custom reporting.** Custom reporting can open many doors for you. In the case of trying to determine your velocity of leads through your marketing funnel, customized reporting can automatically give you the analysis you require when you need it.

  This reporting will be more complex than using a list, and it will give you more data, but it will also require a better knowledge of your tool and your specific requirements. I suggest going with this option only if you know your tool very well and want to take your marketing automation reporting to the next level. Customized reporting does have a few benefits.

You don't want to start out with customized reporting. This type of reporting is for those who want to know how to grow their reporting in the future, and to be able to figure out what can be accomplished with their tool down the road. I suggest waiting for six months at the minimum before you begin messing with custom reporting, because it adds another layer of complexities to your tool and can be very cumbersome to figure out.

- **Using tags or data cards.** A *tag*, also known as a *data card*, is a feature in a few different marketing automation tools that allows you to add unstructured data to a person's database record. *Unstructured data* is data that does not require you to set up a custom field, but is searchable and reportable. You can use tags instead of having to set up a custom field for a lead stage. This approach would be more flexible over time and is compatible with custom reporting.

Many custom reporting tools can keep up with your data and send you an email of the report on a daily basis if you prefer. This method takes time to set up, but over the long run it saves you time over using spreadsheets and doing the reporting manually.

Proving Value with ROI Reporting

Return on Investment (ROI) is a measurement of the money you spend on marketing compared to the money returned by your customers when they make purchases. Sometimes these reports can be very hard to generate because of

- Unclear data
- Multiple tools in use
- Spending and purchases happening over a long time
- Lack of a clear way to attach marketing efforts to an opportunity

When using ROI reporting, make sure that you set up your reports correctly and fully understand their limitations. You can then report on your value more accurately. Before diving into the next sections to learn about ROI reporting, consider the following points:

- **Return does not always have to measure a financial return.** For example, if you have the ability to measure Likes on your Facebook page, you can use that measurement as a return on your marketing investment. You can also assign a financial valuation on a Like, follow, or other engagement so that you can calculate a financial ROI on those actions.

- **Consider large and small reports.** Your measure of ROI can be for large items, such as the total budget this year, or for small items, such as the ROI of a specific campaign. When creating large ROI reports that encompass many smaller efforts, make sure that you use a consistent time frame. When using ROI to evaluate single campaigns, consider all the impact, including backlinks and other social sharing. When adding other outcomes, you should have a standard set of ancillary outcomes to evaluate so that you have a standard way to compare the ROI of different campaigns.
- **Investment isn't limited to money.** Your investments in a campaign are not always strictly financial. Consider the time and other elements that go into the production. Adding your time into the equation helps you look at the campaign in terms of the full production cost, not just what you spent on the campaign.

Beginning with ROI reporting

Most marketing automation tools have built-in ROI reporting for the majority of your marketing campaigns. You want to keep a few things in mind when setting up your ROI reporting. The following ROI reporting is available for the most utilized marketing channels:

- **ROI from email:** I'm not a huge fan of ROI reports on email because many times email is used as a supporting campaign. I prefer to look at how effective my email was at moving someone to the next step in her marketing life cycle.

  If, however, you are being judged on ROI, set up a few reports within your ROI reporting. Set up ROI reports for each type of email you send. This generally includes ROI on nurturing specific campaigns, ROI for newsletters, and ROI set up for other email blasts.
- **ROI from social campaigns:** Tracking the ROI on your social campaigns can be a very tricky task. The best way to track ROI on your social campaigns is to use custom redirects or special URLs for your social assets. You can accomplish these tasks out of the box with some tools or by using UTM parameters.
- **ROI from SEO:** When setting up your ROI reporting for SEO, you must attribute keyword searches to prospects. Doing so ensures that you can run a full ROI report on each key word. To set up your ROI reporting, use your default SEO report in your tool, or use URL parameters to parse this information.

  A person is likely to have many SEO searches throughout his or her research cycle. Keep track of the first SEO search term as well as all other search terms. These terms clue you in to which search terms are the most effective for finding new leads and supporting the buying cycle.

- **ROI from Google AdWords:** You can set up reporting by account, campaign, ad groups, keywords, or individual ads. Looking at each of these levels helps you to prove the value of your marketing. Figure 13-5 shows the structure of an AdWords account so that you can see how the ads are grouped together.

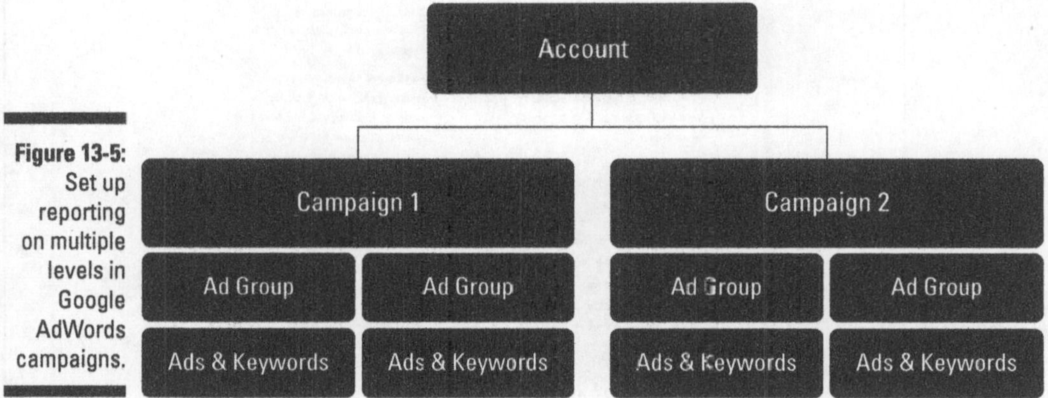

Figure 13-5: Set up reporting on multiple levels in Google AdWords campaigns.

  - *Account:* Evaluating ROI on paid-per-click (PPC) marketing as a whole is best done by looking at the account level. This shows you the total ROI on all Google AdWords so that you can judge the effectiveness of your PPC marketing as a whole channel if you'd like.
  - *Campaign:* Reporting for campaigns controls your settings and your budget. Looking at the ROI of campaigns helps you to understand whether you should refine your targeting. You can set up the ROI on campaigns natively, through your tool, or by passing information in the URL, as Figure 13-6 shows.
  - *Ad groups:* You can set up your ad groups reporting by customizing your reporting tool inside your marketing automation tool, as shown in Figure 13-7, or by setting it up the same way as campaign tracking, using URL parameters.
  - *Keywords:* Evaluating the ROI on the keywords in your paid search programs is accomplished out of the box with your marketing tool, or you can set it up by adding parameters to your URL, as in campaign reporting.
  - *Advertisements:* Setting up the ROI for your advertisements is either a default in your tool or requires setting up custom URL parameters or custom reporting. I do not suggest evaluating the ROI on your ads, but rather the engagement and the amount of opportunities being created. These aspects should be much easier to track than ROI if you do not have this as a standard report in your tool.

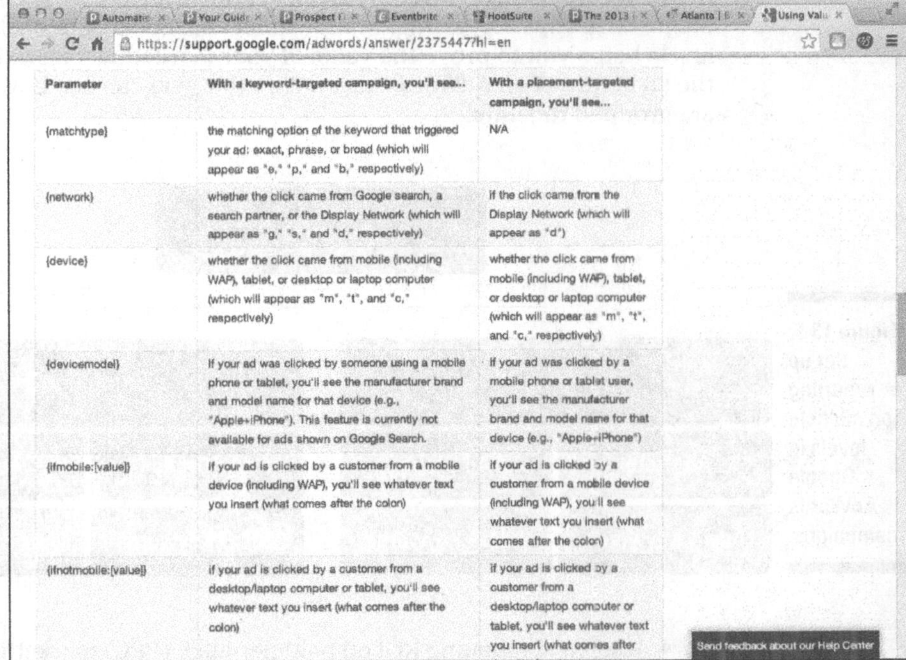

Parameter	With a keyword-targeted campaign, you'll see...	With a placement-targeted campaign, you'll see...
{matchtype}	the matching option of the keyword that triggered your ad: exact, phrase, or broad (which will appear as "e," "p," and "b," respectively)	N/A
{network}	whether the click came from Google search, a search partner, or the Display Network (which will appear as "g," "s," and "d," respectively)	if the click came from the Display Network (which will appear as "d")
{device}	whether the click came from mobile (including WAP), tablet, or desktop or laptop computer (which will appear as "m", "t", and "c," respectively)	whether the click came from mobile (including WAP), tablet, or desktop or laptop computer (which will appear as "m", "t", and "c," respectively)
{devicemodel}	If your ad was clicked by someone using a mobile phone or tablet, you'll see the manufacturer brand and model name for that device (e.g., "Apple+iPhone"). This feature is currently not available for ads shown on Google Search.	If your ad was clicked by a mobile phone or tablet user, you'll see the manufacturer brand and model name for that device (e.g., "Apple+iPhone")
{ifmobile:[value]}	If your ad is clicked by a customer from a mobile device (including WAP), you'll see whatever text you insert (what comes after the colon)	If your ad is clicked by a customer from a mobile device (including WAP), you'll see whatever text you insert (what comes after the colon)
{ifnotmobile:[value]}	If your ad is clicked by a customer from a desktop/laptop computer or tablet, you'll see whatever text you insert (what comes after the colon)	If your ad is clicked by a customer from a desktop/laptop computer or tablet, you'll see whatever text you insert (what comes after

Figure 13-6: Use URL parameters on Google AdWords to track campaigns.

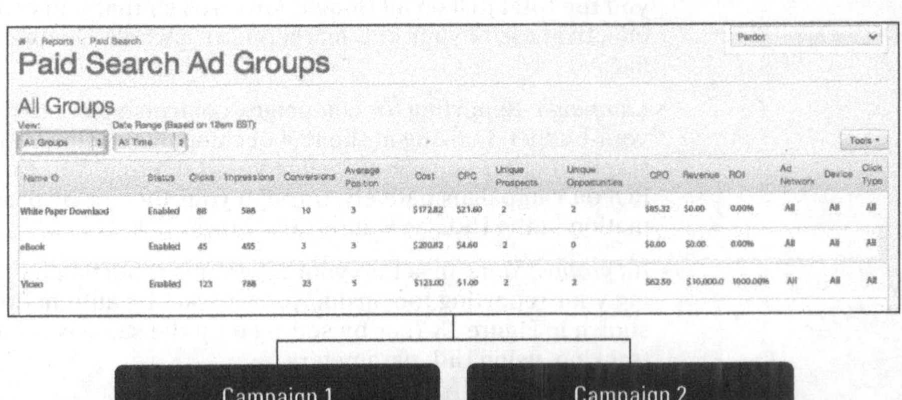

Paid Search Ad Groups

All Groups

Name	Status	Clicks	Impressions	Conversions	Average Position	Cost	CPC	Unique Prospects	Unique Opportunities	CPO	Revenue	ROI	Ad Network	Device	Click Type
White Paper Download	Enabled	88	588	10	3	$172.82	$21.60	2	2	$85.32	$0.00	0.00%	All	All	All
eBook	Enabled	45	455	3	3	$200.82	$4.60	2	0	$0.00	$0.00	0.00%	All	All	All
Video	Enabled	123	788	23	5	$123.00	$1.00	2	2	$62.50	$10,000.0	1000.00%	All	All	All

Figure 13-7: Set up ad groups by customizing your reporting tool.

The easiest way to track any PPC campaign is always by tracking the URL. Learning to use custom redirects and setting up specific campaigns for each is by far the simplest way to track ROI on a paid search campaign. Creating a specific campaign for each keyword is done manually, which is why it does not scale to hundreds of search terms, but works for those who have a limited number of paid search ads. You won't need to create a specific campaign for each keyword if your marketing automation tool is integrated with your PPC channel, but most marketing automation tools integrate only with Google AdWords, which means that creating a specific URL for other PPC channels may be the best and only way to track those PPC channels' effectiveness.

ROI reporting on paid search campaigns will be very difficult to do at scale if you don't have this as a standard feature in your marketing automation tool. I've mentioned the use of parsing URL parameters, but it's not an entry-level task, although tech-savvy marketers can handle it. If, however, you are at this level of reporting, I suggest making sure that you choose a tool that can accomplish parsing URL parameters out of the box. Doing so will remove a ton of manual labor from your workflow.

Limitations of ROI reporting

You have many types of reports in a marketing automation tool to help you evaluate your efforts. ROI is used for a very specific purpose, and it has limitations. Here are a few limitations of ROI reporting to be aware of:

- **Does not account for time.** ROI accounts for only the direct investment of capital, not all your investments of time or your opportunity costs. I suggest looking at time as part of your evaluations concerning where you should be focusing your time. Just because something has a high ROI doesn't mean that it's a great campaign to run. If your time cost is too high, your opportunity costs are high as well.
- **Does not easily prove value of nonrevenue-generating campaigns.** ROI can tell you an exact number only when you have money at the beginning and at the end. In the case of email, I advocate against using ROI as the measuring tool because there is no cost to the campaign and no direct cash in hand as a result. These nonrevenue campaigns are usually supporting a life cycle instead of generating a sale. It is better to use velocity and efficiency reporting to measure the effectiveness of these campaigns.
- **Does not show the full value of a campaign.** ROI puts too much emphasis on a single number, even though marketing is not a singular action. A marketing effort has hundreds of moving parts, and a single campaign might have many positive results. ROI is only one of the benefits to an organization. Branding, funnel management, and thought leadership efforts cannot be measured with ROI.

Adding and parsing URL parameters

Some marketing automation tools include URL parameters to allow for custom information to be passed via a URL. The main reason you need this feature is to have multiple URLs pointing to a single location and tracked at each entry point for each lead. Using multiple URLs to point to a single asset is commonly used for tracking which partner drives the most leads, tracking different channels' effect on driving traffic to a specific event, and tracking multiple paid-search ads to a single landing page.

If your marketing automation tool does not support this feature, you can use the Google URL generator. Some of the more robust marketing automation tools allow you to integrate with the Google URLs to track extra data you want to pass along with your lead to make it easier to track multiple lead source elements such as source, campaign, medium, or type. This allows you to set up a URL from which you can distribute and track leads coming directly from it. The additional information you add into the URL will follow the lead along, making it easier to track where the lead came from, segment more effectively on the additional information, and report more effectively as well.

The main reason to use additional URL parameters is to save time and make tracking and segmenting easier. The URL parameters can automatically add further information to a lead record. For example, if you created a URL that drove leads from Facebook for your white paper, you might want to add on to each lead record that it was a white paper campaign and came from Facebook. All this information can be included in the URL so that when a lead clicks the link in Facebook, and then converts to download the white paper, the lead enters your system with all the information you need to prove the value of your efforts. The following figure shows the Help page from Google to help you set up your URL. Google's tool makes setting up the URL very easy and opens your reporting doors much wider than they were before.

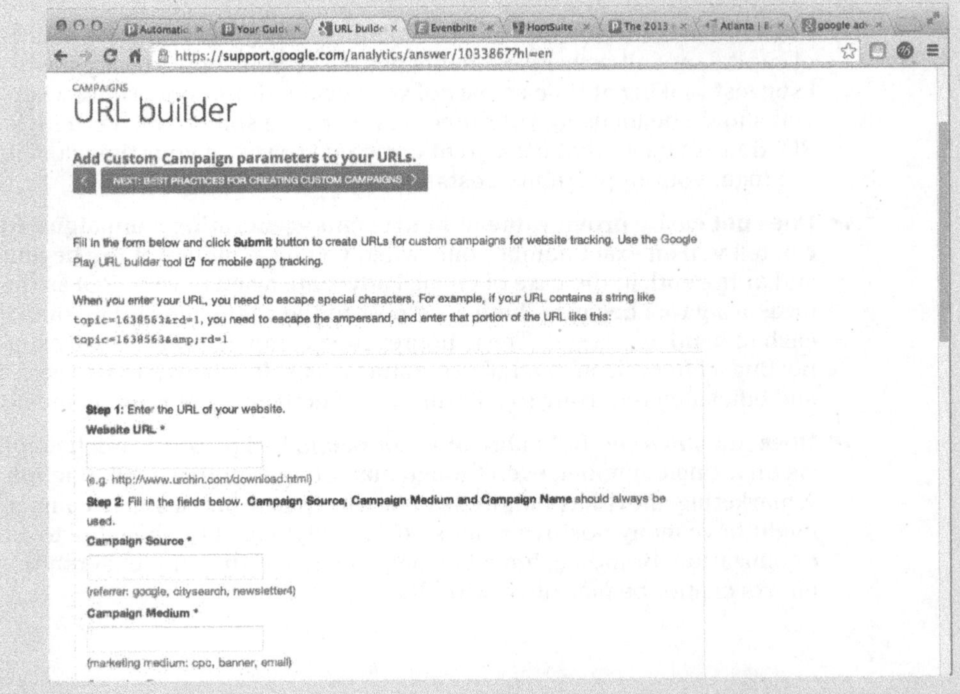

Keeping up with Marketing-Sourced Opportunities

Marketing-sourced opportunities (MSOs) are opportunities that marketing can prove are 100 percent generated by marketing efforts. In other words, MSOs would not have happened if the marketing team had not been involved. Most companies have a minimum threshold of MSOs that they need to meet. MSOs are usually shared with the sales team so that each salesperson knows how many leads to expect to receive from marketing over a given period of time.

MSOs can be tricky to keep up with but also very easy to keep up with if you know what you want to report on. The basic report for MSO leads can be very basic or a bit more complex, depending on your needs. Here are three easy ways to set up a basic MSO report:

- **Using lists:** You can easily set up an MSO report by using lists. Lists are the easiest way besides a prebuilt report that your tool may or may not have. To set up a list, simply use an automation rule to add people to a list after they have been passed along to sales. This approach gives you a list of all sales-ready leads. Then you can get a list of all opportunities the sales team creates and cross-reference the two against each other in Excel. Having the lists in Excel helps you see the number and value of MSOs easily even if your marketing automation tool doesn't have this report as an out-of-the-box feature.
- **Using CRM tools:** Because your CRM has all your opportunity information, you can easily set up a custom field in the lead record to help you with tracking your MSO leads. Figure 13-8 shows an opportunity in Salesforce.com that includes a Lead Source field. The custom field is marked "Marketing" when any new lead is passed from marketing to sales. Having this field marked correctly means that the data will follow the lead to the opportunity stage, giving you the data in your CRM to correctly make your MSO report. Salesforce allows you to automatically populate fields in an opportunity record based on the contact record. Populating fields may require AJAX coding (or any special coding that your CRM may require), depending on your edition of Salesforce.
- **Using automated methods:** If your marketing automation tool is tied to your opportunities in your CRM system, you may have MSO reports automatically created for you out of the box. You should consult your vendor to see whether an automatic MSO report is possible and to find out what you might need to do to set it up. The good news is that this feature is available in most advanced marketing automation tools, so you should be able to have this report without too much work.

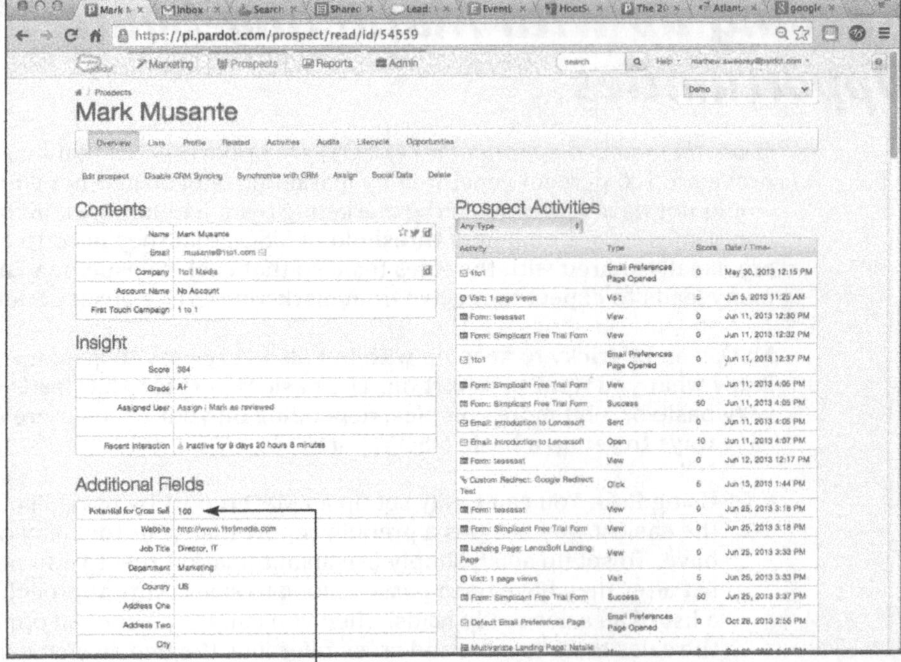

Figure 13-8: You can have a custom Lead Source field marked as "Marketing" when a new lead is passed on.

Looking at Smaller Metrics for Better Campaigns

You can use some very specific reports to evaluate smaller tactics and measure their specific impact so that you can improve the small tactical items for larger gains on the entire campaign. Here are some other types of reports to consider:

- **Completion by goal demographic:** *Completion by goal demographic* is a measurement of a very specific segment of your database. When you can track the people who are not completing your form as well as the people who are, you can get a better idea of how your goal demographic is engaging. Use the following formula to determine your true completion rate by goal demographic. You should target for a ratio of 1:1 completion by goal demographic, which would mean that 100 percent of your conversions are from your goal demographic. So if you had a form that 100 people converted on, and 90 of them were in your core demographic, you would have a ratio of 9 out of 10, or 90 percent. With marketing automation, you'll easily see which of your conversions are in your goal demographic due to your new lead tracking abilities. If you are close to 1:1, your offer and form are perfectly optimized for your goal demographic.

$$\frac{\text{(Total Completion)} - \text{(Non-Goal Demographic)}}{\text{(Total Views)} - \text{(Non-Goal Demographic)}}$$

- **Open-to-click ratio:** Your email open rate on its own tells you how good your subject line is. A click on a link on its own tells you how good your call to action is. Your *open-to-click ratio* tells you whether your call to action meets your prospect's expectation when the prospect opens your email. To get your open-to-click ratio, just divide the number of clicks an email had by the number of opens it had. This is a manual way to run this report; many advanced marketing tools have this feature built in. The goal is to reach 100 percent of opens to clicks. The more congruent your two actions are, the better aligned your subject line and call to action are. The farther away you are from a ratio of 1, the more work you need to do in making sure that your subject line and call to action work together.

$$\frac{\text{(Total Clicks)}}{\text{(Total Opens)}}$$

Evaluating your cold lead nurturing campaign

Evaluating your cold lead nurturing campaign can be very easy or very complicated, depending on what you're looking for. I suggest that you keep things easy at the beginning of your implementation of marketing automation and evaluate yourself on only a few key goals. First, don't think ROI; instead, think value created. I talk more about other ways to prove value other than just ROI in Chapter 10, but to keep this section specific to nurturing, consider my suggestions for valuing your nurturing campaigns.

- **More engagement than before:** If you got more opens and clicks, and fewer bounces, you're taking a step in the right direction. Continue to strive to do better and your nurturing programs will be successful.

- **Found new leads:** Many times, nurturing cold leads will also help you uncover leads you may have missed, or who fell through the cracks. Finding any new leads or opportunities from this campaign should be looked at as a giant win. Many people might use these opportunities to prove ROI, but I recommend against it because you will be training yourself to always value a campaign on ROI, which is not always the best measuring method.
- **Less work to manage your cold leads:** You should also be working less now on managing your cold leads. This should have helped you to set up a process for identifying them, segmenting them, and keeping them engaged. If you can remove these items from your daily tasks, you can focus on higher-priority issues.

Looking at the results of your white paper campaign

After you have made your list, sent out emails, driven people to a form, and completed a white paper campaign, you can choose among a few great and easy ways to measure it. You need to correctly track three basic engagements for your white paper campaign:

- **Form completion rates:** Form completion rates tell you how many people fill out your form after they have it in front of them. You can also track abandonment rates, but for B2B, I don't recommend looking at abandonment rates.
- **Email open rates:** Email open rates are very easy to track, and as I've mentioned before, they're not a great metric; they can, however, generally tell you some good things. You should have close to 100 percent open rates on a white paper campaign. If you are below this number, take a look at your subject line as the reason.
- **Click-through rates:** If you are sending a mass email, expect your click-through rates to be low, well below 5 percent. If you're sending an auto responder email, expect these rates to be very high. It is not uncommon to see them above 50 percent because the lead asked for the email and is expecting it.

Tracking Twitter Engagements

Tracking Twitter engagements can be very helpful in tracking the effectiveness of your Twitter marketing efforts. Here are a few ways to specifically track engagements on Twitter:

- **Basic:** The most basic way to track engagements on Twitter and prove their value is to use a landing page. The landing page should have a form on it and a special automation rule so that anyone who fills out the form is marked as having come in from a Twitter campaign.
- **Moderate:** If you're more advanced and can use custom redirects (or Google UTM parameters), you can create a custom URL for each tweet. These URLs should be taking people to content or another web page that you are tracking. This is where landing pages can come in handy. I talk more about how to set them up in Chapter 9. Your marketing automation tool will be able to pick up the information from people clicking the links and report on where they are in the buying cycle, the effectiveness of your campaigns, and so on.
- **Advanced:** If you are highly advanced with social media and Twitter, you can get into more advanced options for tracking engagements. For example, you can use Twitter Cards and connect them to your marketing automation tool. Currently, Twitter Cards are not easily connected to other applications. I expect this to change in the near future, either through applications that make connecting easier or through Twitter opening a more robust API.

Part V

Putting It All Together

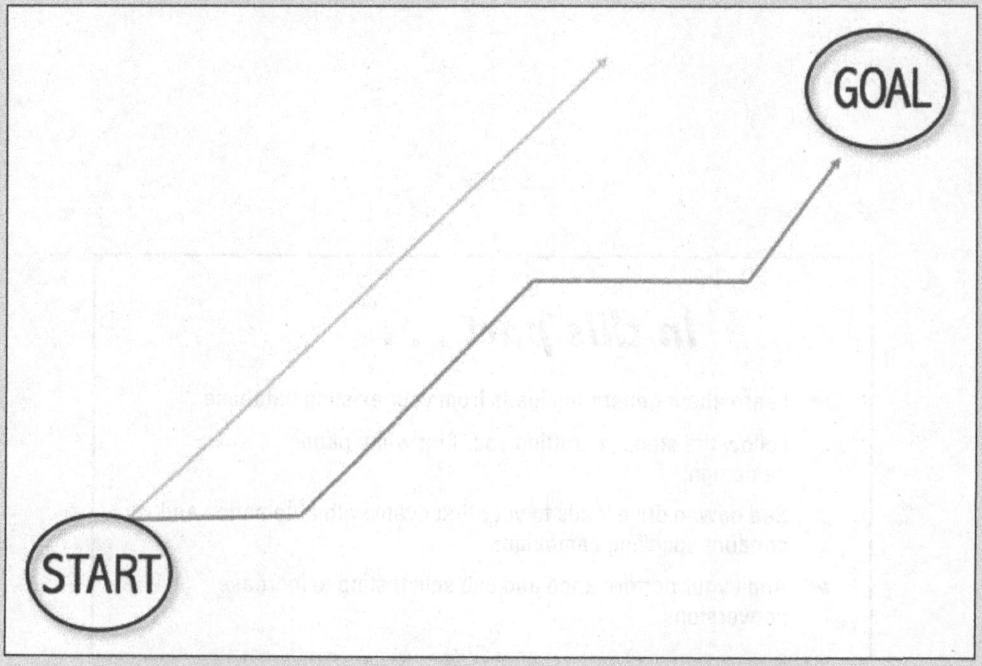

After you have marketing automation and are launching your first campaigns, you'll need to know how to stay ahead of the competition. Visit `www.dummies.com/extras/marketingautomation` for tips on how to always stay at the cutting edge of your industry.

In this part . . .

- Learn about generating leads from your existing database.
- Follow the steps in crafting your first white paper campaign.
- See how to drive leads to your first event with automation and conduct upselling campaigns.
- Audit your performance and use split testing to increase conversions.

Chapter 14

Mastering Your First Campaigns

In This Chapter

- Mining your existing database for leads
- Driving downloads of white papers
- Driving attendance to an online event through automation
- Conducting upselling campaigns

Now the real fun begins. Building your first campaigns is just like everything else in marketing automation in that the more complex your campaigns are, the more time they require in setup and maintenance.

This chapter applies many of the concepts covered in previous chapters to a white paper campaign, a database campaign, an online event campaign, and an upsell campaign. You can find some additional guidance in this chapter for running these specific kinds of campaigns.

Mining Your Existing Database for Hot Leads

You have two ways to get hot leads: You can find new leads, or you can turn a cold lead into a hot one. Most marketers are focused on finding new hot leads, but your database is your best source of hot leads, even if it is highly underused.

Marketing automation opens a new way to mine your database and convert existing database records into new leads. The following sections show you how to find leads in your existing database, keeping in mind that you need to use specific segmentation, special content, and tailored nurturing campaigns to help you do the heavy lifting. I discuss these concepts throughout other chapters in this book.

Finding your hottest leads first

The moment you get into marketing automation, your scenario is as follows: You have a database, but you do not know who is sales ready and who is not. Making this determination is the first thing you should tackle. Identify the most sales-ready leads and get them to the sales team. This is the fastest way to prove the value of your new tool. Figuring out sales-ready leads should be your first campaign. Identifying those sales-ready leads will help you to quickly show value with your new marketing automation tool as well as help you reach your goal of generating more leads with your new tool.

When you first get your marketing automation tool, work on your hottest leads first and then make sure that you can get them to the sales team:

- **Finding your hottest leads first.** Finding the hot leads is easier said than done. To send a targeted email to your hottest leads, you first have to know who the hottest leads are. To find them, I suggest using the stage-based marketing approach that I discuss in Chapter 10. You craft different content for each stage of your buyer's journey. Next, send the email to your entire cold database.

  When sending your emails, be hypertargeted. You send one email to an entire database. This is very similar to email blasting, which I advise against elsewhere in this book, but you must understand the difference. The goal here is to send hypertargeted communication based on a buying stage to help you identify a prospect's buying stage. After you identify that stage, you change your communication to nurture the prospect's specific interest.

  So, for example, if you send an email to your database targeted to the first stage of the buyer's journey, and ten people open that email, you should realize that those prospects are in stage 1 and take appropriate actions. You move those leads on to a nurturing campaign designed for prospects in the first stage of the buyer's journey because you now have a context in which to communicate with them.

  Make sure that you present clear differences between your communications in your stages. This technique is a way to fish for information when you do not have any to start with. People engage with emails that are relevant to them. A recent study I conducted highlighted the need to send fresh, relevant content. Of my 500 survey responses, 76 percent said that they want different content at each stage of their buyer's journey. By sending a series of emails targeted to each behavioral persona, you get some people to engage and tell you which behavioral persona they are at that time. Figure 14-1 shows the data from this report.

  To find your hottest leads first, you can easily target your first email to your database to the last stage of the buyer's journey. For this book, I have identified three stages in the buyer's journey, so this first email should be targeted to the third buyer's stage. I cover what type of content to use for this stage and what this email should look like in Chapter 10.

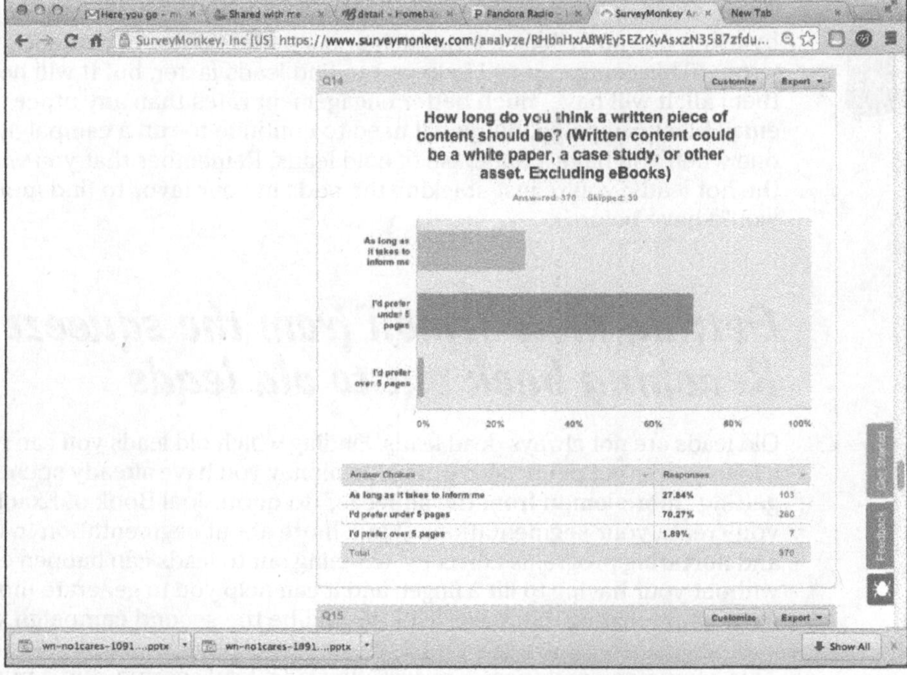

Figure 14-1: Most B2B buyers want different content at each stage of the buyer's journey.

- **Passing leads to the sales team.** This campaign differs from the same campaign without automation in that you can do two things. First, you have a clearer picture of sales readiness because of a combination of lead scoring and email tracking. Many leads may open the email because they find the subject line appealing. For example, a lead who reads the stage-1 subject line "Thought you might like this" and actually enjoys the stage-1 content you sent may be a stage-3 lead, even though your email was not a stage-3 email. However, because you have lead tracking tied to your website, if the lead chooses to continue engagement with you and searches around on your website, your lead scoring can identify that lead as sales ready.

  The second major difference that comes with marketing automation is the ability to get hot leads into the hands of sales instantly. After a prospect engages with your most sales-ready content, you can have an automation rule quality and pass the hot lead to sales in real time. This removes the need for you to do lead triage, or sift through an email report trying to pass on the leads who opened your email manually.

  As part of the campaign, you can also set the task of having the salesperson follow up with his new hot leads. This can happen through automation.

There are no silver bullets. If you think you can have 100 percent engagement by using this stage-based approach and a perfect piece of content, you are wrong. This campaign will help you to find leads faster, but it will never find them all. It will have much better engagement rates than any other type of email blast campaign, but you'll need to continue to run a campaign like this one when you have a database of cold leads. Remember that you won't find all the hot leads; you're just stacking the odds in your favor to find more than you would have before.

Getting more lemon from the squeeze: Reaching back out to old leads

Old leads are not always dead leads. Finding which old leads you can reinvigorate allows you to get more value out of the money you have already spent, thereby getting "more lemon from the squeeze," to quote Joel Book of ExactTarget. If you create your segmentations (I talk more about segmentation in Chapter 6) and nurturing programs correctly, reaching out to leads can happen consistently without your having to lift a finger, and it can help you to generate more leads from your existing database. This should be the second campaign you set up.

This campaign combines an automation rule, lead scoring, and a nurturing campaign. At the beginning, it does not need to be complex. A single nurturing campaign to stay in front of leads you identify in your database works just fine. You can get more granular over time by breaking your campaign into many targeted campaigns for each buyer stage and persona, but a single campaign suffices as a starting point.

Begin your campaign by creating an automation rule to identify the cold leads. Here are a few easy ways to identify the cold leads in your database:

- **No score change.** Leads whose score has not changed over a period of time are ripe to be reengaged. Identifying the correct amount of time to wait before reaching out again is something you should investigate on your own. I suggest waiting 45 days at the minimum, and possibly up to 60 days, past their last engagement before you consider them "cold."
- **No status update.** If the sales team has not updated their Lead Status, you have a great way to identify cold leads. Looking at the Lead Status field is also a much better way to measure than just scoring because it allows you to be even more granular with your follow-ups. So if you know that the lead was passed over as MQL but has not been changed

to a lead status of SQL in the CRM system, these leads are in a very specific stage, and you can craft a very specific message to help move them along. (I talk more about the importance of MQL and SQL in Chapter 13.) You can set up this message using a very simple automation rule. See Figure 14-2 for an example of the automation rule to create.

Rules				
Match type* ◉ Match all ○ Match any				
Automation Rules are retroactive and affect all prospects that meet the selected criteria.				
Prospect CRM status	is	Lead		
and				
Prospect custom field	Lead Status	contains	MQL	
and				
Prospect time	last activity days ago	is greater than	60	
+ Add new rule	+ Add new rule group			
Actions				
Add prospect to list	Cold Lead Nurturing Program			
+ Add new action				

Figure 14-2: Automation rule identifying a cold lead and adding the lead to a nurturing campaign.

When creating the emails for your cold-lead campaign, make sure to keep the following ideas in mind:

- **Dynamic content:** Using dynamic content allows you to create a single campaign and have each email highly targeted to your leads. *Dynamic content* is any part of an email, ad, or web page that is automatically driven by your database. A good example of dynamic content is an email signature. If you are sending an email on behalf of your sales team, and each email comes from a different sales rep, you're using a dynamic signature block in your email. Dynamic content can change words in your emails (think of mail merge fields from other email tools), content blocks inside your emails, and even HTML blocks on your website. The point of using dynamic content is that your marketing strategy changes based on the characteristics of each prospect.
- **Subject lines:** Subject lines should not be sales specific. Consider excluding your brand name or your keywords in your first few emails. Instead, try subject lines such as "Here's a great article I found," or "Thought you would enjoy this."

- **Time between messages:** The general rule is no fewer than six days between nurturing emails, and no more than 45 days.
- **Length of campaign:** Your initial nurturing campaign for a cold lead should not exceed five emails at the beginning. You can add more emails later, so begin with five and grow from there.
- **Using branching in the campaign:** Lead nurturing is effective because you can set up if-then scenarios. If-then scenarios look like this:

  If <condition> is true, ***then*** do <action>

  For example, if an email you send remains unopened, you can use your if-then rule to send a standard follow-up email. So ***If*** <email is un-opened after three days>, ***then*** <send email number 3>. If, however, an email you send is opened, your if-then rule can send an alternative follow-up email.
- **Content:** Refer to Chapter 8 for more on content. For general nurturing emails, make sure that people can digest your content quickly. In the same research project I mentioned earlier in the chapter, only 1.7 percent of respondents said that they preferred their content to be more than five pages long. So keep it *short.*

After you've set up your nurturing program to send emails to leads, you need an automation to identify sales-ready leads and pass them to sales. Ensuring that you have a plan to get the hot leads you find into the hands of sales is the most important step in mining your database of cold leads. Make sure that you follow all the lead-scoring methods I discuss in detail in Chapter 12.

Measuring your early campaigns

Evaluating your cold-lead nurturing campaign can be very easy or very complicated, depending on what you are looking for. I suggest keeping your measurements simple at this stage and evaluating yourself on just a few key goals. Forget ROI; instead, focus on value created. I talk more about this topic in Chapter 10, but to keep this section specific to early nurturing campaigns, here are some ways to value your campaigns:

- **Do you have more engagement than before?** If you got more opens and clicks, along with fewer bounces, you should consider this a step in the right direction. Keep striving.
- **Have you found new leads?** Many times, nurturing campaigns help you uncover leads you may have missed or who fell through the cracks. Finding any new leads or opportunities from this campaign should be viewed as a giant win. Many people might use these opportunities to prove ROI, but I suggest that you don't; otherwise, you train yourself to always value a campaign on ROI, which is not always the best measuring method.

- **Are you doing less work to manage your cold leads?** You should be working less now on managing your cold leads. Your campaigns should help you to set up a process for identifying leads, segmenting them, and keeping them engaged. If you can remove these basic tasks from your daily activities, you can focus on higher-priority items.

Crafting a White Paper Campaign

Content marketing drives the majority of marketing efforts for most B2B companies. In the following sections, I use the term *white paper* as a general term for any marketing asset that is downloaded.

You can use white papers for paid search campaigns, SEO campaigns, email campaigns, and nurturing campaigns. SEO, SEM, and any other paid placement campaigns are called *inbound* campaigns. When you reach out to people via email or social media, you're conducting an *outbound* campaign. Also, one white paper campaign might be part of multiple marketing campaigns. Before you start to build your first download campaign, make sure that you step through the following:

- **Create your asset.** You need to have the URL of the asset ready before you begin. I discuss creating assets and related URLs in Chapter 8.
- **Set aside time to build a few emails.** Make sure to set aside time to build your email templates. If you are running an inbound campaign, you likely need only one template. If you are creating a nurturing campaign, you need three email templates. For a basic outbound email campaign, you need one email template. I discuss building email templates in Chapter 4.
- **Talk to your webmaster.** You may need administrative access to your website if you plan to place a form on any web pages. To minimize your need for IT help, you can easily build a landing page in your marketing automation tool. I discuss building landing pages in Chapter 9.
- **Set a goal.** Whether your campaign is supposed to support the buying cycle, launch a new product, attract new leads, or support other efforts, your goal shapes how, where, and when you execute the campaign. I discuss goal setting in Chapter 10.
- **Send "sets" of emails.** I suggest building nurturing programs in groups of three emails at a time, or sets. At this stage, you don't yet know what works best for nurturing programs, so building any more than three emails is wasted effort because you are likely to have to redo them anyway. So building three emails, sending three emails, and then seeing what worked on those three emails before you build your next set is the best way to begin.

Inbound white paper campaign

For inbound marketing, you need to advertise your white paper and then drive people to its location so that they can download it. You therefore need a URL and a landing page/form. I talk about the importance of forms in Chapter 4, but in this section I tell you what a form should look like for this specific type of campaign to give you an even clearer picture of what this campaign should look like.

- **Keep the form short.** Keeping your form short increases your engagement rates.
- **Keep the content long.** Long-form content performs much higher than short-form content with inbound marketing campaigns.
- **Use progressive profiling.** Progressive profiling is also a wise choice in this instance. I talk about how to set up progressive profiling in Chapter 9.
- **Create an auto responder.** Your auto responder needs to send the white paper requested by a prospect. Using the auto responder ensures that you get the correct email address. An *auto responder email* is an email set up to automatically go out to the person filling out a form. Your forms should always email the content to the person filling out the form. If you offer the content directly, you are missing out on validating an email address. Delivering the content via email guarantees that you're sending to a correct email address because if your content is good, people will give you the correct email address to get it. Auto responder emails also allow you to identify and track the prospect. That way, you can connect email activity with web activity and begin your lead tracking and scoring. Here are some ideas to remember when creating a white paper campaign:
    - *Clearly state what the prospect will receive.* Make sure that the text on your form clearly explains what happens when the form is filled out.
    - *Automate the next steps.* If you are scoring sales-ready leads, make sure that you have your scoring model already set up and the automation rule ready to pass them on to sales. If you are adding people to a nurturing campaign, this is a good time to add people to a nurturing campaign that you have already created.

I say this elsewhere in the book, but it's worth reiterating: Your competition will get your content regardless of what you do, so don't try to create ways to stop them. You'll just create barriers for the people you want to reach.

The importance of short forms with inbound marketing

The more questions you ask, the lower your engagement rates will be. HubSpot recently looked at 40,000 landing pages and determined that the more fields you ask users to fill out, the lower your engagement rates. The study suggests that each question beyond three decreases your engagement rates. The engagement rates were at about 30 percent at only three questions and down to 10 percent when you were asking eight questions. So keep your forms short and use progressive profiling to help you get the information you need.

Progressive profiling is a technology provided by almost all marketing automation tools allowing your forms to change based on what your database knows about a person. This allows your form to change each time a person is asked to fill it out. It only asks two questions per time and allows you to increase your engagement rates by capturing a lot of information over many interactions. You must utilize progressive profiling as much as you can. This helps you to keep your forms short and increases your engagement rates.

Outbound white paper campaign

When you want to promote a white paper to the contacts in your existing database, you have a few ways to go about it. You will typically use outbound campaigns via email as mass email or email nurturing campaigns. Either way, keep the following keys in mind with your first outbound white paper campaign:

- **You don't need a form.** You don't have to create a form or landing page. You already have the prospects' email addresses, so you do not need to require them to fill out a form. If you do, you're likely to decrease your engagement rates.
- **Your subject line should match your content and the goal of your content.** Compose a subject line that's very specific and tailored to each person's interest and level of interest, as shown in Figure 14-3. Your content likely has one of two goals: to stay in front of a person and drive engagement over the course of a long sales cycle, or to nurture a current interest. Either way, make sure your subject line and content fit the goal.

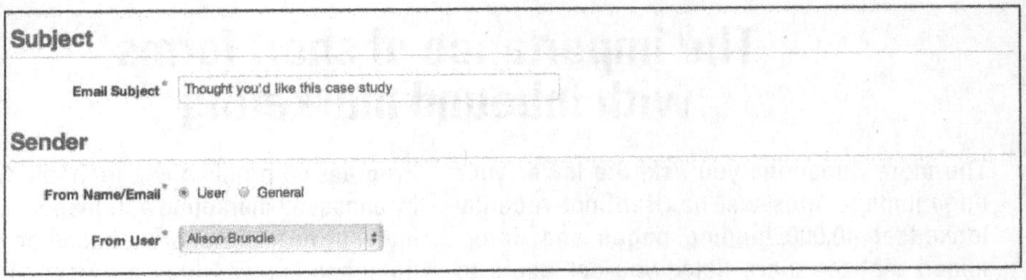

Figure 14-3: Use a specific subject line tailored to interest and level of interest.

- **Your email copy should get to the point.** Keep it short and try to leverage Rich Text instead of heavy HTML. When you feel you must use HTML, use video or other content that is clear, short, and helpful. Figure 14-4 shows a great example of an email from Wistia delivering video content to me.

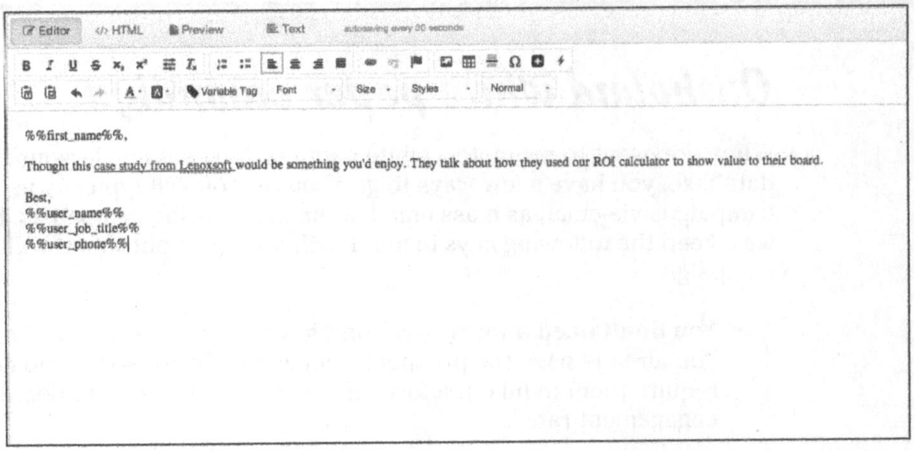

Figure 14-4: Use clear, short, and helpful content in your emails.

- **Your call to action needs to be a hyperlink.** Don't attach your content to the email. Instead, use a link. Links allow you to track the click so that you can report on the content people engage with. Optimize your email for a single call to action.
- **Personalize it.** With marketing automation, your emails can be sent from anyone automatically, so use this feature. Don't just send an email from a company; start to build a relationship with a key person.

How to increase the engagements in your white paper campaign

A white paper campaign is very different with marketing automation than without it. This is because marketing automation gives you a lot more visibility into the full campaign and allows you to optimize it in places you never could before. All these optimizations can also be automated so that you get more leads without having to lift a finger. Here are some simple ways to increase engagements with your white paper campaign:

- **Check form completion rates.** Form completion rates tell you how many people fill out your form when they have it in front of them. You can also track abandonment rates to help you identify those leads who don't instantly connect but do have some level of interest. You can follow up with an email to those leads later with a slightly different spin.
- **Watch email open rates.** Email open rates are very easy to track. Although they don't offer a great metric, they can give you some good information. The open rate can tell you who wanted your content but didn't get it. This information leads to an easy automated follow-up campaign to help you to increase engagement. Because you know these leads wanted your content, you can simply create an automation rule to resend the content to them, helping you drive more engagement from your white paper campaign that you couldn't have done without marketing automation.

Upselling Campaigns

If you sell multiple products, or have multiple levels of service, marketing automation is one of the best ways to upsell your products and services to your buyers. Marketing automation solves the problem of leaving all the upselling responsibilities to an account representative who is trying to manage the relationship.

The next sections show you how using marketing automation for your upsell marketing campaigns can help your account representatives focus on developing relationships while still talking to customers who are interested in buying more of your products and services.

Building your list of possible prospects

Because an upsell campaign is always sent to existing clients, create a target list using the client data in your CRM. Here are the best ways to create your upsell list. It is very similar to mining your database for hot leads, as described earlier in the chapter, yet also very different because all your leads are existing customers. This means that the data points you look at are very different, and the type of communication you will have with your leads is very different as well. Here are some great ways to make your target list:

- **Let the members of the sales team make their own list.** Giving sales the ability to control who goes on and off of the upsell campaign is a good option when your sales team demands 100 percent control over the marketing sent to their leads. You can enable salespeople to make their own lists using the following methods:
  - *A field and a segmentation:* By using segmentation on an extra field in your CRM, you can allow a salesperson to check a box and identify someone who qualifies for upselling campaigns. The downfall of this option is that it requires constant adding and changing of fields. It is not a dynamic solution, so you have to update your CRM system every time you want to change the option.
  - *A list inside the CRM:* If you give salespeople full control over their lists, you remove the need to constantly update your CRM. Some marketing automation solutions allow salespeople to add prospects to lists directly in the CRM. Check with your vendor to be sure, but most mainstream solutions have this feature built in. The benefit of the sales team having full control is that they know exactly which communication their prospects will be receiving, and when.
- **Use a segmentation rule to create your list for you.** If you want complete control over your upsell list, I suggest using a segmentation or automation rule to create the list for you. This option is usually preferred because it gives the marketer the most control over who gets added to the campaign, and it does not require sales to do any work. I discuss segmentation rules in more detail in Chapter 6.

Upselling with special content

The content for your upsell campaign needs to be very specific. I cover general content in Chapter 8, but this section offers some specific tips for creating content for an upsell campaign. There is a very fine art to building an upsell campaign so that you can get your point across without having a negative impact on your relationship with your client. To master this art, keep the following in mind when crafting your content:

- **Emails always come from the owner of the relationship.** If the relationship is owned by an account representative, each email should come from that rep. This approach creates a clear line of communication with your client. Emails from other people confuse clients about whom to speak with. This approach also makes reply to the email easy on the client and ensures that it goes back to the client's main point of contact.

- **Always use Rich Text format.** Because your emails are being sent from a single person, the email should look as if that person wrote it. This is why you should use Rich Text as opposed to full HTML.
- **Keep your emails short.** Your goal is to gauge interest, not sell. If the client is interested, she clicks the call to action (CTA) or asks her account representative for more information.
- **Make your CTA educational.** If you are going to create content, make sure that it is helpful to the person. Try a video series on how to improve clients' work flow or how to eliminate a problem they have. This content is helpful; a one-page product description is not. Let your account representative send the one pager later, if he feels it is appropriate, as a follow-up.
- **Make it personal.** Your email should read as though you're writing to a single person. Don't talk in generalities and don't use bullet points. These traits mark your email as marketing fluff.

Driving leads to the sales team

The final step in the upsell campaign is to get the lead over to the sales team. The lead assignment rules that you use allow the leads to get passed on to sales in real time. You should be thinking about when to pass a lead on, and how. Most leads in upsell campaigns are already in your CRM and assigned to an account rep. Here are the most common scenarios for an upsell campaign:

- **One person owns the relationship and sells multiple products.** When your sales team is relationship based and working with a large book of products, you do not need to do much work on lead assignment. Your leads are already assigned to your account representative, and your rep receives updates when the rep's leads engage with the upsell campaign. Because you don't need to reassign the lead, you just set up an automation to let the account rep know when the client has reached a certain level of sales readiness. You have the following options:
    - **Use your CRM.** Your CRM can take care of alerting the account representative if you want. CRMs can create special lists. So, for example, if you have your lead score synced with your CRM, your sales team can have a list of leads with a score over *X*. The team can then just check this list for any new leads.
    - **Automate a notification.** If you want your marketing automation tool to send out a notification, you simply create a basic automation rule that says when score for product *x* reaches a certain number, send an email to the assigned sales rep.

Sales Support Campaigns

One of the most effective sales support campaigns is a campaign to nurture leads using a competitive solution. For instance, maybe your sales rep has been working a lead who cannot buy today because she is stuck in a two-year contract. Your sales rep still wants to build rapport over those two years but wants to minimize the effort in doing so because he has to close deals this year to hit quota. A nurturing campaign is a great way to deal with this situation. Here are the steps to build a "Competitive Solutions" campaign:

1. **Set up the segmentation.**

   To set up a segmentation, you can create a custom field in the CRM or use a preexisting field. Also, some tools enable segmentation without CRM manipulation. All you really need is a data point to read so that you know when someone should be added to this campaign. I suggest looking at lead status and the field where you mark what tool the lead uses if it's not yours.

2. **Create the drip nurturing campaign.**

   Your drip nurturing campaign for "Competitive Solutions" should be crafted with sales support. The sales team will know the cadence of the emails, what to say, and what pain point the person is likely to have if using that solution. All these aspects are very important.

3. **Train your salespeople on the campaign.**

   Before you launch any campaign, make sure to train your sales team on how to add people to the campaign, what the campaign does, and what they can expect to see as a result.

I highly suggest using this campaign if your industry uses contracts and you have competition. Using this campaign will help lift the sales team's burden of having to follow up every month and let them focus on closing more business. Of all the campaigns I've created for sales teams, this is their favorite by far.

Staying relevant with lost deals

A lost deal happens to the best of us. Once when I was running my first startup, I considered buying two different pieces of software. I chose one and had to tell the other guy no. The funny thing was, the guy I said no to kept sending me nice emails every so often. I received one from him every four to six weeks, just checking in on me. I honestly felt as though I should have done business with him because of how attentive he was. I thought, "If he's this great, imagine how great the rest of that company is."

I expect that something similar has happened to you, whether it was a company using an automated tool or just the world's best sales rep. Either way, marketing automation can do this for you and make all your sales reps look like the best thing since sliced bread.

The reason that you want to nurture a lost deal is easy. You made it all the way to the end with a lead, and a lot of rapport was built. Just because that lead said no today doesn't mean that she won't say yes in the future. Keeping that relationship alive is very important to get to the yes next time. To craft a campaign for nurturing lost deals, follow the same steps outlined in the previous section for the "Competitive Solution" campaign.

Chapter 15

Implementing Advanced Marketing Automation Techniques

In This Chapter

- Auditing your performance
- Split testing to increase conversions
- Saving time with agile techniques
- Integrating marketing automation with offline efforts

I wrote this chapter because I have noticed that after about six months to one year, most marketers are ready for more advanced learning. This chapter gives you some more advanced techniques to consider. Most of these techniques relate to testing and organization, and that's because I've seen these techniques — more so than any other — increase companies' ROI using a marketing automation tool.

This chapter covers topics such as how to structure your team for better efficiencies when using marketing automation, how to better understand the specific testing of your marketing programs, and how to ensure constant improvements in your marketing over time.

This is a more advanced chapter. If you're new to marketing automation, go ahead and read this chapter but hold off on working with these techniques until you master the basics. When first starting with marketing automation, you have a lot to do, so understand that you have room to grow, but don't try to grow too fast. You'll likely just end up going crazy.

Auditing Your Performance for Improved Results

Auditing is a key to improving any process. Auditing marketing automation programs can be eye opening. A simple audit can show you whether your scoring model is correct, your nurturing program has become less effective, or your lead qualification has gone bad. I cover auditing your lead-scoring model in Chapter 12, so in this section I tell you about how to create a sustainable review process and benchmark your performance over time.

Creating a sustainable review process

To put together a sustainable review process, you need to have a few tools already set up and ready to go as well as enough data to make a review worth your while. This is why, earlier in this chapter, I recommend holding off on this chapter's techniques for a while. Before you begin to create a sustainable review process, make sure that you have the following ready to go:

- **Spreadsheet:** As much as we'd all like to do away with keeping spreadsheets, you need one for this review process. I suggest using an online spreadsheet, such as through Google Docs, on which you can collaborate with others. Or use an application like Dropbox so that others on your team have easy access to the spreadsheet.
- **Data:** You need data to do reviews. Without the data, you can't get much value out of your review. Have a minimum of 30 days' worth of data for analysis.

With your data and spreadsheet in hand, you can set up your spreadsheet as follows. Make your first column the name of your asset or program. The second column should contain your benchmark data. (For your first time, this data should be the results of your first attempt at marketing automation.) Figure 15-1 gives a good example of how this spreadsheet should look. Also, although I don't show it in the figure, consider having a column for keeping notes, such as what you changed for this campaign, or what came out differently than you expected. Keeping these notes helps you to quickly look back in time to see what you did to get the results you had, or come up with ideas as to why the results weren't what you expected.

The date column headings in Figure 15-1 are to help you understand that this should be a living document, with revisions expected in the future. Having the dates here helps you note on your calendar the next time you need to review your program.

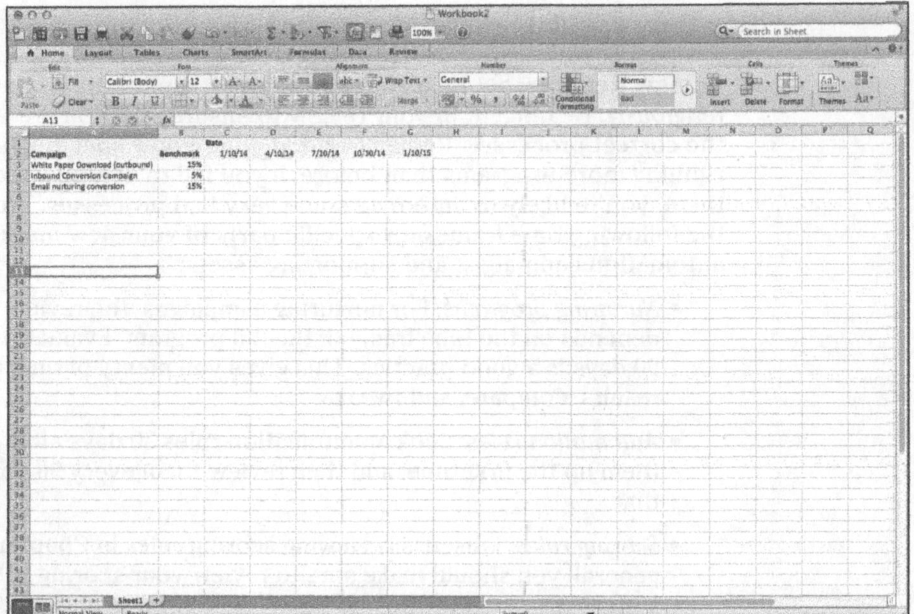

Workbook2
Date
Campaign
Benchmark
1/10/14
4/10/14
7/10/14
10/30/14
1/10/15
White Paper Download (outbound)
15%
Inbound Conversion Campaign
5%
Email nurturing conversion
15%
Sheet1

Figure 15-1: A spreadsheet ready for data.

Be sure to gather all your existing data before you implement a marketing automation tool. If you have an email program, you need to capture your results before you implement marketing automation. Having results on hand will help you benchmark and prove the value of marketing automation over other options, as well as create the baseline for growth. For programs that you haven't run before using marketing automation, use the results of your first attempt as your baseline.

Try to make this process easy on yourself. The spreadsheet is a tool to help you see large trends over time. If you make it a hassle, you won't keep up with it. Try to use only a single number for your benchmark, and use the same number each time. Having multiple benchmarks for a single campaign can add too much complexity to your reporting and increase the time it takes for you to keep up with this data. For a best practice, try to get to where you can fill out the full sheet in only 10 minutes.

Benchmarking your performance over time

Now that you have the data in a single place, you can start to look at it over a long time period, fill it in periodically, and get a feel for how to check out performance over time. I cannot stress enough that this task should not be a time sink. Keeping it quick and easy will ensure that you do it. If you make it hard on yourself, you'll never do it, and you'll fail to improve at the rate you could.

Follow these tips for keeping your review on track:

- **Review timeline:** Set up a standard review timeline and follow it *religiously*. Be diligent in your review to ensure that you are automating the correct processes. Remember that you're now speeding up and running more programs than before. If you fail to carefully monitor them, you're likely to automate some very bad processes. I recommend the following time frames for specific parts of your new marketing automation campaigns and supporting assets:
  - *Nurturing programs:* For nurturing campaigns, the review timeline depends on the time frame of the full program. Evaluating every 90 days is a good practice. This gives you plenty of time to see results, compare, and tweak.
  - *Automation rules:* Look at automation rules 30 days after you set them up the first time, and then review them every 90 days after that.
  - *Scoring rules:* I discuss reviewing scoring rules in Chapter 6, but in general, you should make sure to review your scoring rules once a quarter to begin with, and taper off to twice a year when you have it dialed in. The only time you should do it more frequently than once a quarter is when you notice a high percentage of leads being qualified as MQL but not being accepted as SQL. If you see more than half of your MQL leads not being accepted, you need to reevaluate your scoring as soon as possible.
  - *Lead-assignment programs:* Review these every quarter. Quarterly provides a good time frame to see how the leads are converting into sales. If you have a very long sales cycle, you need to review your programs less frequently because you won't have enough data until you've had time for leads to close out, giving you data to work with. So if you have a sales cycle of six months or more, consider evaluating your models only twice a year.
  - *Content:* I suggest reviewing your content as a whole every 90 days. Lumping your content together into a single number helps you to see larger trends. Consider having a group for all webinars, emails, white papers, and so on.
- **What to look for in your data:** Your data can tell you a lot, and you want to look at both short-term and long-term trends, as follows:
  - *Short-term trends:* Your short-term data reveals trends that you see very easily after you put in a new metric. Seeing that you had a gain or loss over the previous time frame is a good example of short-term data. When looking at short-term data, do your best to understand why the change happened. This is where the real

investment of time comes in. Make sure that you understand what drove the change; this is the key to changing your programs to either capitalize on the gain or minimize the loss.

- *Long-term trends:* Long-term trends reveal themselves over quarters, even years. This type of data is key to your organization as a whole. Studying this data can greatly help with seeing large trends coming down the line. For example, if you notice that your webinar attendance is fading over time, yet your leads from videos are increasing, you get a clue about the importance of a webinar's life span. Many companies have seen this exact trend and are now putting more emphasis on replaying their videos and integrating more inline video CTAs as a result. This is helping them to put more CTAs in the middle of the video while it is playing to help them drive more leads over the life cycle of the video.

A great benefit of tracking your data is the increase in PR opportunities you might get. By tracking your numbers, you can become great case study material. Vendors love to know how their clients improve as a result of their technologies. They will be more than happy to write a PR article with your data if you have good data, providing you with plenty of free PR as well.

Benefitting from Split Testing

Split testing, also known as A/B testing as well as multivariate testing, means to conduct a test by holding a factor constant and testing different outcomes from various scenarios. An example is to have a single paid search ad driving people to two separate landing pages. Testing which landing page has a higher conversion from the same advertisement allows you to maximize the effectiveness of your campaign.

Most of the mainstream marketing automation tools allow for split testing, so you should easily be able to perform this type of test inside your application. Consider split testing your emails, landing pages, and content first. After you have mastered the testing process, you can dive into deeper split testing and test smaller items such as email subject lines, dynamic CTAs on landing pages, and so forth.

The basics of split testing

Split testing goes better if you follow some basics steps. Review the steps in this section and then you can easily use this model to split test many different aspects of your marketing campaigns.

1. **Define your variable.**

   I suggest testing only one element at a time. This makes for the clearest test and removes the subjectivity of most people's opinions as to which email is better. Trying to test more than one element at a time is not good practice and doesn't give you a clear result. Good variables to test are the following:

   - *Call to action language*
   - *Form length*
   - *Type of content (video vs. white paper)*
   - *Email subject line*
   - *Offers*

2. **Create the content you want to test.**

   For example, to test landing page copy, you need multiple variations of your landing page, with each one having a different version of the variable you want to test. Figure 15-2 shows two versions of the same landing page with different call-to-action language in order to test which language converts best.

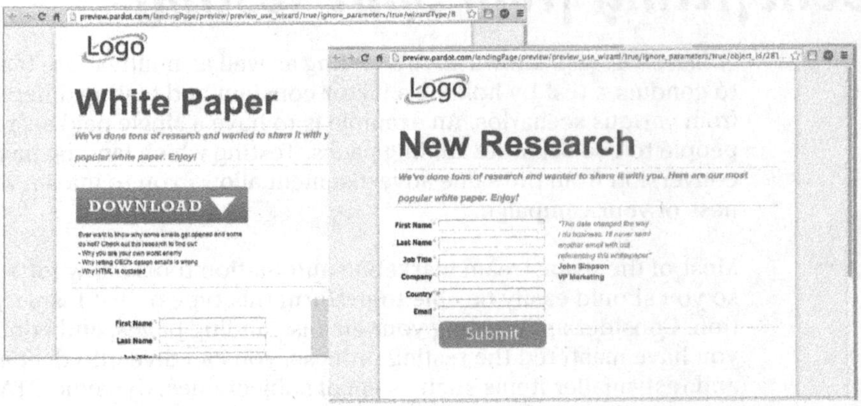

Figure 15-2: Three landing pages with different language.

3. **Create your test.**

   How you create your split test depends on the item you're testing, and the differences between setting up an email split test and a landing page split test are large enough that I cover them in their own sections (coming up).

4. **Run the test.**

   It's time to go live with multiple scenarios to test which one is the best. I suggest testing this with emails with a small segment of your total segmentation, with landing pages only for a short while, and with content for a limited time as well. I get more specific on the time frame for each in the following section.

5. **Review it.**

   If you have a clear winner, first determine why and then end your split test. Next, replace the test group with the single landing page, email, or content that had the highest engagement.

Just because one asset has a higher conversion rate doesn't always mean it's the best one. If you can, look at the leads that converted during your initial split a few months down the road. If one of the lower-performing options has converted more leads into opportunities, you may have found what you really were looking for — that is, not just higher conversion rates on an asset, but more deals at the end of the day. Just remember to take a look back and double-check that the higher-converting asset is converting the leads you really want.

Testing emails for conversions

You can split test emails a few different ways, mostly depending on the tool you use. Here are the two main ways to do a split test:

- **Inline split test:** An *inline split test* is a split test built into your email-creation process. This means that as you are building your email, you can build a few different options simultaneously, letting you streamline your testing and making it easier to do so. Note that this is a very advanced option, so a tool with this feature usually comes with a higher price tag.
- **List sampling:** Sampling has always been a good way to split test. The sampling technique is how Gallup predicts the presidential elections. The sampling method is as follows: Take a few random samples of people from your list, about 10 percent of your total list. From the sample, divide the list into the number of variations you'd like to test. Send a separate email to everyone on each small list. Then send whichever email has the highest engagement to the remaining 90 percent.

Comparing forms, content, and landing pages with split testing

When considering how to improve your conversion rate on a landing page, split testing can easily show you the way. A landing page usually consists of the landing page itself, a form, and content that the form is protecting. You can test all three of these elements using the same type of split test, but not all at the same time. Here is how to split test the different parts of a landing page to increase conversions easily:

- **Have your assets.** To create your split test for a landing page, form, or content, start by creating the different assets.
- **Use only *one* URL.** To test your conversions, you need to have multiple possible outcomes. You want to drive people to multiple landing pages, but you also need to have a way to control traffic so that you spread the traffic to the multiple landing pages evenly, increasing the effectiveness of the test. To spread traffic evenly, you hold the lead source as a constant, which, in the case of a landing page, is its URL. By using a single URL and having your marketing automation tool sending the traffic to multiple pages equally, you can see whether you have a clear winner on conversions from your form, landing page, or content.
- **Run your test.** To create your test, you will most likely use a split testing feature within your marketing automation tool. Most major vendors include this feature. The steps involved to use it vary but the basics are all the same. You'll create or have created the items you want to test already, and have them saved in the marketing automation tool. Your marketing automation solution will create a single URL to promote your content via social, email, online, or any other medium. The results of your test will be found in your marketing automation tool. Some tools can even automatically change your campaigns to optimize for the best outcome. Figure 15-3 shows a split test being set up in the Pardot marketing automation tool.

I've covered how to split test landing pages, content, and forms in the same section because each item lives on the landing page. You just need to change the form on each one to test different form fields, call to action text, or colors. The content presents your offer, so this method easily allows you to test content delivery formats. For example, what do people do more: watch videos or download white papers? Finally, you can test the landing page layout itself with this method as well to discover whether a particular landing page layout works better than your standard website layout.

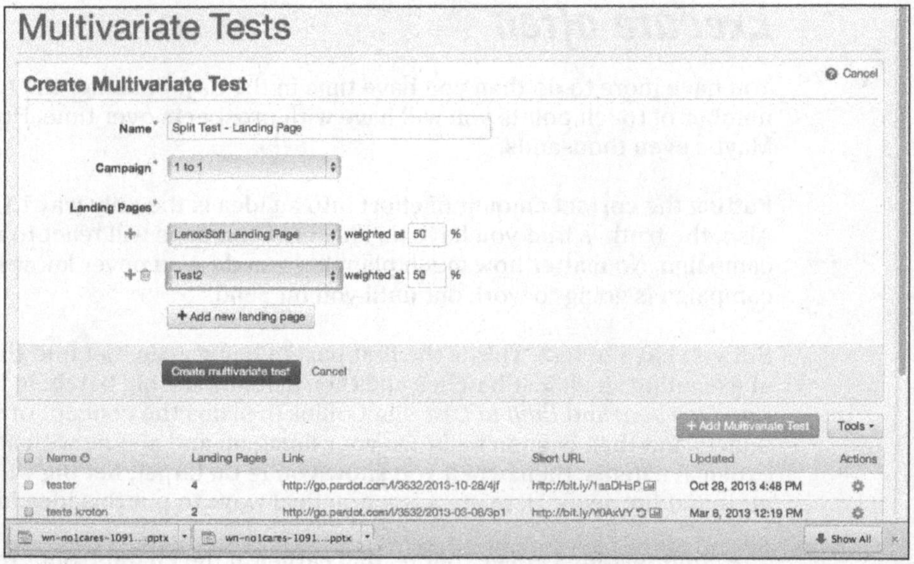

Figure 15-3: Setting up a split test.

Agile Marketing for the Modern Marketer

Agile marketing is a topic I've been studying for a while now. It has picked up steam in the marketing world as a topic of interest to many marketers, and for good reason. During your day, you are probably trying to manage long-term marketing projects as well as react to your sales team's needs and changing market conditions. So, for example, you may have to stop working on a long-term project to put up a blog post defending your position or promoting a new feature release.

Agile marketing is a mindset and framework to help marketers contend with their hectic workloads and better manage a department full of constant change and production. The essence of agile marketing comes down to this: Execute often, test frequently, and be nimble. Maybe these ideas seem too simple to have their own section, but it's worthwhile to explore in some depth how an agile mindset can help you meet your marketing goals faster, easier, and with less effort.

Execute often

You have more to do than you have time in the day. Consider the total number of touch points you will have with prospects over time. Hundreds? Maybe even thousands.

Putting the correct amount of effort into an idea is the only way to survive. Also, the truth is that you have no clue how someone will react to a new campaign. No matter how much planning you do, you never know how a campaign is going to work out until you hit Send.

But you have to test. This is the first part of being agile. Get into the mindset of executing small test batches and then sending the big batch. In his books *Good to Great* and *Built to Last,* Jim Collins explains the concept of shooting bullets and then cannon balls. Do your lining up and aiming with smaller, less expensive items; then, when you know you're on target, bet big with the big guns and fire away. Here are a few practical ways to put this idea into play:

- **Split testing:** I cover split testing earlier in the chapter. Split testing is an agile approach. The next time you want to send an email blast to your full database, take 10 percent of them and split test your emails. You'll find out which one is best and then you can fire that one to the remaining 90 percent for your best results possible.
- **Surveying:** Surveying is an agile approach as well. Before you create your next white paper, consider calling your current prospects, offering them three white paper titles, and asking them which they would rather read. You can even go so far as to draft the first two pages. Use your prospects' feedback to decide which option to move forward with.
- **Beta ideas:** Another great way to test ideas is with beta programs. *Beta* is a term frequently used in technology to identify an early-stage idea. Google is known for using the term *beta* on any new item it releases before launching the full version. Consider trying the same idea with webinars. Case in point: I was working for a software company selling marketing software and wanted to test the waters for a new webinar series on, oddly enough, the concept of agile marketing. So we tested the idea and did a light promotion with a small goal. If we hit our goal, we would spend more money next time on positioning the webinar.

  We did hit our goal, and our last webinar (the third one) had more than double the attendance of our average webinar. Had we not tried the idea, we would never have found those new leads.

Review constantly

Constantly releasing small tests is the first key to being agile, but testing without review doesn't equal good results. You must look at the results of your test to know whether to continue. Set a goal for your test and keep the following in mind when reviewing your results:

- **Baseline:** Use a baseline as the metric you want to beat. If a small test can beat your baseline, you've found a gem to invest more money into.
- **Feedback:** The baseline approach can work well, but sometimes you might be too early to market with your idea. This was the case with my company's agile marketing webinars. Our initial sign-up number didn't come close to reaching our baseline; however, attendees rated the webinar "super helpful," so we decided to do another one after gathering feedback about what worked and what we could do better. This feedback is what led to such a great result in the end.

You have to be okay with failure. Many companies hear the word "fail" and run the other way. To improve yourself and to be a market leader, you have to try new things. This is why I suggest testing ideas on a small scale. Fail on a small scale and you'll learn. Fail on a big scale and you'll be fired.

Getting your boss to buy into acceptable failure isn't easy. Try to get your boss to buy into the concept of small tests. If your company is not progressive with ideas, it isn't likely to adopt this methodology, however.

Eliminate the need for perfect

The best advice I can give you on being agile are the words from my dear friends Scott Armstrong and Nolin LeChasseur of Brainrider: "Always strive for better, not best." There could be no better words to live by in marketing today.

I can easily prove this idea to you. Draw two dots on a piece of paper, one on the bottom left and one on the top right. Now put your pen on one of the dots and close your eyes. Try to draw a straight line to the other dot. This is the "non-agile way." You will find that when you stop drawing your line, you are likely to be a good bit off of your intended target. You can stare at the other dot for hours and you'll get the same results.

The point is that no matter how long you plan, if you don't set up a review loop and change course, you'll never hit your mark. Now try this the agile way.

Go back to the first dot you started on. Put your pen on the dot and close your eyes. Draw a short line and open your eyes. Notice where your line went and then close your eyes and try to continue to draw your line toward the other dot. You can open your eyes and recalibrate as many times as you want. You'll almost certainly hit the dot, with precision and much faster than if you had looked at the other dot for an hour. Figure 15-4 shows what your paper might look like using the two approaches.

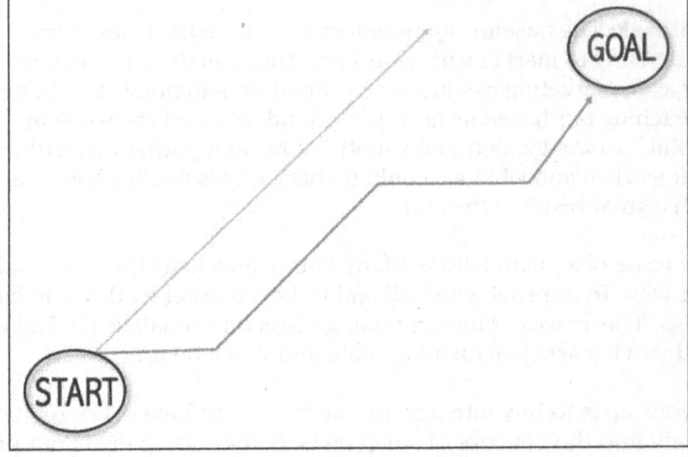

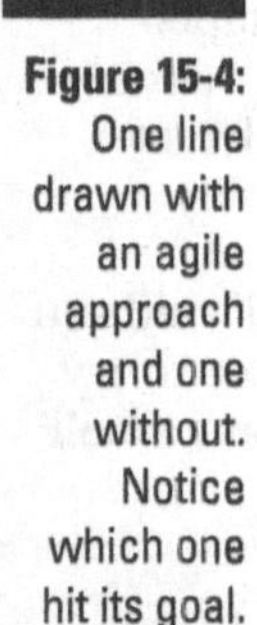

Figure 15-4: One line drawn with an agile approach and one without. Notice which one hit its goal.

The lesson here is to execute often, review your results, recalibrate, and execute again. This process helps you manage more work, get better results, and be happier in general.

Integrating Marketing Automation with Offline Efforts

Marketing automation came about to help manage online marketing efforts, and to give online efforts more power through better visibility, a single prospect record, and automated execution. These purposes are still important, but now you have many ways to integrate marketing automation with offline efforts such as trade shows and direct mail, as well.

Maximizing trade show effectiveness with automation

Trade shows are one thing many businesses have in common. You have to go to them but would rather not. People stop by your booth, get some data sheets, and likely throw them away soon after. Your salespeople usually argue over whose lead was whose, and you can never really get them to put into the CRM the trade show where they found the lead. As a result, all the time you spend setting up and planning is for naught because you can't prove your ROI. Using marketing automation can solve all these issues with trade shows, and it's pretty easy. Follow these steps:

1. **Buy a tablet for each sales representative.**

   Any mobile touch-screen tablet will do.

2. **Create a landing page/form.**

   You need to have Wi-Fi access at your booth for this to work. (There are other ways to do this without Wi-Fi; they require technical skill, however.)

3. **Create automations for your landing page/form.**

   You want to set up a different form for each sales rep and create the following automations for each form to perform:

   - *Autoresponder email:* This form automatically sends an email to prospects when they fill out the form. It also sends them the data sheet automatically so that they don't have to carry it around. You can also now track whether prospects read the data sheet.
   - *Mark lead with lead source:* This form marks the lead with the event that generated the lead, so you don't have to rely on sales representatives to do this.
   - *Add to nurturing campaign:* This form ensures that you add this lead to a follow-up nurturing program.
   - *Assign the lead to the sales rep:* With this form, all leads that come through a specific salesperson are assigned to that person.

4. **Load each tablet with the URL for the specific sales representative.**

   Give all the salespeople their own tablet with their own landing page. Figure 15-5 shows a tablet with an example form and landing page.

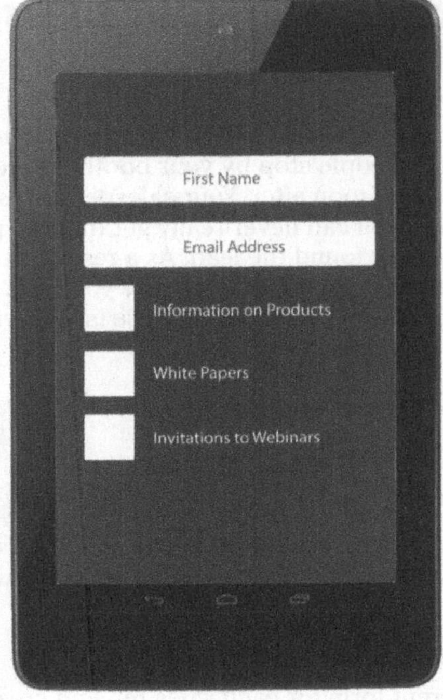

Figure 15-5: An iPad with a landing page and form used at a trade show.

Now your sales team is armed and dangerous. Send the team off to the event and watch the leads get automatically routed to the correct representative, personal follow-ups get sent instantly, and ROI tracking get done — and you never have to do a thing. And your sales reps don't have to input business cards!

Integrating direct mail and automation

Some people think that direct mail marketing doesn't work. I agree that mass-blasting mail doesn't work, with regular mail or email. However, targeted mailings work just as well as targeted email. The main issue that most people have with direct mail is the difficulty in tracking its effectiveness, but with marketing automation, you can solve that issue. Here are the basic actions you need to take to integrate direct mail and your marketing automation tool:

- **Create a specific landing page/URL.** This is the first move you can make to easily track your direct mail efforts. If you give people a special URL to go to for the offer, you know they came from that direct mail piece.
- **Use a PURL if your tool has this feature.** PURL stands for *P*ersonalized *URL*. You can have your marketing automation tool generate a specific URL for each person. If, for example, you provide me, and only me, with

the URL www2.companyname/Mathew-sweezey, and someone goes to this page, you can assume with a high degree of certainty that it was me. This is an older technology but is still useful in integrating the two technologies together. Do note that because this is an older approach, it's no longer a common feature in marketing automation tools. It has been replaced with one URL for the campaign itself and uses the form mentioned in the preceding bullet to track the individual.

- **Direct mail-in automations.** With more people using email, direct mail has little competition in the B2B space. You might want to consider the following options:
  - *Fully integrated solution:* Only a few "fully" integrated marketing automation and direct mail tools exist. This means that the marketing automation tool is tied to a direct mail fulfillment house. So direct mail can be sent as one-off marketing pieces in the way that emails may be sent at triggered times. This fully integrated solution is usually an option only at the very high end of the marketplace.
  - *Semi-integrated:* Many tools have a marketplace through which vendors can add on other technologies. This means that direct mail vendors can add features to your application. This option comes standard with tools that fall below the very high end, as well as on most major applications.
  - *Basic integration:* The most basic way to tie in marketing automation with direct mail marketing is by using a list. This approach requires no integration with your tool; you just have to keep up with a list. When you want to send direct mail, you add the prospect to the list and periodically take the list to your direct mail fulfillment center and have the mail sent. This is by far the easiest for smaller companies.

Part VI

The Part of Tens

Discover ten great tips for creating better content at `www.dummies.com/extras/marketingautomation`.

In this part . . .

- Discover the top ten blogs that you should read to keep you up to date on the latest marketing trends.
- Learn the top ten mistakes most people make when implementing marketing automation. Do NOT to do these things.

Chapter 16

The Top Ten Marketing Automation Mistakes

In This Chapter

- Recognizing common mistakes
- Avoiding common mistakes
- Staying out of big messes

I've worked with hundreds of companies using marketing automation, and some have it down. Others find themselves in a giant mess. This chapter shows you the biggest mistakes companies make with marketing automation.

Biting Off Too Much

This book contains hundreds of pages about marketing automation, and this book is just a beginning. Remember this idea when you're planning your marketing automation strategies. I suggest implementing marketing automation in steps, over a period of time. You're more likely to know what you want when you do get around to building it if you space your efforts out.

Also, make sure that you don't promise too much to too many people in your company. Keeping to exact promises can be tricky. You want to be able to show the maximum value that marketing automation can provide to help you make your case for getting the tool. But be careful: If you promise giant gains in every department, you have to deliver. Instead of making promises, set timelines and goals for the various departments, and let people know when you expect to get to their section so that you can manage expectations.

Skimping on Content Creation

Content is the lifeblood of online marketing. Marketing automation allows you to speed up how fast you can create and execute campaigns. The faster you can create and execute, the more content you need to create. Failing to understand this fact will limit the value you can derive from your tool. Here are a few tips to help keep you cranking out the content you need:

- **Reinvest time.** Simply look at the time you used to spend qualifying leads or importing and exporting CSV files before marketing automation. Take the time you save automating manual tasks and use it all for content creation.
- **Never miss a chance for content.** Creating content is something to keep in the back of your mind at all times. Keep a camera and notebook with you always. Take pictures to use in your blogs, and use your notebook to record quotes and interviews with people you meet. Consider anything as possible content as long as it can be made into something helpful to your audience.
- **Budget for your content.** Most companies don't do a good job at budgeting for content. Consider having a slice of your budget set aside for creating content. You might include sending people to tradeshows to do interviews, or paying for coffee at your local coffee shop for interviews. Regardless, have a budget — and use it.

Having Only One Nurturing Campaign

Nurturing is a skill that requires full understanding of the technique to maximize its effectiveness. Like email, nurturing is something you need to work at over time, and you need to learn new things all the time. Techniques change frequently, with new tricks to try popping up all the time. However, the biggest way to fail with marketing is simply in not thinking small enough about nurturing. Think very small. A nurturing campaign should be focused on reaching only a single goal. The smaller you think about these goals, the better your nurturing campaigns will be.

The trick is something Teresa Amabile and Steve Kramer wrote about in a 2011 article for the Harvard Business Review blog. Years of research helped them prove that constraint is good for creativity. The more constraint you give yourself, the better targeted your content will be, and the better your program will be. Creativity is the key that sets your campaign apart from others. Thinking that you can just automate the emails you already have is the fastest way to fail. Remember, it's a one-to-one medium. If your nurturing campaigns are natural, you will increase the odds of engagement. Keep in mind that a consumer makes a judgment call on your email in 1/20th of a second. So try to put a constraint on your nurturing programs to have a very specific goal, and you'll notice that your emails will be more specific and optimized for that goal and will generally help you reach your goal better than would a campaign with a less refined goal.

Underestimating the Impact of Social Media

Social media changed the way we engage with everything. If you're mad because your cable box is broken, you can tweet and get your cable box fixed faster. When the tsunami hit in 2011, it was first reported on Twitter by citizens of the towns using their cell phones. This was amazing because real-time news was being provided by citizens. Typical news channels usually have a lag between an event like this and the report. Social media is now a huge part of our communications, which means that it's a huge part of how people engage — and how they engage with you, too.

Failing to account for social media in your marketing automation mix leads to failure to correctly score your leads, and you'll fail to use a great medium to generate more leads.

Remember, it's all about the URL. The URL is what a person clicks to access your content, and any marketing automation can track link clicks to allow for scoring, nurturing, and other automations. The buyer's journey isn't just for email. Consider having special tweets sent out and tailored to specific stages in the buyer's journey. Social media is one of your best places to distribute content. It also makes sharing your content very easy for your consumers.

Looking at the Wrong Numbers

Marketing automation tells you how your marketing impacts your organization, but only if you know what you're looking at. Don't think you can just look at ROI for everything. This doesn't work. Consider looking at lots of different reports to determine different kinds of information. The following reports are the ones you should focus on most:

- **Velocity:** This tells you how fast leads are moving through your pipeline. Use the velocity of leads moving through your buyers' stages to see whether your marketing is helping to prove your marketing value. If you can prove that your marketing is generating more leads in less time, you can show a tremendous value. For example, if you have a 45-day buyer's journey, and through your marketing efforts you shorten that by five days, you are actually generating another full month-and-a-half's worth of revenue each year. You can show this fact only if you are looking at the velocity of the leads.

- **Efficiency:** Look at how many leads are created compared to how many are created to closed deals. These numbers tell you whether you're creating the right kind of leads. Improve your efficiency in this area and you'll save money and generate better leads.
- **ROI:** Look at ROI on lead sources such as keywords or paid advertisements. It's impossible to look at the ROI of a lead-nurturing campaign, so make sure that you're not trying to figure that out.

Involving Sales Too Late

Because marketing automation impacts many other departments in an organization, involving those departments at the correct times is key to using marketing automation successfully. The sales team is easily the second most impacted department when implementing marketing automation. Most companies run into issues such as the following when they do not engage the sales team early enough:

- **Missing key technology needs:** If you fail to involve sales early enough, you find out very quickly that you bought the wrong tool. Many sales processes are highly customized, and your marketing automation tool must integrate correctly. If your tool doesn't support the way your CRM system is used, it will not work.
- **Not using the best copy:** If you fail to ask the sales team which of the team's emails are working with leads, you spend a lot of time trying to figure it out. Just ask them and save that time. ***Remember:*** The sales team members are the pros at one-to-one emails, so utilize them as such.
- **Pushback on new tools:** If you fail to get the sales team to buy in to the idea early, you face massive pushback on a "new tool." Salespeople don't like change, and for good reason. They are process based, and changing their process can wreak a lot of havoc for them. Mitigate this attitude by getting them to buy in to the ideas early on, and then to the tool later on.

Overbuying

Overbuying is an issue I see more than I like to admit. Many marketing automation vendors are out there these days. Some do a lot more than others, and some are ranked really well; others are not. A ranking should not matter to you as much as whether the tool actually works for you.

Many tools have awesome features. However, they may not be on your core list of features. A wonderful feature that's not on your core list is okay if it helps you meet your goal, and maybe you just weren't aware of that feature before. Be careful, though. Ask yourself whether you will have time to dig into using the feature over the next 12 months. If the answer is no, it's likely that other tools will have that same feature in a short period of time, so a tool you buy today without that feature is likely to have it one day. Be careful of overbuying for the sake of a single feature; you probably won't be able to use it for a while, especially if you are new to marketing automation.

Also think about how you will use any whizz-bang features. Be honest with yourself: Are you really at that level of complexity? If you're new to marketing automation, you won't be a pro for a few years, and many of those whizz-bang features are made for the pros.

Understand everything involved with a feature. Many features are awesome but take a lot of time to set up. If you're strapped for time, you might not be able to use many of the features, so buying a tool for them is just a waste.

Forgetting to Audit

I used to have a boss who would say, "If it's not measured, it can't be improved." I'm sure this is a saying from the great business writer Peter Druker, and it is 100 percent true. If you are not tracking your progress, you cannot know whether you are improving. I suggest auditing. If you don't audit, you wind up with two main problems:

- **Proving value:** You'll likely need to prove the value of a tool. Even if you've got great numbers now, think about two years down the road when you've used up all your massive gains. You're likely to have to talk about small increases year over year. Auditing shows your progress and helps you prove your value.
- **Knowing whether you're improving:** This is simple. Keep track so that you can get better. You can't argue with that.

Underestimating the Power of a Website

Many companies look at marketing automation as a single way to solve all their problems. These problems may begin with not having a marketing department, not having a content strategy, or not having a good website. All these elements are must-haves to be successful with marketing. Marketing automation just makes marketing easier and opens new doors. If you're looking at getting a new website, you should look at marketing automation at the same time.

If you don't have a website, you'll never get the value out of marketing automation. One of the main benefits of marketing automation is lead tracking. If you don't have a place to track leads, the tool has no value for you.

Most marketing automation tools can build forms, landing pages, and other website features. If you build a new website without knowing how to use your marketing automation tool, you'll probably have to pay someone to build forms and try to tie them into your CRM system for you. These tasks are all done out of the box with a marketing automation tool. So, save yourself the trouble and money and do them together. Have your website administrator sit in on a demo so that the administrator knows what you're planning to do.

Undertraining Sales Teams

You need to train sales teams on the tool they will be using, just as you need to get them to buy in to its value early. If you give a salesperson a lead and show that salesperson the last web page the lead visited, the salesperson is likely to call the prospect and say, "I know you looked at my pricing page." The prospect is likely to find this call creepy and hang up the phone.

Make sure that you train your sales team so that salespeople know how to use the tool they have, understand the data they are being passed, and know how to approach a lead they have intelligence on.

Chapter 17

The Top Ten Marketing Automation Blogs You Need to Read

In This Chapter

- Blogs about content marketing
- Blogs about marketing strategy
- Blogs by individual thought leaders

Marketing automation isn't a single topic but rather a combination of many different topics and disciplines. To be great at marketing automation, you have to be great at many different aspects of marketing. This chapter presents some of the best blogs to read if you want to keep up with many of the underlying topics that influence your marketing automation performance.

Jay Baer

Jay runs an agency called Convince and Convert and released his second book, *Youtility,* in 2013. It was an instant *New York Times* bestseller and quickly caused a stir in the content-creation departments of major marketing organizations. Follow Jay's blog at `www.convinceandconvert.com` and follow him on Twitter (@Jaybaer).

Content Marketing Institute

CMI (CMIcontent) is headed by Joe Pulizzi, who is someone you should be following on Twitter (@joepulizzi). Joe has been working with content marketing since 2001 and is the leading mind in this field. His company, CMI, publishes a blog at `http://contentmarketinginstitute.com/blog` with multiple authors whom I strongly suggest following.

Clickz.com

ClickZ.com publishes information about nearly every marketing tactic and dedicates a section entirely to marketing automation. Many of the posts are written by marketing automation thought leaders. Put `http://www.clickz.com/category/marketing/marketing-automation` in your RSS feed because it offers a lot of high-level marketing automation strategies from many of the industry's best minds.

Brainrider

I've looked up to Scott (@brainrider) and Nolin (@nolin) at Brainrider for years now. Their blog at `http://www.brainrider.com/blog` shows that their passion for marketing and marketing automation is second to none. Both are from Canada and are some of the brightest minds in marketing today. I look to them for the best in content and marketing automation theory.

Joe Chernov: Helicopter to Work Blog

Joe (@jchernov) is a unique man in the world of marketing automation. He has probably been more influential in the marketing automation space than any other person up to this point. He was the VP of Content for Eloqua (@eloqua), the first true marketing automation solution, and he's now the CMO at Kinvey (@kinvey). He has also been quoted in multiple bestselling marketing books, and he's a standard on the marketing automation speaking scene. Check out his blog at `http://jchernov.com`.

SiriusDecisions

SiriusDecisions is one of the foremost marketing automation research firms currently in operation. The company's thoughts are regularly put into its blog, located at `http://www.siriusdecisions.com/blog/new`, where you can keep up with the industry and the trends that are shaping its future. If you're a deep thinker, this is a blog you'll enjoy. The company also hosts a few conferences every year that I suggest looking into as well.

Velocity Partners Ltd.

I'm a huge fan of Velocity's blog at `http://www.velocitypartners.co.uk/our-blog` because of the attention given to visual appeal. This is one of the best-designed blogs I've read, and I'm not the only one who likes it. It was a finalist in the B2B Awards in 2013, and rightly so. Look to Velocity's blog to keep you up to date on new trends in content, design, and strategy.

eConsultancy

eConsultancy (@econsultancy) is one of my favorite research firms at the moment. The firm's blog at `http://econsultancy.com/us/blog` covers a wide swath of marketing techniques and topics. I put it on this list because it needs to be here. If you are not familiar with eConsultancy's reports, you should become familiar with them quickly. The firm's reports are usually the talking points for most speakers in the coming months, and they drive the direction of many larger marketing firms. The insights and research are of the highest caliber, and I urge you to follow the company's blog and check out its events as well.

MarketingProfs

Ann Hadley writes the blog at `http://www.marketingprofs.com`. She is the Chief Content Officer of MarketingProfs, a columnist for Entrepreneur magazine, a keynote speaker, a mom, and a writer. She wrote the bestselling book *Content Rules: How to Create Killer Blogs, Podcasts, Videos, Ebooks, Webinars (and More) That Engage Customers and Ignite Your Business,* which was a *New York Times* bestseller. The MarketingProfs site is full of great content under Ann's guidance and is always a leader in the marketing world.

Mitch Joel

Mitch (@mitchjoel) is known as a digital marketing visionary and is one of the top speakers on marketing topics in general. I suggest following him to keep up on what is changing in the marketing world and to get fresh perspectives on marketing. He may not be talking about marketing automation specifics, but you will definitely be able to create better campaigns from the knowledge you gain from his blog at `http://www.twistimage.com/blog`.

Index

• C •

• D •

• E •

• F •

• G •

• H •

• I •

• J •

• K •

• L •

• M •

• N •

• O •

• P •

• Q •

• R •

• T •

• U •

• V •

• W •

About the Author

Mathew is the head of thought leadership for B2B marketing at Pardot, a Salesforce.com company. A consummate writer, he authors a column for Clickz.com on marketing automation, blogs for multiple companies, and has been featured in publications such as *Marketing Automation Times, Demand Gen Report, ReThink Magazine, MarketingSherpa,* and *ZDnet.* Mathew speaks around the world on the topic of marketing automation and works with Fortune 500, mid-market, and SMB leading companies to help shape their future marketing plans.

Dedication

This book is dedicated to my grandmother, Geneva Bryson, and my grandfather, Sidney Bryson.

Author's Acknowledgments

My name may be on this book as the author, but there are many people who should be given credit. As my good friend Nolin says, "No great idea comes from just one mind. An idea may be hatched by one but is nurtured by many." This is very true with this book. I've been helped by some of the greatest minds in marketing over the course of my career, and the course of this book was set by those conversations of my past. I'd also like to acknowledge everyone who tactically helped this book come to be. There were so many good hands employed to bring this book to fruition, and if you helped on any level, this book wouldn't be possible without you. I want to give a special thank you to all those who supported this effort with their time, thoughts, direction, and guidance.

Publisher's Acknowledgments

Acquisitions Editor: Amy Fandrei

Project and Copy Editor: Susan Christophersen

Technical Editor: Melanie Crissey

Editorial Assistant: Annie Sullivan

Sr. Editorial Assistant: Cherie Case

Project Coordinator: Patrick Redmond

Cover Image: © iStockphoto.com/Tuomas Kujansuu